SIMULATION AND SOCIAL THEORY

Theory, Culture & Society

Theory, Culture and Society caters for the resurgence of interest in culture within contemporary social science and the humanities. Building on the heritage of classical social theory, the book series examines ways in which this tradition has been reshaped by a new generation of theorists. It also publishes theoretically informed analyses of everyday life, popular culture, and new intellectual movements.

EDITOR: Mike Featherstone, *Nottingham Trent University*

SERIES EDITORIAL BOARD
Roy Boyne, *University of Durham*
Mike Hepworth, *University of Aberdeen*
Scott Lash, *Goldsmiths College, University of London*
Roland Robertson, *University of Pittsburgh*
Bryan S. Turner, *University of Cambridge*

THE TCS CENTRE
The Theory, Culture & Society book series, the journals *Theory, Culture & Society* and *Body & Society*, and related conference, seminar and postgraduate programmes operate from the TCS Centre at Nottingham Trent University. For further details of the TCS Centre's activities please contact:

Centre Administrator
The TCS Centre, Room 175
Faculty of Humanities
Nottingham Trent University
Clifton Lane, Nottingham, NG11 8NS, UK
e-mail: tcs@ntu.ac.uk
web: http//tcs@ntu.ac.uk

Recent volumes include:

Michel de Certeau
Cultural Theorist
Ian Buchanan

The Cultural Economy of Cities
Allen J. Scott

Subject, Society and Culture
Roy Boyne

Norbert Elias and Modern Social Theory
Dennis Smith

Development Theory
Deconstructions/Reconstructions
Jan Nederveen Pieterse

Occidentalism
Modernity and Subjectivity
Couze Venn

SIMULATION AND SOCIAL THEORY

Sean Cubitt

SAGE Publications
London • Thousand Oaks • New Delhi

First published 2001

Published in association with *Theory, Culture & Society*, Nottingham Trent University

SAGE Publications Ltd
6 Bonhill Street
London EC2A 4PU

SAGE Publications Inc
2455 Teller Road
Thousand Oaks, California 91320

SAGE Publications India Pvt Ltd
32, M-Block Market
Greater Kailash – I
New Delhi 110 048 ·

British Library Cataloguing in Publication data

A catalogue record for this book is available from the British Library.

ISBN 0 7619 6109 7
ISBN 0 7619 6110 0 (pbk)

Library of Congress catalog record available

Typeset by Photoprint, Torquay
Printed in Great Britain by Biddles Ltd, Guildford, Surrey

CONTENTS

ACKNOWLEDGEMENTS

This book percolated through more than a decade of talking, reading and teaching, and is gratefully dedicated to all those students who hopefully don't need it any more. I owe thanks to all my colleagues at Liverpool John Moores University, but especially Adrian Mellor, whose generosity of heart, infectious enthusiasm and dedication to clarity I have aspired to for years. Particular help with the book, with longer-running discussions and general intellectual first aid came from John Armitage, Warren Buckland, John Caughie, David Connearn, Dimitris Eleftheriotis, Alison McMahan, Maggie Morse, Lydia Papadimitriou, Daniel Reeves, Alison Ripley, Zia Sardar, Vivian Sobchack, Yvonne Spielman and Patti Zimmerman. Chris Rojek and Jackie Griffin at Sage have been a wonderful editorial team. Thanks also to Justin Dyer for judicious copy-editing. None of what follows can be blamed on any of the above.

Part of Chapter 4.iii appeared in a different guise as 'Orbis Tertius', in *Third Text*, no. 47, Summer 1999, 3–10. An earlier draft of parts of Chapter 3.iii appeared as 'Paul Virilio and New Media' in *Theory, Culture & Society*, vol. 16 no. 5, special issue on Virilio, October 1999, 127–42. My grateful thanks to the publishers for allowing me to rework them here.

For Adrian Mellor
and all our students

INTRODUCTION:
THE LONG TERM

tout ne s'est pas perdu, mais tout s'est senti périr.

(Paul Valéry)

In street markets around the world you can buy fake Rolex watches, Gucci handbags, CDs and software, and pay for them with forged credit cards and counterfeit banknotes. A whole new industry has sprung up to counter this anti-industry – an industry dedicated to the protection of brand identities. Bar-codes, holograms, spectrographic analysers and a host of new devices every month are manufactured in an endless spiral of innovation, as the counterfeiters learn to counterfeit the anti-counterfeiting technologies. The leading lights of the anti-fraud world agree: there is no such thing as a permanent solution. As long as customers want Nike, they will buy the least expensive Nike available, whether they come from Nike's offshore factories or an unlicensed workshop round the corner. A favourite strategy to beat the fraudsters is for the luxury brands to provide their own cheap ranges – to counterfeit their own goods. A particular cycle of fakery is complete when the 'original' is only the best imitation. The sad fact is that no-one buys Nike shoes at Niketown unless it's to pretend that they are participating in the last word in consumerism, the original imitation.

Simulation: a copy without a source, an imitation that has lost its original. The theory of simulation is a theory about how our images, our communications and our media have usurped the role of reality, and a history of how reality fades. Though it speaks at length of our mediated world, at its heart simulation is a philosophy of reality and our changing relations with it.

Despite, or perhaps because of, its stunning obviousness, reality has been a profound challenge to human thought since its first recorded stirrings. The very earliest writings we have, from Ur, in the Vedas and in Egyptian papyri, already lament the ephemerality of life's pleasures. When Gilgamesh mourns for Enkidu, Achilles weeps for Patroclus, or Ezekiel prophesies that 'All is vanity', we hear not only the unending demand for meaning that might make the pain of bereavement bearable, but also how our forebears fell to cursing reality's careless cruelty. By the time Socrates drained his cup of hemlock, 399 years before the birth of Christ, the idea that the familiar world we see about us is doomed to disappear had spawned a new belief: that there exists some realm beyond the visible, a world of permanence, home either to immortals or to immortal ideas. Compared with this higher, unchanging realm, ordinary reality faded into pallid insignificance.

The idea of a world beyond or behind the visible is a common but by no means universal belief, and even where it did appear, entry to the higher realms was often restricted to the elect. Kings, heroes and those nominated by the gods made it to the celestial banqueting halls, while the common sort were condemned to an even grimmer post-mortem existence than the one they had endured in life. But around two to two and a half thousand years ago, things began, very slowly, to change. On the one hand, various cults began to offer places in paradise for ordinary merit, rather than epic grandeur: the most successful of these would be Christianity. And on the other, Greek philosophers began to suggest that Reason was not just a method for thinking logically, but was indeed the secret order of the universe. The most successful outcome of this revolution in thinking has been mathematics and the mathematical underpinning of science. Almost as long-lived, though in many ways far less useful, is the tradition of philosophical Idealism.

Idealism (I will use the capital letter to distinguish the philosophical usage from the everyday usage as the opposite of selfishness) is that school of philosophy that believes that the material world, for one reason or another, cannot prove or explain its own existence. For the Idealist, the world is a result of something else that is not the world: either an act of Divine Creation, the product of a universal Mind, the unfolding of an immaterial Reason, or the visible form of an invisible Idea. The opposite mode of philosophy, Materialism, refuses to look beyond the material world for explanations and causes. Instead it follows the scientific model, and restricts its inquiries to what can be physically accounted for, without recourse to the capital letters that tend to decorate Idealism's roster of Mind, Idea, Reason and God. As we shall see, Materialism has its own problems, not least in defining what it means by physical or material reality (for example, is something like the law of gravity physical and material?). But Idealism starts by discrediting reality, and has the job of accounting for its existence by distinguishing it from the really real Idea of which it is in some way an expression. We need to take a detour through this back alley in the history of philosophy because Plato (429–347 BC), who wrote down and schematised Socrates' (469–399 BC) conversational philosophy, introduces the Greek term *eidolon*, which is frequently translated in the Latin style as *simulacrum*. We will have to distinguish late twentieth-century theories of simulation from this Platonic concept if we are to understand two crucial qualities of the modern version: it is not just a theory of reality but a theory of history, and therefore it is (or wishes to be) a Materialist theory.

Socrates' and Plato's *eidolon* or simulacrum is slightly different from, for example, the Buddhist concept of the veil of *maya*. *Maya* is the passionate, sensuous world that stands between us and godhead: not only external reality but our own bodies, our very lives themselves, have value only as stepping stones towards a disembodied, passionless and ascetic freedom from desire.

Socratic reality derives from the pure world of the Ideas, but, like the famous shadows thrown on the wall of a cave which is all its inhabitants know of the world outside, it gives us some inkling of the perfections of that world, even as it hides it from us. As long as we do not get tangled up in the shadows, we are okay. But as soon as we forget that they are only dim reflections of the ideal world, the shadows lose their function of imitating and so directing us towards the Ideals, and become simulations: pictures no longer attached to the ideas, images without originals.

In his famous attack on art in Book X of *The Republic*, Plato makes the distinction clear:

> We have seen that there are three sorts of bed. The first exists in the ultimate nature of things, and if it was made by anyone it must, I suppose, have been made by God. The second is made by the carpenter, the third by the painter. (Plato 1955: 373 [¶ 597])

The ultimate Form of Bed is the idea inhabiting the world of Forms. The carpenter makes innumerable, imperfect particular copies of that one divine Bed, an honest calling, and one in tune with the Ideal Form to which it renders homage. But the painter delivers only an imitation of the mere appearance of the carpenter's particular copy. The link to the divine Form has been lost, and we are plunged into the merely sensuous. That great Original which proceeded from the Mind of God, or from a universal Reason inhabiting the whole universe, has been lost because the artist operates at a third remove from reality (where reality is the ideal Form), imitating the mere (and deceptive) appearance of things which are themselves pale shadows of their Forms. Truth and justice demand that every carpenter's bed should be as like the ideal Bed as possible: as the French philosopher Gilles Deleuze points out, this means making all beds as alike as possible, while the problem with art is that it proliferates different beds (Deleuze 1990). Of course for Socrates and Plato, this sameness is an element of the ascent towards the absolute unity of Reason with itself, the self-identity of Beauty, the self-sufficiency of Truth. If we abandon sameness in favour of difference, we also abandon eternity in favour of history, and with it we will have to sacrifice any belief in that ascent to wholeness.

In Socrates' version, the world already existed in its perfect form: the philosopher's sole task was to bring himself to the condition of being able to perceive it, and perhaps to bring others to a point where they too could share that vision. Socratic philosophy was in the strictest sense conservative: its job was to preserve knowledge of the perfect world of Ideals, to distinguish between legitimate and illegitimate imitations of that ideal Reality on behalf of the population, and to bring the fallen material world back into line with its original model. Two thousand years later, an enormous struggle for the heart and soul of Europe introduced a far more radical understanding of philosophy's job. The process known to its participants as well as to subsequent historians as the Enlightenment brought reason to the service of revolution, sweeping away the shadows of religious (especially Roman Catholic) 'superstition', and turning reason into both the instrument and the goal of social change. In this process, which would culminate in the French and American revolutions, two factors became apparent. Firstly, it appeared that a qualitative change in human affairs was coming about, a change that promised to continue, and which its protagonists recognised first by referring to posterity, and later by invocations of progress. We are by now used to this idea, familiar with it, and even sceptical about it: at this stage of history, it was brand new, bitterly fought for, and equally bitterly attacked by the church, the absolute monarchs and all the local tyrants of a dying feudalism. Secondly, greatly inspired by the classical literature of ancient Greece and Rome though they were, Hume and Locke in Britain, Diderot, Voltaire and Rousseau in France, Goethe and Kant in Germany, realised that the progress of reason had brought the modern world of the eighteenth century to a stage more advanced in terms of scientific and technical knowledge at least, and perhaps also in the arts and philosophy, than the giants of the past. Since it seemed unlikely and immodest to claim that the moderns were individually more intelligent than the ancients, some other factor must have been in play. D'Alembert (1717–83) was still struggling with this issue in his preface to the *Encyclopaedia* of 1751 to 1765, which marks the heroic moment of Enlightenment rationalism (d'Alembert 1963). The Enlightenment, for the first time, confronts the possibility that, in the course of time, a change overcomes the nature either of truth or of our relationship with it. Truth – and therefore illusion – becomes a historical issue.

Immanuel Kant (1724–1804) leaps in. The problem of truth's relativity may seem trivial to us, but it was pressing then, and it demanded of Kant one of the great leaps forward in philosophy. Since truth, in the Idealist tradition to which he belonged, must be by definition unchanging, and since individual philosophers could not be more intelligent in the eighteenth century AD than in the fifth BC, some other condition must have altered. One possibility was Christ's ministry, but even that needed to be translated into a properly philosophical language if it were to provide an explanation of the change. Kant's solution was to propose, in an essay of 1784, a philosophy of history, in itself a novelty, premised on the theses that

> All of a creature's natural capacities are destined to develop completely and in conformity with their end. . . . In man (as the sole rational creature on earth) those natural capacities directed towards the use of his reason are to be completely developed only in the species, not in the individual. . . . The greatest problem for the human species, whose solution nature compels it to seek, is to achieve a universal civil society administered in accordance with the right. (Kant 1983: 30, 33)

Just as an egg is destined to grow into a bird, human beings are destined to become reasonable, but not individually: the species as a whole matures towards rationality, rather like the way individual raindrops are destined to flow together into mighty estuaries. As a species, human beings face the task of building a rational society, the only type of cultural frame in which it will be possible to bring the human race to its rational maturity. The philosophers' job is then to describe the nature of this historical destiny, and to encourage the building of a suitable state, preferably, in Kant's view, a global one.

In a certain sense, simulation theory is a special instance of the philosophy of history, one heavily influenced by the subsequent rise of sociology. The nineteenth-century founders of sociology dealt with a world in which work was compulsory: produce, or starve. But in the twentieth century, a new phenomenon emerged: consume, or be damned. We will come across several readings of this transition from a society of production to a society of consumption, but at their heart is a recognition that capitalism, if it is to continue and to grow, must find new desires to satisfy, new products to consume, and new consumer desires to satisfy. We might take 1929, the year of the Wall Street Crash, as a suitable benchmark. After the Crash, which threw millions into unemployment and starvation worldwide, economists opined that the only way to get the economy started again was to increase demand. The great mechanisms of modern democratic economies – like massive programmes of public works, and the construction of welfare states – increased consumption and allowed the factories to re-open.

But as a result, consumption became compulsory. Where, in production-based societies, hard work was necessary and admirable, under consumerism, possessions and consumption were essential and admired. It is not a case of a conspiracy of manufacturers to make us want unneccessary things: we have internalised consumerism to such an extent that we mock the unfashionable, despise the uncultured and fear the propertyless without any help from outside. And in place of the basic necessities of life, we demand consumer goods purchased not for their intrinsic survival qualities but for their meanings, their added value, their processed nature, their distance from the merely necessary. A whole society, a whole culture, a 'whole way of life', in Raymond Williams' phrase (Williams 1958: 18), is founded on the compulsion to consume. And the objects of consumption are unreal: they are meanings and appearances, style and fashion, the unnecessary and the highly processed. Such at least is the emphasis of simulation theory, which sees in this movement into consumerism the evidence for a new philosophy of history, one without the white light of Reason to guide us towards its fulfilment.

Too much had changed, in the post-war period, for any simple return to the black-and-white politics of the struggle against Hitler. Capitalism was becoming consumerism, while communism, in Russia and in the European communist parties, was becoming a dead bureaucracy. More subtle theories of reality, truth and persuasion were needed than the conceptual apparatus of 'false consciousness' and propaganda that had dominated the war between communism and fascism, and that became the cynical slogans of Cold War politics. Like the concept of ideology, simulation is a political theory, but it has also become a far more pessimistic theory, a theory of the endless reduplication of the same. Though Kant, and after him, as we shall see, Hegel and Marx, saw history as a process with a goal – the cosmopolitan

society fit for philosophers, the realisation of the World Spirit, the establishment of a just and free society – simulation theory would bring a new
philosophy that announced that the end of history had already happened.
Kant, Hegel and Marx thought history would conclude with the realisation
of truth: for simulation theory, it has already ended, and ended in the mass
illusions of the consumer society. For the Ancients then, the world was
already a veil of illusion: Socrates offered a way of distinguishing between
the Ideal, the genuine imitation and the fantastical and misleading simulation. The Moderns, among them Kant, Hegel and Marx, introduced the idea
that truth might be partial, and its realisation postponed into the future, but
that truth and reality would eventually coincide. But after modernity,
simulation theory introduces the possibility that there is no such moment,
and that truth and reality have both already been lost along the way. This
book is the story of that detour of theory, an attempt to understand its
implications for contemporary culture, and an essay into the question as to
whether there is any way forward out of the impasse it has created.

    The first half of the book outlines the theories clustered around the term
'simulation'; the second applies them to some exemplary contemporary
phenomena. We begin with a survey of some of the theories drawn on by
simulation theorists, and then analyse the work of four key figures, all
European, all white, all men, whose pessimism and irony typify the theory.
The major purpose of this section is to help the reader approach the original
writings of Debord, Baudrillard, Virilio and Eco: there is no substitute for
the real thing! This section concludes with a comparison and critique of the
four major theorists of simulation in an effort to establish the limits of the
theories they propose. In the second half of the book, we look at case studies
where these concepts have been applied to the analysis of leisure (theme
park culture), war (particularly the Persian Gulf War of 1991) and work (the
computer). Chapter 8, the conclusion, is an attempt to separate the wheat
from the chaff, in order to see what uses the theory of simulation may have
for us. Its central argument is that simulation theory has concentrated too
much on the relationship between representations and things. Perhaps if we
concentrate instead on relationships among people we can come to a less
gloomy prognosis.

SECTION 1

THEORIES

1

VALUES, SIGNS AND SUBJECTS

(i) Commodities

It is impossible to overestimate the importance of Marx, Saussure and Freud for simulation theory. Despite the fact that all three founding figures of modernism would become targets for major attacks from simulationists, they provide not only key terms for the vocabulary of simulation, but also core concepts of political economy, structural linguistics and psychoanalysis that persist in simulation theory. Thus we need to know something about each of them. Of the three, Karl Marx (1818–83) towers over the twentieth century. At the heart of his revolutionary communism lies a key concept for simulation: the commodity.

The Marxist concept of the commodity, as classically expressed in the first chapter of *Capital*, relies on the labour theory of value: that the value of anything is composed of the amount of human labour that goes into it. Once goods are exchanged with one another, this labour, regardless of whether it takes the form of farming, crafts or manufacture, has to be equivalent to the labour that goes into any other commodity. So concrete human labour becomes an abstract value measured by the average time taken to grow or make the commodity. Every commodity has a use-value – it can be used to satisfy some human desire – but to be a commodity it also has to have an exchange-value, comprising this abstracted value of the labour embodied in it. To have exchange-value and so to be a commodity, a thing has to be exchangeable (something that cannot be exchanged, like air or happiness, cannot be a commodity) and has to have a quantitative value attached to it, a value that arises from the social nature of the relationships between commodities in the process of exchange:

> A commodity only acquires a general expression of its value if, at the same time, all other commodities express their values in the same equivalent; and every newly emergent commodity must follow suit. It thus becomes evident that because the objectivity of commodities as values is the purely 'social existence' of

these things, it can only be expressed through the whole range of their social relations; consequently the form of their value must possess social validity. (Marx 1976: 159)

The 'form of their value' is, of course, money, the universal equivalent.

The commodity form then has the property of abstracting from almost any thing, however unique, an exchange value of a kind which it shares with every other commodity, and at the same time of reducing any work, however different, to a form identical with that of any other. What is more, when producers get together to exchange their commodities, the relationship they form with others is also an abstract one based on the exchange-value of their goods. Human relations are then entirely bound up in the exchange of abstract labour and abstract value embodied in commodities. This leads to the key point in Marx's argument, the concept of commodity fetishism:

. . . the commodity reflects the social characteristics of men's own labour as objective characteristics of the products of labour themselves. . . . It is nothing but the definite social relations between men themselves which assumes here, for them, the fantastic form of a relation between things. (Marx 1976: 164–5)

The processes of abstraction and reduction in the commodification of things results in the 'commodification' of human relationships. This of course leads Marx to his theory of wage labour as the extraction of surplus value (profits) from the purchase of human labour, which has now also become a commodity. More significantly for us, it suggests that humanity, under conditions of capitalism, lives an illusory life measured not in mutual inter-relations between people but in the 'fantastic' relationships between things.

It is on this basis that Marx will build his theory of ideology, the idea that the specific social relationships of an epoch are responsible for producing its characteristic culture and beliefs: capitalist competition, for example, pro-duces the ideology of individualism. We can also notice in the conflict between real and apparent social relations an example of contradiction, the dialectical principle which arises constantly in Marx's thinking. The indus-trial working class or proletariat, for example, experience every day the increasing socialisation of their labour as new machines divide jobs into smaller, more mutually interdependent elements, while at the same time the ideology of capitalism says that mutuality and interdependence are unim-portant compared to individualism and competition. Such contradictions lead, in the Marxist dialectic, directly towards the revolutionary upheavals that produce new social forms. The contradictions of capitalism would lead eventually to revolution, to the establishment of socialism and to the end of history, or what Marx called 'pre-history', the period of social contra-dictions. The question of the goal and the end of human history will reappear in various ways in simulation theory.

Many simulationists would add to the trinity of Marx, Saussure and Freud the German philosopher Friedrich Nietzsche (1844–1900), whom Wyndham Lewis once described as 'the archetype of the vulgarizer . . . he set out to vulgarize . . . the notion of aristocracy' (Lewis 1968: 114). Leader of a splinter faction of the surrealists, Georges Bataille (1897–1962) develops Marx's concept of commodity in the light of both psychoanalysis and Nietzsche's thesis that all contemporary religion and morality is the result of a shameful repression of more ancient, nobler and more savage passions. In the conclusion to *The Genealogy of Morals*, Nietzsche described the 'ascetic ideal' of puritanical religions as 'a will to nothingness, a revulsion from life, a rebellion against the principal conditions of living' (Nietzsche 1956: 299). Bataille, who celebrates the uncontrollable power of life in whatever form, even (and perhaps especially) the most perverse and disgusting, sees in Nietzsche's superman, 'beyond good and evil', the aristocratic connoisseur of the extremes of living. Bataille's contributions to the concept of the commodity form come in two guises: an emphasis on the consumption rather than the production of wealth, and the place of the commodity economy in a 'general economy' that includes the total circulation of energy in the biosphere.

A central concept for Bataille is the idea of expenditure. Some consumption belongs to the production and reproduction of the commodity economy: we consume energy to make things, and we consume food in order to reproduce our labour power. But some forms of consumption are like fireworks: useless, spectacular destruction for its own sake. Inspired by Marcel Mauss' descriptions of potlatch, the ritual giving or destruction of property (Mauss 1967), Bataille looks enviously toward the mass spectacles of slaughter, fantastic funeral and burial rites, communal carnivals of drunkenness and sexual orgies which formerly provided a shared outlet for the destruction of accumulated wealth and the acquisition of power and glory for those who gave them. By contrast, 'In trying to maintain sterility in regard to expenditure, in conformity with reason that balances *accounts*, bourgeois society has only managed to develop a universal meanness' (Bataille 1997: 176).

Encouraged to believe in individualism, people come to experience the world in terms of their own needs. The theory of the general economy, however, stresses the limitations of this vision, emphasising instead the tendency of the planetary ecology to produce excess with wild abundance. From the standpoint of this general economy, the individual is a minor element: death, for example, which terrifies the individual, is part of the life process creating space for new growth from the point of view of the ecology as a whole. Putting his own spin on the theory of entropy (see Chapter 2.iii below), Bataille announces 'that there is generally no growth but only a luxurious squandering of energy in every form!' (Bataille 1988: 192). The bourgeois culture of capitalism seeks to accumulate energy where the general economy seeks to dissipate it, replacing the glory of expenditure with the constraints of accountancy. This classical contradiction produces a series of effects, from the conflict between justice and freedom, to the commodity form's conjunction of the abstract 'thing' with the sensuous experience of consumption. To be human is to be caught in the dialectical relationship between the reasonable individual seeking subsistence and the general economy of sensuality, consumption and destruction. Its effects are visible in all purposeless acts: sexualities, the perverse pleasures of pain and decay, and the insane potlatch of war. Crucial for our argument is the status both Marx and Bataille give to the commodity form, though they differ profoundly in their conceptions of production and consumption. The commodity is in some sense always an illusion, yet nonetheless that illusion has a profound effect on its makers and consumers. In this sense, the commodity forms an archetypal element of the construction of simulation.

(ii) Semiotics, structuralism and signification

> The characteristic which objects of utility have of being values is as much men's social product as is their language.

> (Marx 1976: 167)

Marx's writings offer a number of parallels between the commodity form and language, parallels which were vital to the development of semiotics during the 1950s and 1960s, when this new school of linguistically based social theory took over from the more individualistic intellectual fashion for existentialism in France. The initial impetus came from the rediscovery of a posthumously published collection of lectures by the Swiss linguist Ferdinand de Saussure (1857–1913) in which Saussure replaced the older, chronological or 'diachronic' study of languages as evolving systems with a formal analysis of the state of the language at a specific, 'synchronic' moment in time (Saussure 1974). Rather than pursue the origins and evolution of languages, Saussure recommended the study of their structure as it is employed by a native speaker at a specific time in history. His first step was to look at the material forms of language, the sounds and letters we use. He notes that these materials, the signifiers of a language, have no necessary link to their meanings (the words 'tree', '*arbre*' and '*Baum*' all mean tree, but none of them, spoken or written, have branches, trunks or roots, or shed their leaves in winter). The relation between a signifier and the thing it denotes is arbitrary. But it is also structural: the word 'hut' gets its meaning not from its sound or shape but from its difference from other words – 'hat', 'gut', 'hub' – and from the rules that make other combinations, like 'htu' or 'hhh', illegitimate. From these basic observations, Saussure argued that language is a rule-governed system reliant on the arbitrary but conventional links between signifiers and their meanings or signifieds. Semiotics would extend these linguistic concepts to the widest possible realm of communications, and would develop in particular a critical concept of codes, the additional rule-governed systems required to make a poem rhyme, a sound strike us as musical, an image appear realistic, or an ideology come across as natural.

Saussure's observations opened the gates for twentieth-century linguistic science, which is largely devoted to the structural analysis of language. But semiotics was not content with this achievement. Saussure had disconnected the signifier, the material element of language, from the signified, the mental image which a given word or expression evokes. But he also disconnected both signifier and signified from the referent, the real-world entities like trees and huts which they had previously been presumed to represent. On the one hand, this leads towards a relativist position, according to which there is no necessity to prefer any one system of belief over another (Saussure's lectures were first published the same year as Einstein's Theory of General Relativity). On the other, the disconnection of the codes of language from the real world could be seen as a scientific argument in favour of Marx's concept of ideology: language had the power to create arbitrary structures of meaning with little or no relation to the real world revealed by science, political economy or the general economy of excess and expenditure.

Among the most influential studies of structure were those of the anthropologist Claude Lévi-Strauss (b. 1908), for whom the totality of a culture could be explained through structural analysis. His work on mythologies in North and South America (the best introduction is Lévi-Strauss 1973) partly inspired the most successful of the semioticians, Roland Barthes (1915–80), who, in a collection of newspaper columns later collected as *Mythologies*, undertook a similar analysis of everyday life – the launch of a new Citroën, eating steak with red wine, wrestling matches – and the codes that underpin it (Barthes 1972). Crucial to both was the concept of a certain overarching structure guiding every instance of ordinary life. Barthes in particular developed the distinction between denotation – signs pointing towards specific referents – and connotation, a second-order and ideological coding of the first: in a famous example, he looks at a photograph which denotes a young black soldier saluting the French flag, which in turn connotes the ideological principle that in French civilisation, all races serve the flag equally (Barthes 1972, 1977).

Though such studies were impressive in their ability to make sense of both exotic and everyday cultures, they were far less successful at explaining how such structures change over time. The inference of structuralism was clear: in Barthes's words at his 1977 inaugural lecture at the Collège de France, 'language is fascist'. We have no choice but to speak with the language we are given, a language that structures our consciousness. A crucial addition to the vocabulary of semiotics came from the rediscovered work of the Russian linguist V.N. Vološinov (1895–1936), who used the term 'polysemy' to point to another quality of signs: their ability to carry several layers of meaning simultaneously. Vološinov also argued that this ambiguity was compounded by multi-accentuality – the way a speaker can inflect a word or phrase so as to alter its meaning – and heteroglossia – the ability of listeners to re-translate what they hear so that it means something different again. For Vološinov, this made language a site of struggle rather than a system of oppression (Vološinov 1986). But Vološinov tended to stress actual speech (*parole* in French), where structuralism tended to emphasis the system of rules internalised by any native speaker (*langue*). In the work of the philosopher Jacques Derrida, this distinction would be expressed forcefully in the idea that the system of writing was more fundamental than the act of speaking, but even in less literary circles, the emphasis lay on texts and textuality. This was not at all an unproductive line of inquiry – we will see how the concept of intertextuality, the relations between texts, is important for simulation theory. Yet it would suffer from its suggestion that all production of language – be it spoken or written, visual or auditory, the language of flowers or the language of advertising – is done by the language itself, with the 'author' a minor clerk obeying its commands, and the 'reader' reduced to the role of passive dupe of the whole system.

More importantly for our discussion, semiotics hits a problem with the theory of representation. If we accept that any particular utterance – be it a sentence, a photograph or a website – is the product of the language system – of writing, photography or web-design – we should also accept that it is subject to certain kinds of structuring constraints: the sentence will be grammatical, the photograph will be flat, the web-page will be rectangular. Let's take the example of film, which for some critics of the 1940s and 1950s (Bazin 1967, 1971; Kracauer 1960) had been seen as the exemplary medium for the depiction of reality. The ability to capture light mechanically, to record movement and sound and to synchronise them, and in Bazin's case the specifically cinematic techniques of deep-focus and the long take, contributed to film's destiny, the revelation of reality stripped of the banal familiarity with which we normally view it. But from a semiotic perspective, the system of film – its techniques of camerawork and editing, its tricks of the trade, its codes of story-telling and comprehension – means that it can never capture reality. Reality is not flat, or black and white, or ninety minutes long; it does not have a story; crime isn't always punished, nor virtue rewarded. It is not that cinema lies to us. It is that by its very nature, any re-presentation does more than present: it cannot only denote, it must also connote.

It is only a short step from the semiotic accusation that all representations are ideological to the simulation theory statement that representation is impossible. To some extent, that final step is prefigured in the semiotic response to psychoanalysis.

(iii) Psychoanalysis: Freud, surrealism and Lacan

The human infant is an unusual creature. Most of our fellow mammals can look after themselves within days or even hours of birth, but the human child lives for years before it can walk, feed itself and reproduce. Sigmund Freud (1856–1939) based his radical interventions in psychology on the assumption that the mental life of children lives on in the adult psyche. Translations of Freud into English (the *Complete Works* appeared in English translation before their German publication) confound two words embodying an important distinction, the word *Instinkt* or instinct, a biological, innate quality, and

'*Trieb*' or drive, the developed form of the instinct as it becomes socialised. The new-born infant is instinctual: as it grows, it passes through various stages in which these biological instincts are forced to take socially acceptable forms. These stages, such as the Oedipus Complex, when the child must learn that it cannot possess its mother, are experienced as psychic traumas, shocks to the child's mental life which it can either adapt to, for example by taking on one of the gender roles offered by society, or react against, usually resulting in some sort of unhappiness or even mental illness. However, adults are rarely aware of such reminiscences shaping their behaviour. Freud therefore argued that, alongside the conscious mind, unconscious processes still governed by the sexual and destructive drives of infancy can be observed, not only in the symptoms of mental illness, but also in dreams, slips of the tongue, jokes and other everyday occurrences.

The discovery of the unconscious was and remains highly contentious, even though many Freudian concepts have entered into common-sense discourse: the Freudian slip, of course, but also the idea of being traumatised by abuse in childhood. Certainly Freud retains his significance not only because of the widespread interest in his work among, for example, Hollywood filmmakers, but also because psychoanalysis is the most significant discourse before feminism to address gender as a central issue in human life and because it instigates the idea that the human mind is neither unified, nor wholly conscious of its actions and motives.

Psychoanalysis rests upon a practice of interpretation (see Ricoeur 1970), so it is not surprising to find that Freud's work has been the object of intense scrutiny and debate among psychoanalysts. By the 1950s, the general consensus was that illness arose from the unconscious, and it was the job of psychoanalysis to bring unconscious material into consciousness in order for the conscious mind to take control once more. Interpreted in this way, psychoanalysis seems to be the exact opposite of semiotics, which argued that meaning was created not in the individual consciousness but in the social world of language. The invention or discovery of the unconscious seems to drive us back to the mental world of individuals. This definition of mental health as conscious order, however, did not strike a spark with the French psychoanalyst Jacques Lacan (1901–81), whose life work can be read as a reconciliation of semiotics and psychoanalysis. In the wake of World War I, official culture in France tended to frown on German ideas, and Freud especially suffered from the prevailing climate of anti-semitism. Perhaps in reaction against an academic culture which saw France as the home of rationalism and Germany as the centre of wild imaginings and lurid passions, a key artistic and cultural avant-garde of the inter-war years, surrealism, swept through the French intelligentsia. The surrealists drew on Freud for techniques of random association, chance collisions, dreams and hallucinatory states, to which they added a fascination with popular culture, a rather macho heterosexism and eventually a version of Marxism in which the revolution would also bring about the liberation of the unconscious (see the selections from surrealist manifestos in Harrison and Wood 1992: 432–50, 474–81, 526–29).

Lacan was deeply involved with the surrealists, especially with Bataille, whose widow Sylvie was to become Lacan's second wife. But he also brought into psychoanalysis a strong philosophical background and an important interest in Saussurean linguistics which would become central to his re-interpretation of psychoanalysis. Lacan is an even more controversial figure than Freud, not least because of the increasingly bizarre jargon in which he couched his seminars and writings, and his eccentric personality. But he is important for us because he gives influential expression to a set of terms which will be vital for the understanding of simulation theory.

The new-born child feels itself to be an amorphous mass of sensations. Unable to distinguish inside from out, touch from light, hand from mouth or dribble from speech, the infant has yet even to understand that it is a separate entity. This, according to Lacan, takes place at the 'mirror phase'. Imagine a child recognising itself for the first time in a mirror. What it sees is itself, but somehow more clearly defined, more distinct, more coordinated than it feels itself to be. This image in the mirror is the child's first self-image, an ideal version of itself which forms the basis of the Imaginary, the mental realm of all those images of ourselves that we carry around with us, that populate the culture of fandom, and which allow us to empathise with other people and identify with fictional characters. But the mirror phase is also the first splitting of the psyche, severing the infant from its union with its mother.

The second great split occurs in the Oedipal phase, when the child is presented with the first of the myriad laws which it will have to obey, the prohibition against incest. In Lacan's version, the prohibition is backed up by the threat of castration, the fear that the punishment for its desire will be the removal of the symbol of desire, the phallus. So not only is the Oedipus the introduction of a new character in the child's psychic life, the powerful and forbidding (in the sense of nay-saying) father, it is also both the first intuition of law, and the first use of symbols. The first code that the child learns is thus the code of sexual difference, a code learnt in fear and anxiety and under threat, a violence which remains as trauma, and which structures all subsequent signification and socialisation, the domain Lacan describes as the Symbolic. It is at this moment that we can first really describe the child as a subject, in three senses: of subjectivity, of the subject of a sentence, and the subject of a state. For Lacan we are not simply active subjects, we are also passively subjected to the systems of meaning that form both society and our conscious life.

In this process the child also becomes the subject of its own desire (the more recent and more accurate term for that rendered as 'eros' by Freud's English translators). Desire for Lacan has a dialectical structure. What you desire is always something you do not have, a lack, something other: he uses the term *objet petit 'a'*, object little 'a' (for the French word *autre*, other), to denote the object of desire. We reach beyond ourselves to try to grasp this other, and come back with something, but never with the otherness that we desired. This is because the true object of desire is neither Imaginary nor Symbolic, and so can never be part of us. Instead, it is Real, a topic on which Lacan has little to say, save only, *le réel, c'est l'impossible*, the Real is the impossible. Total satisfaction, like total knowledge, is unavailable. Fulfilment is not an option for human beings. But neither is stasis: desire constantly returns and returns in pursuit of its impossible object.

Thankfully, children lack the skill and strength to turn their immensely powerful desires into action. Socialisation is the necessary process of learning to control those desires. Where the control breaks down, we also lose control of both the Imaginary – self-image in relation to the surrounding environment – and the Symbolic – the ability to communicate, to form sentences or behave according to social codes. Yet it is those very codes, especially as internalised by the growing child, that stand between us and fulfilment. In place of real satisfactions, we can only grasp the palest shadow, the merest representation of them, the signifier but never the referent. In this way, Lacan brings into psychoanalysis the extraordinarily complex and influential philosophy of Martin Heidegger (1889–1976). Heidegger traces the gradual disappearance from the world of a fullness he believes it had once, in the days of the earliest Greek civilisation. For Lacan this becomes a sense of loss and lack native to humanity which he describes as a *manque à être*, a lack in being. The movement from instinct to drive, and the subsequent tangling of desire and representation, make this condition of lack the human condition. To be human is to suffer a divorce from reality, not only the world's reality but our own. The profound pessimism of the Lacanian dialectic both haunts and is contested by theories of simulation.

2
TECHNOLOGY, INFORMATION AND REASON

(i) Canadians in the global village

The late nineteenth and early twentieth centuries are full of mammoth attempts by cultural historians to answer the question, posed with irrefutable violence by World War I: 'What is civilisation?' Probably the most negative response came from the Dadaists, artists who had fled to neutral Zurich at the height of the European conflagration: civilisation was over, and it was rubbish anyway. Like the images of Auschwitz and Hiroshima a generation later, the blind, shell-shocked, gassed and mutilated victims of the trenches cast a pall over the claims of culture to lead towards morality, justice, beauty and happiness. If European civilisation was the pinnacle of human achievement, why was an entire generation put to slaughter in its name? One of those who returned wounded from that war was a young Canadian officer, Harold A. Innis (1894–1952), who, unlike the Dadaists, sought some kind of redemption for the cultured life (see Angus 1993).

Innis wrote several major works on economic history before turning his hand to a communications theory of civilisation. The global histories of Spengler, Toynbee, Marx and others gave Innis models for an all-embracing account of human history, a story which he would tell in terms not of religion, economics or concepts of time, but of communication technologies. His fundamental thesis is briefly stated in an essay on 'The Bias of Communication':

> A medium of communication has an important influence on the dissemination of knowledge over space and over time. . . . According to its characteristics it may be better suited to the dissemination of knowledge over time than over space, particularly if the medium is heavy and durable and not suited to transportation, or to the dissemination of knowledge over space than over time, particularly if the medium is light and easily transported. The relative emphasis on time or space will imply a bias of signification to the culture in which it is embedded. . . . We can perhaps assume that the use of a medium of communication over a long period will to some extent determine the character of the knowledge to be communicated and suggest that its pervasive influence will eventually create a civilization in which life and flexibility will become exceedingly difficult to maintain. (Innis 1951: 33–4)

Thus civilisations like the Babylonian, reliant on clay tablets and monumental sculpture, are destined to orient themselves towards permanence, time, destiny and continuity, while those which use lightweight materials, like the papyrus-based military empire of the Romans, would tend towards geographical spread, speed in communication, conquest and mobility. A typical example of Innis' innovative approach to histories of communication is his recognition that it is not just carved stone or paper that constitutes a technology, but the types of writing which were used. Innis believed, with many of his generation, that classical Greece had been the highest flowering of human culture. This he relates not only to the technology of writing as such, but to the technological advancement represented by the invention of the alphabet:

> The powerful oral tradition of the Greeks and the flexibility of the alphabet enabled them to resist the tendencies of empire in the East towards absolute monarchism and theocracy. They drove a wedge between the political empire concept with its emphasis on space and the ecclesiastical empire concept with its emphasis on time, and reduced them to the rational proportions of the city-state. The monopoly of complex systems of writing, which had been the basis of large-scale organizations of the East, was destroyed. The adaptability of the alphabet to language weakened the possibilities of uniformity and enhanced the problems of government with fatal results to large-scale political organizations. (Innis 1972: 84)

Like the brief flowering of Elizabethan England, when 'Restrictions on printing facilitated an interest in the drama and the flowering of the oral tradition in the plays of Shakespeare' (Innis 1951: 55), the Greeks benefited from the balance they managed to achieve between the claims of literacy and the traditions of speech – dialogue, discussion, drama, participation and the arts of memory, like the oral tradition we know as Homer's epics.

This distinction between the oral and the written is central to Innis' discussions of communications history. In an essay on 'The Problem of Space' he is quite explicit: 'The oral tradition implies the spirit but writing and printing are inherently materialistic' (Innis 1951: 131), to which he added elsewhere, 'A writing age was essentially an egoistic age' (Innis 1951: 9). Innis sees the spiritual and communal virtues of the oral overcome by the selfish, profit-oriented world of the written. These great general theories touch closely on the development of simulation theory when Innis develops them towards a critique of the contemporary mediascape:

> . . . the art of writing provided man with a transpersonal memory. Men were given an artificially extended and verifiable memory of objects and events not present to sight or recollection. Individuals applied their minds to symbols rather than things and went beyond the world of concrete experience into the world of conceptual relations created within an enlarged time and space universe. The time world was extended beyond the range of remembered things and the space world beyond the range of known places. Writing enormously enhanced a capacity for abstract thinking which had been evident in the growth of language in the oral tradition. (Innis 1972:10)

Thus Innis indicates that the problem of simulation – of a divorce from experience, and thus from reality – is initiated in the first fall from grace represented by the rise of writing. This might remind the reader of the strange mourning for the loss of Being which forms the central theme of

Heidegger's philosophy and haunts the work of many leading French post-structuralists like Lacan, as we saw in Chapter 1. For Innis, the world after oral culture is torn between the temporal, monumental and conservative cultures of ecclesiastical cultures like Egypt and Babylon, and the spatial, swift, imperial cultures of military empires like Rome and, in our time, the print-based empires of the European and North American powers.

For Innis, broadcasting follows and amplifies the powers of print, and in the aftermath of World War II, the urgency of the problem of communication is even greater than after World War I. 'Large scale mechanization of knowledge', he warns, 'is characterized by imperfect competition and the active creation of monopolies in language which prevent understanding and hasten appeals to force' (Innis 1951: 28–9). Thinking of the regionalised structure of the US news industry of the time, but also of European nationalism, he notes that:

> The newspaper with a monopoly over time was limited in its power over space because of its regional character. Its monopoly was characterized by instability and crises. The radio introduced a new phase in the history of Western Civilization by emphasizing centralization and the necessity of a concern with continuity. The bias of communication in paper and the printing industry was destined to be offset by the bias of the radio. Democracy . . . was destined to be offset by planning and bureaucracy. (Innis 1951: 60)

Here Innis notes the similarities between the USSR and the USA, both ostensibly committed to equality and some form of democracy, but both equally gripped by the necessity of planning. A crucial test for any theory of modern communications is the notorious use of radio by the Nazi Party in Germany before and during World War II. Innis' observations are crucial:

> Political boundaries related to the demands of the printing industry disappeared with the new instrument of communication. The spoken language provided a new base for the exploitation of nationalism and a far more effective device for appealing to larger numbers. Illiteracy was no longer a serious barrier. . . . In some sense the problem of the German people is the problem of Western civilization. As modern developments in communication have made for greater realism they have made for greater possibilities of delusion. (Innis 1951: 81–2)

In the Nazi period in Germany, Innis, like the members of the Frankfurt School (see section iii below), sees not just the result of an aberrant and temporary mass hysteria but the focused shock of a global crisis of modern culture. The processes that abstracted human thought from human experience through the invention of writing have produced, through the mechanisation of knowledge in the print industries and the centralising powers of broadcasting, an extreme disruption even of the logical, rational structures associated with abstract thought, to leave us prey to a planned world without democracy, and a culture as easily composed of illusions and irrationality as of community and care. 'Mass production and standardization are the enemies of the West', he concludes his book on *Empire and Communications*. 'The limitations of mechanization of the printed and the spoken word must be emphasized and determined efforts to recapture the vitality of the oral tradition must be made' (Innis 1972: 169–70).

The oral/literate distinction would also be of central importance for Innis' fellow Torontonian Marshal McLuhan (1911–80). McLuhan would extend the distinction, towards an audible–tactile/linear–visual distinction in the first of his key works, *The Gutenberg Galaxy* (1962), through cool and hot media in *Understanding Media* (1964), to end up with a biological account of right and left hemispheres of the brain associated with the different families of media in the co-authored and posthumous *The Global Village* (1989). Though McLuhan presents the first of these books as 'a footnote of explanation' to Innis' work (McLuhan 1962: 50), his emphasis after *Gutenberg* is much more on the contemporary scene, with extensive discussions of photography and film as linear, fragmented and mechanised forms that mimic the printed media, while television, radio and, latterly, computer networks are the emblematic media of a new communications order in which the lost community of oral society is reintroduced electronically, this time on a global scale. The main outlines of this theory are well known and widely debated by media scholars (an influential early critique is in Williams 1974; Winston 1998 doesn't mention McLuhan by name, but is a sustained critique of his legacy among media historians). For McLuhan, 'cultural ecology has a reasonably stable base in the human sensorium, and . . . any extension of the human sensorium by technological dilation has a quite appreciable affect in setting up new ratios or proportions among all the senses' (McLuhan 1962: 35). Culture is based in the biology of the human organism, but any new technology acts as an extension of the basic organs – the wheel is an extension of the feet, radio is an extension of the ear. So each new technology alters the relationship between human senses, exaggerating one, diminishing the relative importance of another. And this, in turn, impacts on the culture based on the ratio of the senses, skewing it towards the feet or the ear. McLuhan also dips into information theory (see section ii below) with the idea that any medium is more important *as a medium* than the messages which it is used to transfer. That is, the nature of the medium – oral, visual, auditory, tactile – influences so profoundly the kind of message that can be framed in it that it is far more important to investigate the medium than its messages – cinema rather than films, printing rather than books, television rather than programmes. The medium is the message (McLuhan 1964: 15).

Within this overarching description of human history as something determined by its technologies, rather than by God's will, economics or politics, McLuhan lays some of the foundations for later simulation theorists. The present day is for him, as for Innis, a battleground between the powers of the literate culture associated with Gutenberg's invention of printing, and the new oral cultures of the electronic global village. He locates the 'great paradox of the Gutenberg era, that its seeing activism is cinematic in the strict movie sense. It is a consistent series of static shots or "fixed points of view" in homogeneous relationship. Homogenization of men and materials will become the great program of the Gutenberg era' (McLuhan 1962: 127). 'Print created national uniformity and government centralism, but also individualism and opposition to government as such'

(McLuhan 1962: 235); that is, print media are responsible for the egoism described by Innis, and both for the anti-democratic movement towards centralisation, and for the resistance against it: both are aspects of the same world-view, 'The new time sense of typographic man . . . cinematic and sequential and pictorial' (McLuhan 1962: 241).

McLuhan is, however, profoundly optimistic. Having dealt with the history of print in *Gutenberg*, he announces at the beginning of its companion volume:

> After three thousand years of explosion, by means of fragmentary and mechanical technologies, the Western world is imploding . . . abolishing both space and time. . . . Rapidly, we approach the final phase of the extensions of man – the technological simulation of consciousness, when the creative process of knowing will be collectively and corporately extended to the whole of human society. . . .
> (McLuhan 1964: 11)

Yet this experience of implosion, so important to simulation theory, is not entirely without adverse consequences:

> Electric speed in bringing all social and political functions together in a sudden implosion has heightened human awareness of responsibility to an intense degree. . . . This is the Age of Anxiety for the reason of the electric implosion that compels commitment and participation, quite regardless of any 'point of view'.
> (McLuhan 1964: 13)

Again, the sense of compulsion towards participation will be picked up in later simulation theory as a crucial aspect of postmodern societies.

McLuhan believes that the anxious years of accommodation to the new media will soon be achieved, bringing with them an almost ecological sense of 'total human interdependence' (McLuhan 1962: 276). At the same time, however, 'The effect of electric technology had at first been anxiety. Now it appears to create boredom' (McLuhan 1962: 35), or indeed worse: there are many passages where McLuhan points up frightening prospects for industrial civilisation. 'Once we have surrendered our senses and nervous systems to the private manipulation of those who would try to benefit from taking a lease on our eyes and ears and nerves, we don't really have any rights left', he argues (McLuhan 1964: 79). Instead we become victims of myth, which he defines as 'contraction or implosion of any process, and the instant speed of electricity confers the mythic dimension on ordinary industrial and social action today' (McLuhan 1964: 34). Computerisation brings an intensification of these processes, for good or ill. 'The poet Stephane Mallarmé', McLuhan recalls, 'thought "the world exists to end in a book". We are now in a position to go beyond that and to transfer the entire show to the memory of a computer' (McLuhan 1964: 70). While this process might lead towards a unification of all humanity into a single consciousness, there are also issues of power and oppression to confront. In the context of a discussion of the behavioural psychologist B.F. Skinner in *War and Peace in the Global Village*, McLuhan suggests that,

Unlike animals, man has no nature but his own history – his total history. Electronically, this total history is now potentially present in a kind of simultaneous transparency. . . . We have been rapt into 'the artifice of eternity' by the placing of our own nervous system around the entire globe. The first satellite ended 'nature' in the old sense. Nature became the content of a man-made environment. From that moment, all terrestrial phenomena were to become increasingly programmed artifacts. . . . (McLuhan and Fiore 1968: 177–8)

This programming of the planet is thinkable because of the rise of networked consciousness in the age of electronic media, especially the computer, whose

true function is to program and orchestrate terrestrial and galactic environments and energies in a harmonious way. For centuries the lack of symmetry and proportion in all these areas has created a sort of universal spastic condition for lack of inter-relation between them. In merely terrestrial terms, programming the environment means, first of all, a kind of console for global thermostats to pattern all sensory life in a way conducive to comfort and happiness. (McLuhan and Fiore 1968: 89–90)

The spasms that have afflicted the fragmented, print-dominated consciousness of Gutenberg Man like the flickering of a poorly projected movie can be soothed and homogenised, programmed by the new media-conscious social science. Yet, as McLuhan observes in his most famous book, *The Medium is the Massage*, actuality does not bear out the more utopian aspects of this safe, calm, post-historical programme. Instead, according to McLuhan, because of a failure to adapt to the new media, governments have pledged their new technologies to the old purposes of empire: 'Real, total war has become information war. It is being fought by subtle electronic media – under cold conditions, and constantly. The cold war is the real war front – a surround – involving everybody – all the time – everywhere' (McLuhan and Fiore 1967: 138). As we shall see, such words of warning in Innis and McLuhan's work – despite the general optimism of the message – as well as their emphasis on the formative role of the media in contemporary society, have been major inspirations for the development of simulation theory.

(ii) Information and efficiency

It was not only sociologists and historians who turned to media analysis after World War II. Huge numbers of engineers were involved in the development of the new electronic networks which would transform the mediascape in the years after 1945. Few have had a more impressive impact on both social theory and the design of new technologies than Claude E. Shannon (b. 1916), an engineer with Bell Laboratories. During the 1940s, Shannon noted the similarities between the symbolic algebra devised in the mid-nineteenth century by the Irish mathematician George Boole, a mathematical language for expressing logical statements, and the types of switches used for connecting and disconnecting elements of a network. As the use of telephones boomed in the post-war years, Bell were faced with the economic imperative to replace human switchboard operators with switching technology. Shannon's mathematical theory of communication (Shannon and Weaver 1949) not only allowed them to make their human switches redundant but also paved the way for the logic gates of contemporary computers.

Though he set out only to provide a basis for the efficient delivery of messages, Shannon's method of abstraction actually furnished a general theory of information. The theory deals with order and disorder: how does an ordered message survive in a disordered or 'noisy' environment? How certain can we be that what we receive is what was sent? To deal with these issues mathematically, Shannon developed a vocabulary widely used today: sender, receiver, encoding and decoding, channel, noise. To do their mathematical job, these terms have to be considered at their most abstract, so that Shannon and his colleague Warren Weaver had to argue that the nature of the channel did not matter: the unique factor of the channel was the ratio of signal (message) to noise, and the amount of redundancy involved, where redundancy refers to those elements of a message unnecessary to its sending and reception, such as repetition. Information theory also introduced statistical approaches to probability in describing communication: after the first few words, you can probably guess how this sentence will end. On the other hand, a message with a lot of new material in it will not be so easy to predict, and its conclusion will be more uncertain. Surprisingly, Shannon's central equation takes the same form as the famous law Second Law of Thermodynamics, the 'law of entropy' that states that energy tends to dissipate over time (Campbell 1982: 16–19). Shannon's information theory holds likewise that information tends to disintegrate over time, or, to put it another way, it takes energy to maintain order, and therefore information, in a system. The human body requires food and water so that the information holding its molecules together can be maintained. Take away the energy, and the body dies and its molecules go their separate ways.

Shannon's ideas were developed by the mathematician Norbert Wiener (1894–1964), who coined the term 'cybernetics'. The word derives from the Greek word for steersman, and Wiener argued that any homeostatic system, that is, any system which maintains itself in a stable form, must have some form of steersman to correct any deviation from its internal order and its relation with its environment. This mechanism is feedback, named for the effect generated by holding a microphone in front of a loudspeaker, so that input and output reinforce and interfere with one another. A typical feedback device is the thermostat attached to central heating: sensing the ambient temperature, it responds by switching the heating on or off. Likewise riding a bike or photographing a bird in flight demand constant muscular readjustments (Wiener 1961: 112–15). According to Wiener, such feedback loops govern not only such small-scale events as our interactions with the environment, but also the way in which species evolve, ensuring that the environment feeds back to variant organisms the message of their success or failure (Wiener 1950: 28–47). In social terms, Wiener, dreading the return of social catastrophe in the wake of World War II, saw communications as the war of order against entropy. With these fundamental tools, Shannon and Wiener effected a revolution in science: no longer would matter and energy be enough to describe the universe – we would also have to take account of information (see Hayles 1999 for a recent account of the cultural impact of information science).

Indeed it is the reconceptualisation of genetics in the light of information theory that has led to the extraordinary flowering of the life sciences at the turn of the millennium. Shannon's work on the idea of codes focused on their efficiency. The alphabet, with twenty-four symbols, could easily create uncertainty, whereas the zeros and ones of binary code used in computers were much less ambiguous. When Crick and Watson deciphered the double-helix structure of DNA, they did so clambering on the shoulders of hundreds of scientists who had already worked out that DNA, the molecule responsible for inheritance in all living things, was composed of chains of only four substances, adenine, guanine, cytosine and thymine, A, G, C and T for short. Combined into three-element 'bases' (AGT, CCA . . .), these four components can be understood as a code, in this case one for switching on or off the manufacture of proteins in the cells of the living body. Human DNA has about a hundred thousand genes, and around three thousand million As, Gs, Cs and Ts. The breakthroughs that have allowed the development of gene mapping, of genetic engineering, DNA finger-printing and biotechnology all rest on the theory of DNA as an information system. Among our key theorists, Jean Baudrillard, in particular, draws on the concept of the DNA code in his writings, especially the concept of recombination, the process of shuffling genes when organisms reproduce, mixing the genetic heritage of the parents (Jones 1994: 58).

This new concept of the molecular structure of inheritance, of DNA as communicating a message from one generation to the next, relies on a further development in information theory, the concept of systems. Shannon's theory was essentially linear, addressing the process of sending and receiving. Wiener added the feedback principle to provide a cyclical structure. Systems theorists like Gregory Bateson (1972) insisted that communication was always complex and inter-related, cyclical rather than linear, and that breakdowns in communication revealed systemic flaws in social relations as a whole, as in cases of culture shock or misunderstandings between the sexes. Systems theory, with its interest in homeostatic systems, can be linked to the new conditions of the Cold War and the ideologies of the balance of power, collective security and mutually assured destruction (Mattelart and Mattelart 1998: 48; see also Edwards 1996). As we will see, systems theory also plays powerfully into the discourse of simulation, and develops further with its successor theories of chaos and complexity, which argue that under certain conditions, turbulent, chaotic and apparently entropic systems can generate new levels of order spontaneously (see among others Dyson 1988; Gleick 1987; Prigogine and Stenghers 1998; Waldrop 1992).

Information and systems theory has had an enormous impact on our understanding of natural and human phenomena from meteorology to the global economy, and it forms the basis of the kind of computer modelling which we will investigate in the case studies in Section 2. Computers themselves are unthinkable outside the history of information science: courses in computing are frequently called 'Information Technology', and it is not at all unusual to hear our period of history described as the information society. It's a little more surprising to realise that the most powerful school of psychology in the contemporary world, cognitive science, is also based firmly in information theory. Cognitive science developed as a reaction to the dominant behaviourist school of psychology during the 1950s, a line of thought that believed only what could be seen and measured in humanity: its behaviour. Since 'mind' cannot be observed, the behaviourists did without a concept of mind, and instead tried to develop a stimulus–response theory, based on observing how our environments confront us as stimuli, and how we respond to them (see Skinner 1971). One of the first to break with this tradition was the linguist Noam Chomsky (b. 1928).

Chomsky noted two central facts about language. Firstly, just about every sentence anyone ever speaks or writes is unique. And secondly, children learn not only how to imitate, but also how to develop new sentences from the limited list of available words and grammatical constructions available in the language they pick up. On the basis of these facts, Chomsky insists that language is not a set pattern of responses which the infant learns to imitate, but that there is an innate capacity for language which children learn to use in the context of the actual language spoken around them (Chomsky 1957, 1965, 1972). In pursuit of the universal grammar inborn in human beings, Chomsky and his associates analysed the structures of many different languages, in each case seeking out the fundamental logical structure, the system of the language itself, and the way in which it uses a small group of transformations to express the deep structure of thought in the actual words and syntax of a real sentence.

Chomsky's approach not only revolutionised linguistics, it suggested to a generation of psychologists that there must be similar models innate in the biology of the brain which shape our capacity for perception, calculation and all the other factors which make us human. A characteristic of cognitive science is to argue that the human brain itself is hardwired in such a way that it gives rise to such typical human activities as speech, story-telling, investigation and planning. In this way, cognitive science links together linguistics, neurobiology, psychology and information theory to produce a concept of the mind as a biological organ characterised by its ability to create models of the world it inhabits. These models might take the form of mental maps or they may look like presuppositions. The film critic David Bordwell, for example, explains our interest in movie narratives as a result of our habit of forming hypotheses about the characters and the events we see, and guessing what will happen next (see, for example, Bordwell 1985,

1989). We create models of the likely outcomes, and measure our map of events against what we are shown next. In this sense, cognitive science is not only a child of information theory, but a clear relative of at least certain forms of simulation.

Cognitive science is also deeply involved with the comparison between the human mind and computers. The comparison works both ways: computers are today being designed taking into account what we know about the workings of the brain, especially the idea of parallel processing, according to which the brain splits tasks into smaller subroutines which are parcelled out to different parts of the brain to process simultaneously. This concept has been especially influential in the development of artificial intelligence research (see Minsky 1985), but also in at least some influential accounts of human consciousness (see Dennett 1991, 1996; Johnson-Laird 1993). As Howard Gardner observes, 'Since the first generation of cognitive scientists, the computer has served as the most available and the most appropriate model for thinking about thinking' (Gardner 1987: 385), but by the same token the computer as model has emphasised only the most highly structured and orderly elements of consciousness, like Chomsky's rules of transformational grammar. The most important factor, from our point of view, is that cognitive science has tended towards a definition of the human mind as an information-processing system, and one which, moreover, uses representations, models or simulations of the world in order to solve problems and plan actions. In this way psychology joins biology, social science and communication studies in focusing on information systems as the hallmark of our world and our contemporary understandings of it. But simulation theory, inspired as it is by such developments in the scientific culture, has also taken a great deal from critiques of scientific discourse, critiques to which we now turn.

(iii) The retreat from utopia

In the same way that technological historians and information theorists were influenced by the histories through which they lived, so sociologists and philosophers who turned their gaze towards the changing nature of mass society in the twentieth century had to cope with war, genocide and technological nightmares. Where nineteenth-century thinkers wanted to understand how things could be made better, their twentieth-century counterparts had to address fascism, nuclear arms and ecological disaster, and ask themselves why people collude in their own oppression. Intensely concerned with such questions, and very significant to the development of simulation theory, the Frankfurt School was established in the 1930s in Germany but driven into exile by the Nazis, eventually spending the war years in the USA. Max Horkheimer (1895–1973), Theodor W. Adorno (1903–69), Siegfried Kracauer (1889–1966), Walter Benjamin (1892–1940) and, in a second generation, Herbert Marcuse (1898–1979) and Jürgen Habermas

(b. 1926) were among the leading figures of the School, which developed Critical Theory, an attempt to marry Marxism, Freud (and later cognitive psychology) with the late nineteenth- and early twentieth-century social theories of Max Weber and Georg Simmel as a way of escaping the narrow confines of 'vulgar' Marxism in pursuit of a political analysis of contemporary culture.

As befits a group so heavily persecuted themselves, the Frankfurt School are by and large frankly pessimistic about human civilisation, Adorno, for example, going so far as to argue that 'To write poetry after Auschwitz is barbaric' (Adorno 1967: 34). His friend the mystical Jewish radical Benjamin had argued in an immensely influential essay on 'The Work of Art in the Age of Mechanical Reproduction' (Benjamin 1969a) and in other essays written before his suicide while fleeing Nazi persecution (see Benjamin 1973, 1979) that the new media technologies were instruments for the democratisation of culture. Adorno countered in a letter that high and low culture were 'the two torn halves of an integral freedom, to which however they do not add up' (Adorno 1977: 123). Avant-garde art had pursued its autonomy from the claims of church and state to such an extent that it no longer addressed real life, while popular culture was slave to commerce and the mechanisation of daily life. Adorno and Horkheimer's experiences in the USA confirmed their worst suspicions: Nazism was just an exaggerated form of a culture which now embraced the whole of the industrialised world, a culture characterised by standardisation and repetition.

Though now unfashionable, Horkheimer and Adorno's critique of the 'culture industry' (Horkheimer and Adorno 1973) instigates an important line of criticism implicit in simulation theory concerning the nature of technology. Science and technology have fallen under the control of capitalism, and the enlightened rationality that underpins them has become an instrument of oppression. This 'instrumental reason', the highest powers of the human mind turned into an instrument of power and exploitation, characterises the modern period so thoroughly that, in Adorno's case, the only response is pure 'negativity', the refusal of everything about our time. Not even social sciences are immune: sociological -analysis has itself been turned into the instrument of opinion polling, market research and advertising. In the writings of Herbert Marcuse, especially his *One-Dimensional Man* (Marcuse 1964), this extension of technological and instrumental reason into every area of society has generated a total rationalism in which freedom – of worship, of speech, of enterprise – has been reduced to the freedom to conform. In this sense, he can argue that contemporary society is in fact totalitarian.

This critique of totalitarianism and of reason would be one of the great themes of the postmodernist critics who emerged during the 1980s. The philosopher Jean-François Lyotard's essay on *The Postmodern Condition* (Lyotard 1984), for example, argues that the modern period had been dominated by rationalism, the idea of technological progress and faith in the emancipation of human beings from superstition and political oppression.

The postmodern, by contrast, no longer believes in these 'grand narratives' of history. Largely inspired by the failure of the social movements of the late 1960s to secure a revolutionary change in society, this postmodern critique replaced the Frankfurt criticism of capitalism with a bitterly anti-Marxist stance, blaming Marxism and socialism for their belief in planning an administered society, for the repression of women, migrants and ex-colonised peoples, for a faith in technology that had produced ecological catastrophes, and for a rationalist mindset whose faith in the future had trampled over the aspirations of the present. An important ingredient of this postmodernisation of theoretical discourse was the concept, first voiced by the US conservative sociologist Daniel Bell (1973), of the post-industrial society, in which the powers of production which formed the centre of Marxism are replaced by an economy based on information.

Bell had made his name with a work arguing that class could no longer be seen as a clear-cut division in a society of consumers, and that therefore we were living after the 'end of ideology' (Bell 1962). Building on this theme, Lyotard argues that there is therefore no clear goal for class struggle, the central historical engine of Marxist histories. The US critic Fredric Jameson would extend this argument to suggest that postmodernism is characterised by the loss of 'depth' models (for example, the idea that truth and reality are available under the surface of false ideological knowledge) and the consequent collapse of any sense of authentic experience or expression (Jameson 1991). Postmodern culture revels in the superficial and the artificial. Information technologies have been seen as instrumental in this historical development. A society based on information is one based on representations, but those representations are not images of authentic reality: they are more like the entries in the catalogue of a planetary archive. Postmodern cultural production is then not about representing the world, but about reordering the catalogue of existing representations. In a world saturated with media, the media mediate not reality but other media, representing representations of representations in an endless chain lacking the older, modernist belief in an ultimate grounding in objective reality. A central question for simulation theory in this context would then be whether this is a necessary or a happy result.

Many themes in contemporary thought feed into simulation theory. The critique of representation raised by semiotics initiates the new doubts raised by simulation theorists concerning the nature and standing of reality and subjectivity. Marx's critique of the commodity shows how a certain unreality inhabits everyday life. Psychoanalytic concepts undermine the centrality of the conscious, rational mind. Semiotics places consciousness as the effect of the matrix of social and cultural structures. Innis' concern with the spatialising tendencies of contemporary media and the consequent loss of temporal perspective leads towards the 'end of history'. McLuhan's technological determinism leads towards a belief in the powers of the media to alter the consciousness of a whole epoch. Information theory and concepts of the information society not only underpin computer simulation, but also provide crucial understandings of the systemic nature of human relationships. And the critique of instrumental reason among the Frankfurt School leads directly to the attack on Marxism as the last great historical liberation movement. We might have dwelt on other themes: obvious candidates are the sociology of consumerism and the fragmentary, montage methodology developed by Walter Benjamin as a way of understanding the growth of urban cultures (see Buck-Morss 1989). What I hope to have achieved in these opening chapters is an account of the intellectual roots of simulation theory which grounds it in the history of the twentieth century, and provides the reader with some of the tools necessary to grapple with the often dense and allusive prose of simulation theory proper.

3

THE POETICS OF PESSIMISM

(i) Guy Debord: dialectics and spectacle

> Daily life is governed by an economic system in which the production and consumption of insults tends to balance out.
>
> (Raoul Vaneigem, *The Revolution of Everyday Life*)

Sometime during the afternoon of Wednesday, 30 November 1994, a reclusive 62-year-old alcoholic committed suicide in the Haute-Loire district of France. By his own estimate, more than half of those Guy Debord (1931–94) knew well had been in prison, sometimes more than once. An 'uncommonly high percentage' of his friends had died violently (Debord 1991: 16). Revolutionary, drunkard, director of obscure films, pamphleteer, prose stylist of 'chill eloquence' (Macey n.d.), Debord brought the savagery of the post-war avant-gardes to the philosophical critique of politics in one of the most influential books of the later twentieth century, *The Society of the Spectacle*, a short, brilliant and devastating attack on the enormous lie of contemporary social life, seen at the time as the script for the near revolution of May 1968. *The Society of the Spectacle* is the opening salvo of simulation theory. And though its dialectical method and belief in eventual emergence from the 'pre-history' of capitalism were to become the targets which later simulationists, especially Baudrillard, would try to defuse and destroy, it is impossible to understand them without understanding Debord's 221 theses, the series of aphorisms that make up his book. At the heart of the book is a theme aptly summarised by Steven Best:

> Marx spoke of the degradation of *being into having*, where creative praxis is reduced to the mere possession of an object, rather than its imaginative transformation, and where emotions are reduced to greed. Debord speaks of a further reduction, the tranformation of *having into appearing*, where the material object gives way to its representation as sign. (Best 1994: 48)

To understand how Debord's sometimes cryptic, always thorny arguments arrive at this radical, and in some ways radically pessimistic, summary of the existing state of affairs, we will have to take a brief course in dialectics.

You could say that modern European history, especially World War II and the Cold War that followed, was a struggle between political tendencies over the correct interpretation of Hegel (see Cassirer 1946: 249), the most politically influential philosopher of modern times. Georg Wilhelm Friedrich Hegel (1770–1831) based his mammoth philosophical system of interconnected ideas on a very particular concept of history. The entire universe and all its doings since the Creation are the unfolding of Reason. God, the Absolute, is the universal Reason, and the world is not just a reflection of that World Spirit, but also the historical map of its evolution, the living process of Reason becoming manifest in the history of the world. Before the creation, God was radically incomplete: by creating the world and especially in creating human beings, God can make his abstract, purely logical rationality known in its fullness as a process of development and eventual fulfilment. In the innumerable events of human history, Hegel perceives vast conflicts not between individuals but within the historical movements of thought, reason and the Absolute:

> These vast congeries of volitions, interests, and activities constitute the tools and means of the World Spirit for attaining its purpose, bringing it to consciousness and realizing it. . . . Reason governs the world and has consequently governed its history. In relation to this reason, which is universal and substantial, in and for itself, all else is subordinate, subservient and the means for its realization. (Hegel 1953: 31)

Whatever happens in history is ultimately for the good, since history is the process of God's becoming real ('being realised'): in the end, everything which is irrational (and therefore both inessential and evil) will simply have ceased to exist. So God, the World Spirit, moves from raw, abstract existence to the full reality of self-knowledge through his materialisation in Nature, his unfolding through History and his eventual self-knowledge. But how can Reason know itself? At the end of the historical process, human reason recognises in the historical record the tale of Reason's self-revelation, in a moment in which human and absolute reason become the same. Hegel was in the enviable position of discovering that the whole universe had existed solely so that he could discover, in his mighty philosophical system, the purpose behind history.

Hegel may have thought he had the secret of the universe wrapped up, but there was still the problem of how to interpret his philosophical legacy. The 'Right' Hegelians, politically conservative, admired Hegel's belief in the fundamental rightness of the world as it now exists; the 'Left' Hegelians, by contrast, were far more interested in the revolutionary method by which, according to Hegel, the world spirit progressed through a series of twists and turns, moves and countermoves, assertions and negations, theses and antitheses: the process of the dialectic. According to Hegel, God, finding his abstraction incomplete, alienates himself from himself as his creation, Nature. Here a second contradiction comes into play, between the natural and the supernatural. Man is the next step of this dialectic, resolving the spatial problem of a God set face-to-face with himself in the form of nature. Man arrives as the *temporal* being, overcoming the pure power of *space* with the machinery of *time*. But this too creates a gulf between the human and the divine conceptions of time, and we are set for the next twists, the next overcomings, the next syntheses, of a process of perpetual conflict, contradiction and innovation. History then has not only a goal – the realisation of the Absolute's self-knowledge – but also a logical structure comprising thesis, antithesis (the contradiction) and synthesis (the resolution or, more properly, the overcoming) that instigates the next stage of the process.

In a reading of Hegel which would be extremely influential among French intellectuals, Alexandre Kojève argues that the guiding principle of the Hegelian dialectic is its negativity (Kojève 1969: 169): the principle that everything must be in some way 'overcome' if it is to realise its full potential. An apple, for example, must cease to be an apple (by being eaten) in order to fulfil its destiny. Even the highest human achievements, or the loftiest natural phenomena, only achieve their true significance when we understand that they have to overcome and be overcome: forests must be cleared for cities to be built, the religion of the cathedral builders must be annihilated before the cinema can be invented. Likewise, common-sense ideas must be overthrown in the pursuit of science, and science ploughed under in the cultivation of truth. Just as the laws of thermodynamics take us away from everyday understandings of how things work, so dialectical philosophy takes us beyond science, most especially because, as Herbert Marcuse has it, 'All facts embody the knower as well as the doer' (Marcuse 1960: viii). In other words, in dialectics, the scientific separation of the viewing, knowing, acting subject and the passive, known object is dissolved: a 'fact' is as much a subjective as an objective event, a moment of a process in which world and mind move slowly towards one another.

This dialectical process, however, is not a calm and stately progress but a matter of conflict, struggle and contradiction. It was this aspect of dialectical thinking that inspired the young Karl Marx. Here, for example, are his thoughts on money:

> Money, which is the external, universal means and power . . . to turn imagination into reality and reality into mere imagination, similarly turns real human and natural powers into purely abstract representations, and therefore imperfections and tormenting phantoms, just as it turns real imperfections and phantoms – truly impotent powers which exist only in the individual's fancy – into real essential powers and abilities. (Marx 1975a: 378)

Here in the 1844 Manuscripts, Marx tussles with the material basis of the distinction between demand and need: demand, supplied with money, can take active possession, even of things it does not really require, while need without money remains entirely in the realm of thought. Money can thus turn the rich man's passing fancy into reality, but the poor man's urgent requirements into torturing, ungraspable figments of imagination. Money, for Marx, is dialectical. But it is also, vitally for us, the basis of the simulation.

Dialectical thinking brings with it two more fundamental premises: firstly, that it is possible to consider the existence of a partial truth as well as an absolute one, that is, a truth which is good for a certain duration or occasion but inadequate at another time or place. And, secondly, that ideas have a role in the making and changing of history. This second statement is true even of Marx, for whom it is not the Absolute Spirit who creates the world in an act of self-alienation, but humanity. As Hegel writes, 'philosophy should understand, that its content is nothing other than *actuality*' (Hegel 1977: ¶ 6: 8): experience forms the basic content, but philosophy works on this raw material to form ideas, which in turn have the status of raw material for the next level of dialectics. Likewise, in consuming and negating the natural world by transforming it into goods, people also transform themselves, under the conditions of class society, as the goods they have made escape them to become an alien reality, no longer part of them but bought and sold as separate objects over which their makers have no further power (see Taylor 1979: 140–54).

Fresh from the neo-Dadaist avant-gardes of lettrisme and COBRA, Guy Debord took all these heady concepts – of history as dialectic, of money as the origin of an illusory economy, of conflict and contradiction, of the worker whose products have become strangers to him – and threaded them into a new theory of society. During the post-war years, France had been the home of existentialism, a philosophy of life whose big question concerned how to retain one's individual freedom. During the 1950s a new school developed, structuralism, which asked how it was that people colluded in their own oppression. It is almost possible to distinguish them by saying that existentialism was a philosophy of the resistance, trying to understand how people fought on without hope; structuralism wanted to understand the mentality of collaboration, why people assisted their oppressors during the war and succumbed to political and social norms after it. Intriguingly, one influential aspect of structural thought came from Louis Althusser, leading ideologue of the Communist Party of France, whose crusade was against the young Marx and all forms of Hegelianism. It was against all of these that Debord set out, in 1967, to write the definitive tract of contemporary revolution, against both communist and capitalist, proposing instead of individual freedom or social submission a revolution of social freedom. In the process, he would lay the foundations for the contemporary theory of simulation in the politicised concept of the spectacle.

It is nearly impossible to summarise *The Society of the Spectacle*. Already an intensely compressed, aphoristic, fat-free book, it contains only the lean, tough meat of a brutal probe into the falsity of contemporary society. France especially had already confronted this inauthenticity in the work of the influential philosopher Jean-Paul Sartre, who not only had the benefit of an audience whose schooling included compulsory classes in philosophy, but who chose to write some of his most important attacks on the diminishing of human freedom in the form of novels and plays. For Sartre, the absolute freedom of the individual was paramount, even though that freedom entailed the collapse of all moral systems and the risk of making existence itself meaningless. The fundamental choice for Sartre lay between total commitment to one's own actions, or suffering events to happen to you: the inauthentic existence of someone who has never chosen. That inauthenticity was a hallmark of modern society, and in later years Sartre would identify it with the alienation described by Marx as a fundamental result of the capitalist mode of production. The same recognition, channelled through a vivid and original political philosophy, animates Debord's extraordinary little book.

The existentialist themes of meaninglessness and alienation initiated by Sartre are taken to a new level with Debord's insistence that the spectacular society, 'the autonomous movement of the non-living' (Debord 1977: ¶ 2),[1] the dominance of a consumer capitalism governed by the circulation of images, is now the unifying characteristic of all contemporary societies, East and West, North and South. In 1967, under the conditions of the Cold War, Debord saw two varieties of spectacle, respectively endorsed by capitalism in the West and communism in the East, the two forms battling for the souls of Third World bureaucracies (Debord 1977: ¶ 113). In 1988 when he wrote his *Comments on the Society of the Spectacle* (Debord 1990), after the advent of perestroika and glasnost, he saw both forms of spectacle amalgamated in a single 'integrated spectacle', global in its aspirations. The spectacle is the dominant form of social regulation, he argues. Seen from within, it was the regime of images, the replacement of reality by pictures of it (Debord 1977: ¶ 36). Seen from without, it was the dominant form of social relation between people (Debord 1977: ¶ 4). As we saw in Chapter 1.i, Marx had written of the commodity in exactly these terms: human relations seen in 'the fantastic form of a relation between things' (Marx 1976: 164–5). Debord sees this relation metamorphosing into a relation between images of things: no longer objects, but the images associated with them; not a car but an image, the false image, of freedom; not clothes but an image, the false image, of fashion.

To argue his case, Debord draws explicitly on the work of the young Marx, then only recently available to Western readers, and already hemmed in with Communist Party warnings that the dialectical Hegelianism of the *Economic and Philosophical Manuscripts* was juvenile work, incompatible with the full-blown materialism over which they claimed sole ownership. Debord derives from Marx the lightning logic of the dialectic, a constant stream of statements and counterstatements, reversals and perversions of clichés and dogmas. At every turn, Debord notes the partial truths that allow the spectacle to appear plausible and even wholly true, while in fact, he argues, it proceeds by a process of '*détournement*', of turning a legitimate historical tendency towards separation into a means for dehistoricising the present. And once the present has been isolated from history, it can stop changing: the status quo can replenish itself endlessly.

His response is to apply the same principle of *détournement* to the language of the spectacle itself, turning familiar phrases inside out, upside down and back to front in order to reveal the poverty, hypocrisy and deviousness of the spectacular society. For example, in a critique of the

---

1. Because Debord claims no copyright in his own work, there are innumerable versions of the English translation and the French original available, including at least one online. I therefore give references according to Debord's numbering of his paragraphs.

reforms campaigned for by the Communist and Socialist parties of the 1960s, Debord argues that the proletariat, the industrial working class, 'cannot recognise itself in the righting of a large number of wrongs . . . but only in the absolute wrong of being relegated to the margin of life' (Debord 1977: ¶ 114). Here we get a typically double movement. Firstly, the righting of wrongs in the plural – a task we all rally to – confronts the absolute wrong, in the singular, of the spectacle itself. The inference is left implicit: that reformists who want only to improve local and specific problems through free education, pubic holidays and union representation are only lending more credibility to the domination of the spectacle. As a revolutionary, Debord will not accept this kind of bribe, in any case designed to ensure the continuation of the same old alienation and regimentation. Instead, he says, the working class demands a total change in the whole conduct of society: nothing less than reality itself will suffice.

But, and once again this is typical, there is a third movement of the dialectic lurking in this sentence. Its place is marked by the word 'recognize', a crucial term for dialectical thought, as we have already seen in Hegel's World Spirit seeking to recognise itself in history. The spectacle is the great lie: it involves the misrecognition of needs and desires. If the working class is ever to recognise itself, that is, if it is ever to come to know its own reality, it will have to overthrow the social conditions that currently produce its alienation from 'life', its own, real demands. Thus Debord is describing at one and the same time the state of affairs in which the mass of the population are content to be duped by the spectacle, and the more profound dissatisfaction and unhappiness that comes from living a lie. It is not therefore a question of believing that individual workers are demanding a revolution, and more a case of arguing that the proletariat will never be truly at home in the world until it recognises its own alienation by bringing an end to it.

What then of the ruling class? Surely they benefit from the society of the spectacle? In ¶ 143, Debord writes that the ruling class is 'made up of specialists in the ownership of things, who are themselves a possession of things'. Once again we see the technique of *détournement* redirecting the sense of a sentence by reversing the order of its words. Those who are most enamoured of possession are themselves possessed. To grasp the full impact of this apparent paradox, we have to go back to one of the more radical claims of modern philosophy, one we have already come close to in the writing of Herbert Marcuse (see Chapter 2.iii): the claim that things appear to us as things because they have been socially constructed to appear that way. Things or, to use the correct philosophical term, objects only exist for the dialectician because they have become separated from the people who look at them as objects. This process of separation produces both objects and the people who are separated from them, described in the technical language of theory as subjects. Subjectively, then, the world is full of objects, and the ruling class is specialised in a particular relationship with objects, a relationship of ownership. But by becoming subjects that own objects, they define themselves as the subjects of those objects and that relationship, as purely and only their owners. They cannot, for example, meet their objects as equals but only as things, only as items to be counted, consumed, wasted, ignored, hoarded. Whatever they do with their objects must also happen to them, since subject and object come into existence as the torn halves of a single relationship. Even though they have been artificially separated in the society of the spectacle, subject and object are still the matching parts of a primary unit, and their unity still controls the way in which whatever happens to one of them will happen to the other. In this sense even the rulers are victims of the spectacle from which they appear to benefit, and even the rulers are profoundly alienated from the world they control.

Asked why Sartre had not been arrested for his later Marxist escapades, President de Gaulle, comparing Sartre to the scandalously witty protagonist of the French Enlightenment, replied 'One does not imprison Voltaire', thus dealing in a single phrase a death blow to the cause of authenticity. No matter how often he was brought into police custody, no matter how radical his thought or his life, Sartre had become, from that moment on, a brand name. The authenticity which he sought was now a kind of chic, which came with the books and the public image, just as it comes with Yves St Laurent jackets. In the society of the spectacle, even authenticity becomes a marketable *image* of itself. Think, for example, of the 'authentic' voices of inner urban rap artists blaring from the in-car stereos of white suburban youths. Under the terms of the society of the spectacle, you can be as authentic as you wish, indeed it is encouraged in the pursuit of marketable products; but your authenticity can always be recuperated by the simple ploy of patronising it, employing it, redirecting it towards the circulation of images that constitutes the spectacle itself, no longer rage but the spectacle of rage.

Debord looked elsewhere than the tiring mythology of freedom that the existentialists embraced. Instead he turned towards another somewhat unlikely source, the Hungarian philosopher Georg Lukács (1885–1971). A minister in Béla Kun's short-lived revolutionary government in Hungary after World War I, Lukács was deported to Austria, where he wrote *History and Class Consciousness* (Lukács 1971). Later in the 1930s, he would champion the cause of socialist realism against Bertolt Brecht (Bloch et al. 1977), only redeeming himself by taking the post of Minister of Culture in Imre Nagy's once again short-lived government during the Hungarian Uprising against the Soviets in 1956. In particular, *History and Class Consciousness* contains a long, dense, brilliant essay on 'Reification and the Consciousness of the Proletariat' (Lukács 1971: 83–222), inspired, like Debord, by the writings of the young Marx, which would help set Debord on a course apart from the existentialist avant-gardes among whom he had come of age.

Starting from Marx's analysis of the commodity, Lukács turns to the nature of factory work, governed by mechanical time and the division of labour, subordinated to both machinery and 'market laws' over which the worker has no control, a process of specialised tasks in which 'the fragmentation of the object of production necessarily entails the fragmentation of its subject' (Lukács 1971: 89). Because the products of labour appear as discrete objects, disguising the real social relations that produce them, the relationships between objects also disappears, leaving an atomised universe such that neither subjects nor objects, people nor commodities, have either genuine relationships or, for lack of relationships, any genuine individuality. The workers can only contemplate the objects which they have produced.

The word 'contemplation' has a strict philosophical sense in Lukács. Contemplation belongs to the world of pure thought, and Lukács identifies in the classical German philosophical tradition an unavoidable tendency for pure thought to aestheticise the objects of contemplation, a tendency which then either promotes aesthetic contemplation in place of *action* or, as with Hegel, suggests that the world of objects is purely aesthetic and therefore incapable of *change*. The 'immediate' nature of aestheticised facts becomes a kind of moral imperative, so politicians can claim to be 'respecting the facts' when all they want is an alibi for maintaining the status quo. Precisely because it sees itself as the *end* of a historical process of mediation, the dialectical process of thesis, antithesis and synthesis, the capitalist world order presents itself as immediate (Lukács 1971: 156). But if it is immediate, it cannot undergo further mediations: it has left history.

The purpose of the Hegelian dialectic was to reveal that all 'things', all 'facts', are really mediations, moments of a historical process of change (Lukács 1971: 179) in which relations are every bit as important as objects. The Marxist dialectic, Lukács argues, goes further. It demands more than just the new contemplative relation with objects that Hegel had brought about. Instead it demands a new practical relation with objects – not only to observe change but to cause it. 'History', Lukács concludes, 'is the history of the unceasing overthrow of the objective forms that shape the life of men' (Lukács 1971: 186). Like Marx, he believes that contemplative knowledge can only achieve the analysis of individuals in society as it exists today, but that practical knowledge ('praxis') can address the reality of social humanity: in Marx's famous thesis on Feuerbach, 'The philosophers have only *interpreted* the world, in various ways; the point is to *change* it' (Marx 1975b: 423).

The objective nature of objects – including the objectified person of the worker turned into a mechanical connection in a factory and a mechanical consumer of commodities at home – is the first sketch of the spectacle. The world we inhabit is constructed socially in such a way as to appear like a mass of unconnected commodities, including the commodity form of labour which each of us has to sell in order to make a living. Debord makes two significant additions to this analysis of Lukács: he moves from the factory to the world of the post-war consumer, and from the factory worker to the mass of the population. The reach of the spectacle is even more extensive than even Lukács had described it: it inhabits every waking moment, and perhaps even our dreams.

Lukács' translators use the term 'reification' (from the Latin 'to turn into a thing') to describe the worker's experience of becoming an object. Debord takes this reification in the workplace as read. His aim is to show how the same process embraces 'the main part of the time lived outside modern production' (Debord 1977: ¶ 6). The new conditions of consumerism in Europe of the 1960s seemed to promise a better life ahead, and a healing of old social divisions. Sociologists would describe it as the affluent society and would point towards the statistical decline of manufacturing and the rise of service and information sectors – such areas as retailing, local government, education and the management of data in banking, insurance and utilities industries. More leisure time, better social welfare, wider opportunities for education, more and more varied goods in the shops were all taken at the time as evidence of a brave new world: the consumer society. Debord's task was to show that all of this was a cheap sham.

But Debord wanted to do more than this: he wanted to demonstrate that the sham derived from the commodity form at the heart of capitalism, and to show how dangerous and how destructive it had become. Most of all, he wants to show the way in which the spectacle has invaded daily life to such an extent that the very possibility of 'authenticity', of a real experience of reality, has been stolen away. Not only have our subjective experiences been turned into false imitations of real experience, but reality itself has been turned into an imitation of itself: 'reality rises up within the spectacle, and the spectacle is real' (Debord 1977: ¶ 8). There is no outside of the spectacle, no residual reality to which we can appeal. Thus it is no use claiming that the disabled, for example, are misrepresented: to be represented at all is to become spectacular, to sacrifice the claim to truthful experience that could be misrepresented, that there exists some reality fundamentally different from its spectacular representation. The whole of human life is spectacularised, including lived reality. This is why every picture of a wheelchair user becomes at once either a narrative of tragedy, or a narrative of triumph over tragedy, regardless of the actual person and his or her real experience of disability. Nor can we try to contrast the spectacle with some 'genuine need or desire which is not itself shaped by society and its history' (Debord 1977: ¶ 68). The enormous accumulation of commodities is too great for any 'authentic' desire to remain unchanged by it. Instead, we confront within and without 'unlimited artificiality' (Debord 1977: ¶ 68).

Debord's example is someone who collects key chains given away as 'free gifts' in some promotional campaign. Since these key chains have only been made in order to be collected, the collector, by becoming a collector, subjects himself to them, becomes the subject of these objects, submitting himself to these meaningless gadgets. So the collector gathers 'the indulgences of the commodity', a reference to the acquisition of indulgences, for example in the shape of little 'mass cards', by Roman Catholics which promise an alleviation of punishment in the afterlife. From Debord's atheist standpoint, the two practices share the qualities of submission to an unknown mystery and the trivial objects by which that intimacy with the non-existent is celebrated and advertised (Debord 1977: ¶ 67). A contemporary equivalent might be wearing sweatshirts embroidered with their manufacturer's logos, proof, on the one hand, of your loyalty to the brand, but, on the other, of how the brand possesses you, persuading you to act as a spectacular advertisement for its products, and accepting the fetishised commodity which has replaced genuine desire, genuine art and genuine self-expression.

To get to the heart of the spectacle, however, it will be useful to go back one more time to Marcuse's introduction to the revolutionary legacy of Hegel:

> The progress of cognition from common sense to knowledge arrives at a world which is negative in its very structure because that which is real opposes and denies the potentiality inherent in itself – potentialities which themselves strive for realization. Reason is the negation of the negation. (Marcuse 1960: x)

In Marcuse's reading of Hegel's majestic philosophy, reason equates not with the Absolute but with the science of social life, the scientific understanding of how we live as social beings, the science, ultimately, of revolution. This, of course, has nothing in common with Hegel's divine Absolute – nothing, that is, except the concept of negation. The real world is, for Marcuse as it was for Marx, the real world of mass production and the factory workers whose labour supports it, the world of the poor, a world of dirt, danger and disease. That grim reality is a denial of the immense potential of all those lives crushed and wasted by oppression and exploitation. Reason, the reason of revolution, refuses to accept the miserable conditions of the day. By the time Marcuse was writing, only a few years before Debord's book, nothing seemed to have changed in the state of oppression since Marx's times except the machinery for producing it. Beneath the apparent blessings of the consumer society, humanity has still not achieved its potential. We are still unhappy and the source of our unhappiness is still the same: capitalism. Only the means of oppression has changed. Alongside the basic reality of the factory life described by Marx, a new reality has colonised even our unconscious, our dreams and fantasies. That new reality is the realm of the mass media.

But the spectacle is more inclusive than the media we normally think of. It includes not only TV, radio, cinema and pop music; it embraces the fine arts and education, advertising and architecture, packaging and industrial design, fashion, sport and festivals. As a result of these new forms of communication, the contemporary world is doubly unreal. It is unreal first, as it was for Marx, because of the brutality with which it extinguishes the creativity of those who work in the factory system and live in its slums. But it is unreal a second time because everything we see and understand has been given a false gloss of the image, the hypocritical glamour of the spectacle. These unreal realities are negative, in the sense that they negate not once but twice over the human possibilities they have covered over with exploitation and lies.

The initial task of the spectacle is to encourage consumption. By the time Debord came to write, however, that task had been more than fulfilled: people were already skilled, even compulsive, consumers, and it was this aspect of life that drove him to revolutionary rage. Consumption has become compulsory, he argues (Debord 1977: ¶ 42–3). Consumerism was needed at first to cope with a curious crisis that capitalism undergoes from time to time: a crisis of overproduction. It's not that unusual to hear of butter mountains, wine lakes and the dumping of 'excess' harvests at sea: this morning as I got ready to write, there was another report of 'overproduction' in South Africa's vineyards, as if to emphasise the point. Dumping and hoarding are two ways of coping with the crisis, keeping the product scarce and the prices high. But consumerism achieves a more regulated solution to the crisis, by encouraging us to buy more things, even when we don't need or even want them, and preparing us to throw them away again in order to replace them with new commodities. What consumerism seeks to supply is a regulated programme of overconsumption designed to cope with industrial overproduction. A simple example is the plastic bag. There cannot be a home in the industrial world that isn't plagued by an infestation of packaging, wrappers and carrier bags, yet every time we shop, we accumulate more of them. Many serve no purpose at all: why wrap an orange? The packaging industry produces almost nothing but pure waste. A second example is junk mail. When consumer protection groups attempted to curb the quantities of unwanted advertising that has so swamped the US Mail as to earn it the nickname 'snail mail', their case was eventually thrown out by the Supreme Court, who ruled that unsolicited papers thrust though your letterbox are protected by the First Amendment to the US Constitution, the law that protects freedom of speech. Again, unwanted and useless products that go straight into the bin. The one purpose of these products, plastic wrappers and junk mail, is to keep their industries – and incidentally the recycling industry – in business. Here capitalist production has gone way beyond any attempt to respond to human needs for clothing, food and shelter, and entered a cycle of pure waste whose only function is to keep on functioning. At the same time, we have learnt to believe that any job is better than none, that the functioning of even the most inane and stupid industries is better than increased leisure time, that it is the function of factories not to manufacture things we need, but to manufacture jobs. This is why Debord is able to say that the whole of society, even factory production, has become spectacular. It has lost any sense of reality in the circular logic of industries that produce jobs and the absurdity of compulsory consumption.

The spectacle can be considered in the light of political economy as a kind of value added to the basic requirements of survival. Not only are advertising, promotion and marketing additions to the basic content of the commodity, but at times they even supersede any possible use-value that the commodity might have, at its purest in wholly useless objects that will be instantly consumed and recycled, such as advertisements themselves, occasionally amusing the first time they are seen, but inevitably repeated beyond the point of interest or even promotion of the product. A curious example of this was the campaign for Chanel No. 5 perfumes that was so successful in attracting ordinary buyers that Chanel began to lose their core elite market and had to launch a new, 'artier' campaign to alienate this larger customer base. One thinks too of those products marketed on the added-value selling point that they require further work from the consumer: half-baked bread and microwave popcorn that advertise themselves as needing the special homemade touch that comes from messing about in the kitchen. Then there is the KitKat chocolate bar which you are supposed to refrigerate: below a certain temperature, its packaging changes colour, a purposeless, inane, wasted effort. Perhaps the ultimate example of the purely spectacular commodity is the television programme itself, which, as television research-ers have been pointing out since the 1970s, requires our creative input to make sense, but which is consumed and thrown away in the time it takes to view. Even news programmes, with their invitation to 'make up your own mind' on the day's events, are simply products whose main function is to keep the television stations going and to keep us watching.

The tendency to urban sprawl in the 1950s had, Debord believed, produced a 'technological pseudo-peasantry' (Debord 1977: ¶ 177) whose isolation in their suburban new towns was meat and drink to the pseudo-communities constructed by the media. Here in full play is the most complete form to date of the society of the spectacle. And here the theme of the spatialisation of social life – through suburbanisation and through broadcasting, as well as the myriad forms of tourism and the 'dictatorship of the automobile' (Debord 1977: ¶ 174) – spells the end of that movement of change which is history.

> When ideology, having become absolute, through the possession of absolute power, changes from partial knowledge into totalitarian falsehood, the thought of history is so perfectly annihilated that history itself, even at the level of the most empirical knowledge, can no longer exist. (Debord 1977: ¶ 108)

Entrenched in dominance, ideology ceases to be a partial account of the world and becomes the only account, a lie because we are unable now to recognise that it is only a partial version. And having achieved this dominance, ideology as spectacle deprives us of change. The perpetual present of the totalitarian bureaucrat, the perfect system, the endless status quo, may have arisen from the crises of fascism, but they have become the stock in trade of everyday political management since the second half of the twentieth century. Debord gives a brilliant account in Section V (Debord 1977: ¶ 125–46) of the administration of time, as the bureacrats' static, empty time at the end of historical change, as the mechanical time of the factory and the timetable, and as the pseudo-cyclical time of the spectacle. The pseudo-cycles of television schedules, department store seasons and fashion turn time into a consumer good: not just something needed in order to consume, but a commodity in its own right to be squandered in splendid, vacuous pursuits like sunbathing. Perhaps he misses the sense in which time can also be hoarded – as family albums, but also as TV memories, when you remember the doings of soap stars rather than the events of your own life. Instead, Debord believes that individual life is deprived of time, excluded from the spectacular time of TV's simulations of experience, and left to wither. Real living is constantly deferred to those vacations and leisure hours which are presented to us as commodities, and in which therefore 'what was presented to us as genuine life reveals itself simply as *more genuinely spectacular* life' (Debord 1977: ¶ 153).

Individuals in the spectacular society cannot recognise others or know their own reality. They are profoundly and doubly alienated, once from others, and again from themselves. Culture presents itself as a way back to the lost unity of the self, and the lost community with others, a negation of the isolated and schizophrenic individual. But if culture is the pursuit of lost unity, what happens to culture when it achieves the unity it seeks? It negates itself! Culture has come to an end, and there are two directions in which it can go. It can become the ossified archive of past achievements endlessly recycled in a sham imitation of the cultural life of the past; or it can seek to annihilate itself through the kind of revolutinary critique that Debord offers. But even this must be done right: sociology as a university discipline has become the spectacular critique of the spectacle, a pessimismistic science which, glorifying the system to the point of destroying all alternative realities, can be recycled in the society of the spectacle as another spectacular performance. If theory is to avoid turning the critique of the spectacle into another commodity, a kind of coffee-table theory, it must move, once again, away from philosophising about how the world is, and towards an activist praxis designed to change it, 'where dialogue arms itself to make its own conditions victorious' (Debord 1977: ¶ 221).

Debord was a revolutionary. His belief that the working class, defined in strict Marxist terms, is the vehicle of a revolution in the meaning of history as well as the overthrow of the spectacular lie of contemporary social order is no longer fashionable, and the leading intellectuals of our times tend to be those who argue that revolution is impossible and the working class are the last people to bring it about. Indeed, the word 'revolution' has become a standard term in advertising to denote any minimal differentiation between products. The first great theorist of simulation would be the last utopian. From his bleak vision of the present, only the pessimism survives into the development of the theory since the 1960s.

(ii) Jean Baudrillard: simulation and seduction

> Was he wearing a mask? Was anyone wearing a mask? Was anyone anything? . . . Was there anything that was apart from what it seemed? The Marquis had taken off his nose and turned out to be a detective. Might he now just as well take off his head and turn out to be a hobgoblin? Was not everything, after all, like this bewildering woodland, this dance of dark and light? Everything only a glimpse, the glimpse always unforeseen, and always forgotten. For Gabriel Syme had found in the heart of that sun-splashed wood what many modern painters had found

there. He had found the thing which the modern people call Impres-
sionism, which is another name for that final scepticism which can find no
floor to the universe.

(G.K. Chesterton, *The Man Who Was Thursday*)

I am a nihilist.

(Baudrillard 1994a: 160)

In 1988, amid the breakup of the old Soviet bloc, Debord revisited his theses
in *Comments on the Society of the Spectacle*. The processes described in the
earlier book had, he argues, accelerated to reach the level of what he calls
the integrated spectacle, characterised by 'incessant technological renewal;
integration of state and economy; generalised secrecy; unanswerable lies; an
eternal present' (Debord 1990: 12), a state characterised as 'an eternity of
noisy insignificance' (Debord 1990: 15). With a typical dialectical twist on
an initial statement, Debord sees that, in the collapse of the Cold War
opposition between the capitalist state and state capitalism (Stalinism), 'the
globalisation of the false was also the falsification of the globe' (Debord
1990: 10). In the work of the French sociologist Jean Baudrillard (b. 1929),
this more radical thesis of the integrated spectacle, 'that has integrated itself
into reality to the same extent as it was describing it, and that it was
reconstructing as it was describing it' (Debord 1990: 9), becomes the more
general thesis of simulation. In Debord's earlier analysis, there was always a
residual reality, human nature or the proletariat, against which the perversion
of the spectacle could be measured. In his *Comments*, and throughout
Baudrillard's major works, reality itself has been so profoundly altered by its
infection and ultimate integration into spectacle that there is no outside, no
remaining reality, to compare the simulation with. We inhabit a world with
neither truth nor history, and for Baudrillard therefore permanently divorced
from that historical truth which alone, in Debord's revolutionary version,
could bring an end to the endless spectacle. In the world of the simulation,
there will be no revolution. Not only is truth debarred from us in the present;
we cannot even look forward to its revelation in the future.

In his earliest books (Baudrillard 1968, 1970, 1972), Baudrillard, in the
tradition of Lukács and Marcuse, tried to update Marxism to deal with the
changes wrought by the consumer society. But in a series of books originally
published between 1973 and 1981 (Baudrillard 1975, 1983b, 1990a, 1993a,
1994a), he broke with Marxism, and especially with the dialectic, establishing in their place the theory of a society not even of spectacle, but of
simulation. Although the last of these, *Fatal Strategies*, and his more recent
writings of the 1990s, as we shall see, turn towards a more universal and
metaphysical account of simulation, in the most persuasive and influential of
his books from the 1970s, simulation describes a specific historical period in
the formation of societies: the contemporary world that begins with the Wall
Street Crash of 1929 and its political and economic aftermath (Baudrillard
1983b: 27; 1993a: 33).

It is perhaps easiest to situate Baudrillard as an anti-Marxist. *The Mirror of Production* completes his earlier work by offering a major critique of economic determinism, while later works offer an alternative to the theory of the dialectic (while at the same time in many respects using dialectical methods to overthrow the dialectic). Marx, he argues, was right when he wrote of the centrality of the commodity form, but because he wrote only of an earlier and now superseded moment in the history of modernity, his analysis has become mere ideology (Baudrillard 1975: 117). The situationists correctly grasped the movement from commodity to spectacle, but by insisting that the commodity came first, and could only be analysed by political economy, they fall for the Marxist ideology (Baudrillard 1975: 120). Today, he argues:

> The super-ideology of the sign and the general operationalization of the signifier – everywhere sanctioned today by the new master disciplines of structural linguistics, semiology, information theory, and cybernetics – has replaced good old political economy [bringing about] the symbolic destruction of all social relations not so much by the ownership of the means of production but by *the control of the code*. Here there is a revolution of the capitalist system equal in importance to the industrial revolution. (Baudrillard 1975: 122)

The sign, a term Baudrillard uses here in the transition from spectacle to simulation, is more than ('super') ideological. In separating the signifier – the material used to create meaning – from the signified – the thing it means – signification has undergone a revolution equivalent to that brought about by the separation of exchange-value from use-value. Because it is now autonomous, the signifier can function, as it does for example in product design, not to refer us to the value of the product, but as a value in its own right: we consume things not for their use-value or their meaning but simply for their appearance. The triumph of linguistics and information theory is then a reflection of a change in the operation of society, which no longer depends on production and consumption of commodities but on the circulation and consumption of signifiers. The look of things is now even more important than their exchange-value, and the system that governs their circulation is no longer that of the economy but what Baudrillard refers to as the code.

The code is a dominant concept in the major works of the 1970s, but unfortunately Baudrillard never gives a simple definition of it. Clues, however, are scattered through *The Mirror of Production* and the following books. The first thing we have to grasp is that the code is pervasive: it pervades not only society but theories about it, and those theories return into circulation as elements of the code – as Debord had noted, the sociology of the spectacle itself becomes spectacular and ends up supporting the system it came to criticise. Information theory, for example, not only describes but produces the situation it gives an account of. By draining messages mathematically of meaning, it aids a system in which meaning evaporates. The term 'operational' in the last quotation gives a sense too of what the code does: it operates. Its sole interest is in continuing to operate: this is why it opposes change and eventually divorces itself and everyone caught up in it from history. The code functions, it appears, like the code of language, the underlying grammatical rules that, according to contemporary linguistics, generate every spoken sentence; or like the mathematical codes for compression and transmission that govern modern communications technologies; or, most tellingly perhaps, like the genetic code, forming and shaping the body of every living thing and 'operating' the body like a remotely controlled robot.

Conceptualising society as the functioning of the code has some extremely important and ultimately devastating consequences. In his next book, *Symbolic Exchange and Death*, Baudrillard advances his analysis to introduce the concept of simulation. The natural law of value, based on use-value, was also founded in the relationship between signifiers and their referents, the things to which they refer. Use and meaning gave previous societies a certain fullness, although Baudrillard does perceive even in the Renaissance, when capitalism first began, a kind of simulation, which he calls 'counterfeit'. The Industrial Revolution brought with it a second order of simulation when it introduced the commodity form. Under this regime of the market law of value, commodities were produced as equivalents for one another, equivalents which included the industrial worker's labour power. By the same token, signifiers were now freed from the necessity to refer to reality, their equivalent of use-value, and instead were produced endlessly as equivalents, one for another. The third order of simulation, our own, is dominated by the 'structural law of value', which is also the code.

Summarising these changes in *Simulation and Simulacara*, Baudrillard starts from the 'natural law of value' of early societies, and then defines for the Renaissance, the Industrial Revolution and the contemporary world the successive phases of the image:

> it is the reflection of a profound reality;
> it masks and denatures a profound reality
> it masks the *absence* of a profound reality
> it has no relation to any reality whatsoever: it is its own pure simulacrum
> (Baudrillard 1994a: 6 [1983a: 11])[2]

The referential value of signs – the ability of words to refer to real things, or of commodities to refer to their use-values – is ultimately replaced by the structural value of exchange and the systematic coding of language as a system of pure differences, as conceived of by Saussure. The regime of production which dominated between the Industrial Revolution of the 1790s and the Wall Street Crash of 1929, the system described by Marx, no longer exists. It has evolved into a system in which production no longer has a goal – such as the historical emancipation of the workers, or technological

---

2. Reference is to the Glaser translation. The chapter from *Simulation and Simulacra* on 'The Precession of Simulacra' was previously translated as 1983a. Since this is widely used, I will provide references to this version when citing from the more recent translation.

progress, or the sharing of wealth. It does not even have the rationale of providing for our needs. Instead, under the rule of the code, it produces only more and more signifiers without referents and commodities that do not match our needs, ultimately producing the circulation of e-cash, no longer tied to 'real' wealth, as speculative capital on the world's stock exchanges. Recognising this new shift in *The Transparency of Evil*, Baudrillard adds a new order of simulation to the three proposed in the earlier works (though by now he has joined the Renaissance and Industrial orders into a single 'commodity' stage):

> At the fourth, the fractal (or viral, or radiant) stage of value, there is no point of reference at all, and value radiates in all directions, occupying all interstices, without reference to anything whatsoever, by virtue of pure contiguity. . . . this kind of propagation or chain reaction makes all valuation impossible. (Baudrillard 1993b: 5)

In this latest permutation, messages and money are indistinguishable from one another, both being composed of digital transmissions. The orders of simulation based on nature, on commodities and on meanings dissolve when even signs cannot be differentiated from one another.

Baudrillard captures the essence of this vast historical movement in brilliant, aphoristic statements rather than by consistent argument. Here, for example, he condenses the histories of production techniques and communication in the concept of

> the series: the very possibility of two or *n* identical objects. The relation between them is no longer one of an original and its counterfeit, analogy or reflection, but instead is one of equivalence and indifference. In the series, objects become indistinct simulacra of one another and, along with objects, of the men that produce them. The extinction of the original reference alone facilitates the general law of equivalence, that is to say, *the very possibility of production*. (Baudrillard 1993a: 55)

Saussurean linguistics had been based on the constitutive differences between sounds and letters – such that we never confuse 'hat' with 'hut', not because they sound or look like headgear or houses, but because of the difference between 'a' and 'u'. But in serial factory production, there is no difference between one gizmo and the next, and under the laws of exchange-value, no difference even between one overcoat and twenty bags of nails, if they can be exchanged for an equivalent amount of money. Not only manufactured goods, but the people who produce them become exchange-able, and lose any sense of specificity or, in Baudrillard's terms, of reality. This is the point of the phrase 'the extinction of the original reference': in serial production, there is no original to be copied, because each item rolling off the production line is an identical copy of the previous item, and the next, not of some original thing. Likewise in language: words follow words in endless succession, each equivalent to the next, with no original to which they refer.

This is why Baudrillard feels free to say that we no longer live in an era of production. Production has been superseded by the general law of equivalence (the structural law of value) in which all differences are repressed, since the only one that matters, the difference between the real and the copy, no longer holds. The code is ultimately indifferent to anything but its own reproduction. It cares not a whit if the circulation of signs involves battleships or bath oil, only that the circulation continue. While Debord had still been able to locate some residual reality in the life of the workers, for Baudrillard that moment of history too is over, so that now 'The end of the spectacle brings with it the collapse of reality into hyperrealism' (Baudrillard 1993a: 71).

And it is into the giddy realms of the hyperreal that we now must ascend: the realm of 'the *hallucinatory resemblance of the real to itself*' (Baudrillard 1993a: 72), where 'the very definition of the real is *that of which it is possible to give an equivalent reproduction.* . . . At the end of this process of reproducibility, the real is not only that which can be reproduced, but *that which is always already reproduced*: the hyperreal' (Baudrillard 1993a: 73). It is not quite accurate to describe simulation as that state of affairs in which the real is lost from view; rather, the real is infected by the principle of equivalence and indifference. If there can be an equivalent to the real – in the form of reproduction – then the real enters the indifferent circulation of signs. And the reproduction in which it is caught is not simply the reproductive technology of photography and film, but the code's own system of self-replication. For Debord and the dialectical tradition, reality was always deferred, always waiting to be fully realised, against the deadweight of everything that denied its full potential. For Baudrillard, recalling Lacan's idea of the Real as the domain of the impossible object of desire, the real which we inhabit is no longer full of its own reality, where 'reality' points us towards Heidegger's argument that being has faded from the world, and towards Lacan's *manque à être*. So Baudrillard argues the inverse of Debord's case, that the real has already out-realised itself, becoming in the process excessively (hyper)real. The example he uses here is that of opinion polls. The public scarcely exists as an entity: we can't see it gathered together, it doesn't go down to the pub or off to the soccer match. Yet it has an opinion, scientifically measured. But, argues Baudrillard, on the one hand, opinion is simply an artefact of the questions which are asked, and, on the other, its publication gives to the ideal, imaginary concept of the public a reality it would not otherwise possess. In the effort to describe this imaginary public, the pollsters have brought it into existence: a typical effect of the code in operation.

Thus public opinion, as constructed in the polls, becomes more real than the people whose opinion is supposedly expressed in it: 'not an unreal but a hyperreal political substance' (Baudrillard 1993a: 64). Unreality would suggest a simple exile from a reality still existing elsewhere, as in Heidegger's philosophy. Hyperreality suggests that we can no longer refer to an external, validating reality, but only to the excessive obviousness of the real, Lacan's domain of desire, in the hyperreal. Thus what we desire is no longer a real satisfaction, but a hyperreal simulation of satisfaction that begins with the desire for commodities but ends in desire for the hyperreal glamour of their simulation. So the social relations that began their downward spiral in Marx's perception of relations between people take on the fantastic form of relations between objects, only to become a relation between the signs of objects, and ultimately between signifiers without objects. The hyperreal is then the product of simulation as the most extreme form of socialisation.

Here we face one of Baudrillard's disorienting revaluations of familiar terms. Baudrillard distrusts all socialisation, seeing the social only as the operation of the code in the age of mass media, something which, like public opinion, is pure display. This 'obscene' display – obscene because it reveals everything to the point of overwhelming us with its brutal obviousness – is characteristic of the hyperreal. Moreover, hyperreality is coded through the media, though not specifically by its content. The familiar analysis of ideological messages is of no interest to Baudrillard, since it rests on a theory of misrepresentation of the real. Instead, the media in the age of information operate, as McLuhan had argued, in such a way that 'the medium is the message'. So for example, there are no historical events any more, only media events, the medium alone manufacturing the event. The job of spin doctors, for example, is not just to manage interpretations, but to provide the news stories which will then be interpreted, to stage the meetings and even the wars which will fill the media with images and sounds, but which, strictly speaking, have no reality outside the media. In this sense Baudrillard can argue that there has been an *implosion of the medium and the real* where even the definition and the distinct action of the medium are no longer distinguishable' (Baudrillard 1983b: 101). This gives Baudrillard a means to argue that there can be no radical intervention in the media: there cannot be, for example, a radical news agenda. We cannot make the dominant forms of media carry politically progressive messages, since all messages become pure signifiers, elements of the code; nor can we intervene in the forms of the media themselves, since they have become indistinguishable from the hyperreal.

This lack of distinction is a further aspect of the indifference of the mode of simulation: 'a single *model*, whose efficacy is *immediacy*, simultaneously generates the message, the medium, and the "real" ' (Baudrillard 1983b: 102). As in serial production, there is no 'original' product of which all the others are copies: there exists only a model to which they are all identical. The code's model operates without the distinguishing differences (for example, the spatial distinction between between sender and receiver, or the temporal difference between an event and the report of the event typical of pre-television media) of communication, that is, without mediation, immediate. Thus the model, which permeates the social and indeed constitutes it as a code, having eradicated the need for mediation between distinct poles of the communication process, can manufacture at one and the same time the medium, its content and the real which has been superseded by the media. Crucial to this argument is the way in which the hyperreal is not only a heightening of reality to the point of excessive obviousness, but the loss of those distinctions which used to make it possible to think of the social as a field of conflict heading towards some historical destiny. All the terms of dialectical thinking – the signifier and the signified in linguistics, the sender and receiver in information theory, the infrastructure and superstructure of Marxism, the conscious and unconscious in psychoanalysis: all these dialectical opposites have become indistinguishable in the era of the hyperreal. This, once again, is why the dialectic can no longer function, and dialectical thought appears, in Baudrillard, as hopelessly nostalgic. We simply do not live in a world in which discrimination between opposites is possible.

For simulation theory, the relation between media and hyperreality is of immense interest. Baudrillard gives a very clear example in a discussion of quadraphonic hi-fi players, which provide

> The technical delirium of the perfect restitution of music (Bach, Monteverdi, Mozart!) *that has never existed*, that no one has ever heard, and that was not meant to be heard like this. Moreover, one does not 'hear' it, for the distance that allows one to *hear* music, at a concert or somewhere else, is abolished. . . . Something else fascinates (but no longer seduces) you: technical perfection, 'high fidelity' . . . one no longer knows what object it is faithful to, for no one knows where the real begins or ends, nor understands, therefore, the fever of perfectibility that persists in the real's reproduction . . . the real becomes a vertiginous fantasy of exactitude lost in the infinitesimal. (Baudrillard 1990a: 30)

Contemporary recording and playback technologies are devoted to realising the perfect version of the score. To do so, they will cut together a half-dozen performances, electronically manipulating stray noises or bad notes, even substituting the high notes from one singer for the less clear tones of another. Typically, especially in classical music recordings, there is a tendency to avoid the acoustic signatures of concert halls in favour of the 'dead' sound of studios. Everything is done to give the most perfect possible rendering of what the producers have determined to be the authentic score of the piece. But this search for perfection, says Baudrillard, misses the point of performance, the distance between performer and audience, the particular sound of this hall or that church, the risk of someone failing to hit a note. In place of the 'real' event, with all its flaws, we are presented with the commercial and flawless product of the CD, which no longer provides us with a sense of participation in the event, but 'seduces' with its seamless perfection. The recording is then not a recording as such: it doesn't document an original event that took place at some definite place and time. It is a pure product, made according to a model of perfection, in which reality itself has been turned into the concept of the music, the ideal score played by ideal musicians through the magic of the medium. In this way 'real' music has been transformed into a perfect simulation of itself, and we will never be satisfied with a less than perfect rendition in the future.

In these earlier works, it is television which, in particular, bears the brunt of Baudrillard's contempt. Yet he argues too that we can scarcely blame the media for the ills of our society, because 'there is now no longer a medium in the literal sense: it is now intangible, diffused, and diffracted in the real, and it can no longer even be said that the latter is distorted by it' (Baudrillard 1994a: 30, translation amended [1983a: 54]). Since the implosion of the real and the diffusion of media into reality are synonymous, we cannot blame the media for distorting reality. To do so would be to accuse the media of acting ideologically, but today

> Ideology only corresponds to a corruption of reality through signs; simulation corresponds to a short-circuit of reality and to its duplication through signs. It is always the goal of the ideological analysis to restore the objective process, it is always a false problem to wish to restore the truth beneath the simulacrum. (Baudrillard 1994a: 27 [1983a: 48])

In place of the familiar complaints of ideological analysis – complaints of racism and sexism and distortion of the facts – Baudrillard here argues that we must recognise that the code of simulation exists only to maintain itself, and that in order to do so it maintains, quite indifferently, not only the television stations but also science, universities, journalism and every discourse that asks us to place our faith in facts. It is not so much that the facts are dissembled in bad reporting, as that all mediation, including all reporting, radical or conservative, serves to reproduce the regime of objectivity. That very modern desire for objectivity is part of the scientific rationality born with capitalism in the Renaissance, entrenched in the technological rationalism of the Industrial Revolution, and achieving its most intense contemporary dissemination as the administrative rationality of social welfare. Objectivity is, then, another aspect of the hyperrealisation of reality: its conversion into the object of scrutiny, of manipulation, of signification, and of exploitation.

It is in this sense that Baudrillard can talk about the media not as persuasive but as dissuasive. On the one hand, media in the age of simulation act to dissolve and render indifferent. No longer charged with conveying scientific or political, or even economic, truth, their purpose is to dissolve all the oppositions which, in the previous era of production, promised to bring about the renewed movement of history. Trapped into a perpetual present, the media can only circulate. On the other, the media want not to encourage us into historical action, but to discourage us from any action whatsoever. Baudrillard is not unaware, however, of the cultural studies research into television viewing which argues for an active viewer participating in the creation of meaning (see, for example, Ang 1991, 1995; Morley 1987, 1992; Seiter et al. 1989). He notes that such passivity was at a certain stage – notably under totalitarian regimes – a characteristic of modernity, but that we have passed 'from obligatory passivity to models constructed from the outset on the basis of the subject's "active response", and this subject's involvement and "ludic" participation towards a total environment model made up of incessant spontaneous responses, joyous feedback and irradiated contacts' (Baudrillard 1993a: 71). Even our apparent activity in such new recreations as electronic games (1990a: 59) are a kind of somnambular re-creation of real interactivity, ludic (playful) only in the

sense that they are governed by rules which demand compulsory involvement which, however, is not genuine communication between people but
merely a response to stimuli, a feedback loop through which the code checks
out that it is still functioning and we are still connected to it.

We are now in a position to read Baudrillard's clearest statement of his
theme, the opening pages of *Simulation and Simulacara*. He begins with one
of Jorge Luis Borges' fables, concerning the emperor who commands the
making of a map so detailed that it is eventually the same size as his
kingdom. In the Borges story, the map rots gradually away; in Baudrillard's
re-telling, it is the kingdom that disappears, leaving only vestiges of itself in
tattered remains scattered across the desert (the desert which will form a
central metaphor of his essays on *America*, Baudrillard 1988a). Today, he
tells us, the map precedes the territory, logically and in the time of
experience, so much so that the territory has disappeared, or more correctly
is created in the process of map-making. Simulation does not involve the
imitation of a pre-existing real: 'It is the generation by models of a real
without origin or reality: a hyperreal' (Baudrillard 1994a: 1 [1983a: 1]).
Note here the distinction between the real and reality: the hyperreal is an
extreme form of the real, but it lacks that quality of fullness to itself that
characterises Heideggerian being, the quality of reality. The hyperreal is not
generated by the reality of class conflict, production, the psyche or any other
explanatory mechanism: it is generated by models of itself.

Baudrillard then takes us a step further: 'it is no longer a question of either
maps or territories', he notes. 'Something has disappeared: the sovereign
difference, between one and the other, that constituted the charm of
abstraction' (Baudrillard 1994a: 2 [1983a: 2]). The process of abstraction,
whereby we create an abstract version, like a map, from the bones of the real
has itself a kind of poetry, but it is also a charm in the sense of a magic spell.
The difference between the map and the ground used to make the map
fascinating, but it also charmed the real into existence. The dream of a total
map is an allegory for the modern drive towards total knowledge, a complete
scientific description of the universe. But in simulation, that ambition to
create an abstract knowledge of the whole of everything is lost in an
upheaval that leaves us without a real to know. We lose, in simulation, the
grounds of our metaphysical certainty concerning the difference between the
real and the abstraction, the real and the representation, the real and
knowledge about it. The difference is the crucial thing we have lost, since
without that difference that separates the two poles of any of these systems
of truth, picturing or science, we cannot distinguish one from the other. This
is the profound implication of the indifference of simulation, its assimilation
of all separations into an indefinite cloud of self-generating models. Unlike
Debord, Baudrillard can no longer appeal to the real potential of human
beings, since they too have lost their reality as something distinct from their
socialised position in society and the discourses that circulate in it. Humanity is subjected to a regime of codes that synthesises them as neither real nor
false consciousness, but as statistics, citizens, consumers. But there is no

human nature left to appeal to or to wish to restore. The negation of human potential addressed by Debord can therefore no longer be negated: there can be no historical movement in which, through the dialectical negation of the negation, we might arrive at the synthesis of the idea of humanity with its actuality. This is because the dialectic depended on the separation between the idea and the actuality in order to work, but they are now indistinguishable from one another. There are no separations now – a theme Baudrillard pursues in a number of books in which he castigates Freudians, Marxists, Saussureans, sociologists and scientists for believing that there is a way of distinguishing the real from the representation. Under simulation, no distinctions are possible, and therefore no history. Reason itself collapses for lack of distinctions with which to work, and the rational is replaced by the operational (ope*rational*), in which simulation reproduces itself endlessly through the control codes lodged in databanks, in the structures of grammar, in the rules of social behaviour.

We can tell that the real has lost its reality by the way in which it is no longer embraced by the Imaginary – Lacan's word, once again, for the psychological domain made up of all our images of our relations with our self and our environment. The distinction between self and environment has gone – caught up in the general indifference – so that we have difficulty isolating a sense of self apart from the flow of simulations that engulf us. Individuality, already trapped into conformity when we first learnt to define our personalities by the commodities we associated with, has now become a simulation too. Each of us is a simulacrum of an individual, while the 'real' individual has dissolved into the masses. And since one job of the imaginary is to establish the relations between the self and the real, the imaginary itself has been dragged into the loss of distinctions, and is no longer separable from the real which it once described and distinguished as that which lay outside the self. Where the imaginary once was, there is now a code operating which simply replaces the real with signs of the real, such that we can no longer see a patch of ground without seeing it *as*: *as* a landscape, *as* a map, *as* a resource. The days in which we could see it for itself are over: now we only see it as an extension of ourselves, and ourselves as an extension of it.

In its own way, this can sound like a sort of zen utopia. The difference is that in simulation, the simulacrum corresponds not to some deeper underlying order or a divine state of integration, but to the final divorce between human society and the world of things as they might be said to exist without us, things in and for themselves. That world, as it might be imagined to have existed, was indeed inhabited by divinity, since only a God could know it. But in the following sections, Baudrillard looks specifically at the theological wars that began in Byzantium over the picturing of God (and which, incidentally, also led to the almost total destruction of the mediaeval heritage of painting and much statuary in England in the fifteenth and again in the seventeenth centuries). The iconoclasm, the destruction of images, began because of the accusation that iconolaters, those who worshipped using images, were in fact worshipping not God but the image of God. Baudrillard, always ready to take the least expected side in an argument, sides with the iconoclasts, arguing that they understood the fatal error in iconolatry: that worshipping the image of God actually brings about the disappearance of God from the worship. Worse still, he argues, is the realisation that God has never existed except as an image, that 'God is his own simulacrum' (Baudrillard 1994a: 4 [1983a: 8]). The appalling, deliberately blasphemous argument suggests that with the disappearance or death of God, something final occurs in the world of the image. Whenever there was a dispute over the truth, or a need to distinguish between true and false, God was the ultimate arbiter: even if I could be fooled, God would know. But if God himself is no longer available to judge, then the whole system according to which signs could be in some sense exchanged for their meanings also collapses. In the absence of God, as the final arbiter of truth, the distinction between true and false disappears, and the world descends into a state in which signs are exchanged no longer for real things but for one another: the vast simulacrum of the code.

Throughout these pages, and on into those that follow, in which Baudrillard discusses the case of anthropological knowledge, the realm of simulation is often allied with the idea of death. We no longer need the Last Judgement, he says, because 'Everything is already dead and resurrected in advance' (Baudrillard 1994a: 6 [1983a: 12]). Death is another of the complex terms in Baudrillard. Here he refers to death in the sense of the Marxist theory of technology and capital as 'dead labour', in the sense that the skills of living workers are transferred to machines, and their earnings transferred into investment capital to pay for them. The code is mechanical in operation, and therefore can also be said to be run by the dead: the dead labour of technologies and techniques, money and ideas, that were created in ages past and accumulated to the point at which they have begun to run the world of the living. In the historical processes of production, the real itself has died, but like those dead labourers whose craft went into the design of machine tools, the image of the real has been resurrected posthumously in the form of images and stories, the mass media production of data and evidence, news and 'objectivity' in place of the dead real.

Capitalism's drive to accumulate has by now infested every aspect of life. Our drive to knowledge is actually a drive to accumulate things, but things have a way of taking their revenge by refusing to be accumulated. What we strive to know and preserve disintegrates as soon as we discover it, like Egyptian mummies that begin to decay from the moment the tomb is opened. We believe that there is something profoundly moral about our will to knowledge, just as we do about our democratic institutions or about our resistance to and attacks on them. But capital is 'a monstrous, unprincipled entreprise' (Baudrillard 1994a: 17 [1983a: 32]) to which principles of good and evil, another polar distinction, do not apply. Even the left's attack on capital's immorality functions in terms of good and evil, and therefore serves to bolster the belief in the good and the laws of morality. But those laws are themselves another simulacrum, another layer of the self-regulating code.

What is truly scandalous about the Watergate burglary, during which Republican Party operatives broke into Democratic Party offices, is that there was no scandal. This was neither a case of a few bad apples in the barrel, nor proof that capital is immoral in general and should be replaced by a moral order like socialism. On the contrary: what the media, left and right, failed to acknowledge was that there is no basis left on which to make a moral judgement. The last task of social critique is to expose this lack. But perhaps it is too much to say that morality has disappeared, since clearly we do refer, in however confused a way, to moral principles in daily life. Baudrillard offers us another metaphor, describing the 'Hell of simulation' (Baudrillard 1994a: 18 [1983a: 34]) as a Möbius strip – the paradoxical geometrical figure easily made by giving a strip of paper a half-twist and joining the ends together. The Möbius strip provides an analogy with the fundamental undecidability of moral issues. Looking at the strip, it is impossible to say which side is inside and which is outside, because they alternate as you move around the paper. Likewise the politics of manipulation (did the Watergate journalists manipulate their sources, or were they manipulated by them?) never allows a final decision. Similarly with meaning: it is not so much that meaning has disappeared as that it has become the undecidable circling of endless potential (and potentially contradictory and mutually destructive) interpretations.

How are we to get out of this endless loop of undecidability? Baudrillard imagines a scenario in which simulation – the simulation of a crime, for example – is used to expose the order of simulation, arguing that simulation dissolves the differences on which the law is based. But this strategy fails when power responds with an injection of the real – with crisis, effects and consequences. This 'hysterical' or 'panic' attempt to restore the real, however, only ever results in further overproduction of the real that otherwise escapes the system, and so only manufactures further hyperreality. And power itself, the central concern of the philosopher and historian Michel Foucault, is like money or meaning – a floating simulation of itself that requires an occasional (simulated) assassination attempt to restore to it the signs of power, but which has otherwise lost its reality along with every other explanatory system. Just as employment has become a struggle for jobs, not for the production of needful things, jobs that hide the unreality of work, so power exists only to conceal its own absence (Baudrillard 1994a: 26 [1983a: 54]).

Perhaps the most terrifying and the most absurd sign of the operation of the code lies in nuclear deterrence. Here the resources of the two most powerful nations in the world are brought into play in order to assure that something does *not* happen. The Cold War antagonists, the USA and the USSR, apparently entirely at loggerheads, are actually colluding with each other to ensure that the historic event of mutual destruction never occurs. The whole global system is an immensely expensive, degrading, mutely violent structure designed to ensure that nothing changes. There is tension, drama, activity, hyperactivity, but nothing happens. Communism and capitalism, long before the fall of the Berlin Wall in 1989, were already indistinguishable on the stage of global politics. All the morality, all the meaning, all the politics of left and right, all the distinctions between freedom and tyranny, peace and war are collapsed into the balance of terror. No more fitting symbol could summarise the appalling scale, the total dominance, of the simulacrum in the contemporary world.

(iii) Paul Virilio: speed and transappearance

> I try to forget what happiness was and when that don't work, I study the stars.

> (Derek Walcott, *Omeros*)

It was not until 1945 that the young Paul Virilio (b. 1932) discovered the sea. The seashore was forbidden to the French under the German occupation, but his first sight at twelve or thirteen years of age was all the more impressive for the delay. What impressed the boy most was the emptiness of the horizon. Holidaying in 1958 on the coast of Brittany, he became fascinated by what was later to become the subject of his first book, the absurd conjunction of the concrete blockhouses, remains of the German Atlantic Wall coastal defences, with the directionless vastness of the ocean (Virilio 1994b: 10–11). As a leading architect and urbanist, director of the prestigous École Spéciale de l'Architecture as well as a cultural critic, Virilio began his analysis of modernity under the summer sun, amazed at the military attempt to guard a territory without a map.

That first book, *Bunker Archeology*, is valuable not only as a major text of architectural and cultural analysis, but also as an introduction to Virilio's major themes, most of all the relation between warfare and the conduct of daily life. Its special interest lies in the description of the ways in which military thinking is conveyed into the everyday via the invention and remaking of media. The parallel progress of warfare and cartography, for example, suggest to him a fundamental premise of his thought: 'the function of arms and the function of the eye were indifferently identified as one and the same' (Virilio 1994b: 17), since seeing your opponent is the necessary prerequisite to aiming a weapon directly at him. The speed of vision becomes a model for the speed of communication, transport and weaponry (Virilio 1994b: 17). As a result, there is a trend towards miniaturisation as an aid to speed (since the smaller a piece of equipment is, the faster energy and information can travel around it), and another tendency towards a desire for omnipresence, for being able to be and to see everywhere simultaneously (Virilio 1994b: 18). As a result the distinction between a weapon, a vehicle and a medium diminishes to nothing, and sea, air and ground are blended together in a single operational structure. In an equal and opposite direction, there is the tendency towards camouflage and dissimulation, and towards mobile resources as a way of combatting the instantaneous, omnipresent vision of your opponent. Finally the world is constricted to an ever shrinking scale, and its geography of landmarks and journeys transformed into '*a carpet of trajectories*' (Virilio 1994b: 19). In a sense very close to Baudrillard's, Virilio can begin to speak of a time of implosion, in which the 'reality' of even such constructs as national boundaries has been superseded militarily by '*the area of violence*', the time of energy (Virilio 1994b: 21). As for Baudrillard, with Virilio we are introduced to the contemporary world as a time out of time: the final reduction of the world.

It is always flattering to be told that you inhabit the ultimate moment in history, and that your own time witnesses the definitive crisis of your civilisation. Much of the interest and attraction of Virilio's writings comes from his belief that we inhabit today a crisis of perception, precipitated through the militarisation of visual technologies and the embedding of these technologies in the familiar environs of the street, the home and the architecture of daily life. This crisis of the solid geometry of buildings, as they give way to the fluid transparencies of media, just as they do to the ultra-rapid surveillance, transport and weapons technologies of war, he sees inaugurated in the time-lapse chrono-photographic experiments of Étienne Jules Marey in the late nineteenth century (for example, Virilio 1994a: 60–1; see also Braun 1992; Dagognet 1992), the beginnings of cinema, and the inauguration of a tendency towards dematerialisation that will culminate in digital technologies. The history of the twentieth century is then a tale of the gradual encroachment of a militarised mindset into everyday life through the forms of the media, especially their acceleration of perception, their miniaturisation, and their gradual eradication of the distances which have, until now, provided the grounds, not so much of representation, as in Baudrillard, but of perception, as in the philosophy of phenomenology. This deeply melancholy account of the world is reminiscent of the pessimistic Marxism of Theodor W. Adorno, but where Adorno is concerned to discover the origins of the administered society in the history of Nazism as an outcome of Enlightenment rationalism, Virilio's burning concern is with a contemporary apocalypse. That catastrophe is ultimately an ethical one, since the progress of media technologies leads to the destruction of the grounds for human choice: the human will, the basis of ethical decision-making.

An aphorist like Baudrillard, Virilio composes his books out of allusions and epigrams, but he is a more meticulous historian than his contemporary, and is deeply informed by current media and communications scholarship. According to his central thesis,

> With the supersonic vector (airplane, rocket, airwaves), penetration and destruction become one. The instantaneousness of action at a distance corresponds to the defeat of the unprepared adversary, but also, and especially, to the defeat of the world as a field, as distance, as matter. (Virilio 1986: 133)

The militarisation of society at large and of the media in particular (the 'airwaves' of telecommunication) produces an acceleration of communication which demolishes the temporal and spatial distance between action and the world. By erasing that difference, the militarised media destroy the materiality of the world and our relations with it. It is into this trajectory of media history that Virilio inserts his concept of picnolepsia, the medical term for those momentary lapses in attention that arise from stress or boredom. The cinema as an invention employs those lapses and encourages their development, both since the machinery of projection requires that we ignore the spaces between frames when the screen goes dark, and since it depends on the active participation of the audience in constructing the continuity of film, which, being made up of discrete frames, is otherwise, like Marey's chrono-photographs, fundamentally discontinuous. In the end, this acclimatisation to the discontinuous sampling of reality will lead to 'the authority of electronic automatism, reducing our will to zero' (Virilio 1991a: 104). Virilio spends little time analysing the films of the Lumière brothers, often seen as the originals of the documentary and realist traditions of cinema, and instead repeatedly returns to the illusionistic magical tableaux of Georges Méliès. Marey's chrono-photography, Virilio argues, established a science of the invisible, revealing what the eye is too slow to catch, an analysis very close to that of Walter Benjamin, who described the same mysterious beauty of images of water splashing or bullets striking wood as 'the optical unconscious' (Benjamin 1969a: 237). In Méliès's trick films of the 1890s,

> What science attempts to illuminate, 'the non-seen of the lost moments', becomes with Méliès *the very basis of the production of appearance*, of his invention, what he shows of reality is what reacts continually to the absences of the reality which has passed. (Virilio 1991a: 17)

The problems addressed here, of the ability of the eye to establish continuity between frames ('persistence of vision') and even more so the ability to effect the transition from shot to shot, have been central to the discussion of cinema since the earliest times. But he introduces another theme: that what is actually shown in a Méliès film like *The Man with the India Rubber Head*, where the director's head appears to expand, is, on the one hand, characters reacting to the absurd and impossible events engineered through manipulating the cinematic apparatus, and, on the other, the bizarre autonomy of objects and characters freed from the chains of reality by the same cinematic devices. A technology that had begun by trying to reveal a world too small or too fast for human perception ends up as a medium for inventing things with no ties to reality at all.

   Virilo's picnoleptic theory assumes the subordination of the viewer not to the text of a film and its ideological messages, but to the medium of cinema itself. Harking back again to McLuhan, for Virilio, the medium is the message. And that message is that subjectivity is whittled away by the picnoleptic events to which the cinema has accustomed us. Cinema's production of a reality effect – the way it allows us to believe that what we see is a record of some real event – itself relies on an absence from reality: picnolepsia, a lapse of attention. Reality disappears in our absent-minded inattention, and in the same loss of connection between perceiver and perceived, so does our subjectivtity. The process has only speeded up with the expansion of military surveillance technologies into the vast reaches of outer space.

> Where the *passive* small-scale optics of the space of matter – air, water, lens glass – was happy to serve up the **great world** of appearances for our contemplation, the *active* large-scale optics of the time of the speed of light opens, beyond any horizon, on to flickering perception of the **small world** of the transparence of waves bearing various signals: a 'transappearance' that eliminates the normal boundary of the horizon line, exclusively promoting the screen frame, 'the square horizon'. (Virilio 1997: 41)

The older optics used to give us a simple one-to-one relationship with things on a human scale: even the lens glass of telescopes and microscopes only introduced us to worlds of a scale at the threshold of our own. But the immense orbiting machinery of contemporary military science, inhabiting the absolute timescales of the speed of light (absolute because, according to Einstein's theory of relativity, nothing can travel faster) and installed beyond the horizon of human vision (they see us, but we can't see them), has shrunk the world. Our seeing was once passive and contemplative: we saw things as they were, and we could enter into philosophical dialogue with them. But in the big optics of the new order, we see only waveforms, not things: today we measure quanta of light. Cinema's flickering twenty-four frames per second, a rate established to match human perception, has been superseded by the staggering, inhuman transmission rates of gigabytes per second that only another machine can interpret. In the vast agglomerations of minute observations made at incredible speeds, the world gradually vanishes, turned into the pure datastreams, so that the old horizon (not just the limits of human vision but philosophically the bounds of human perception) is replaced by a new and entirely artifical one: the 'horizon' of the VDU (visual display unit).

The appearance on which our relations with the world once were based has been replaced by a combination of transparency and disappearance, a 'transappearance' (a word we could perhaps retranslate into English as 'virtuality') into which the old, familiar world is evaporating. Where analogue media like photography and film could still claim at least a resemblance to actual objects and actual vision, the digital image is now entirely abstracted from material reality and especially from the reality of human perception. Marey's chrono-photographs relied on the eye (persistence of vision) and the brain (the phi-effect, in which the brain fills in the missing flow from image to image). The digital media work at rates that go beyond what we can sense or even what we can think. The analogue makes a picture that is analogous to what it depicts; the digital transforms its objects into numbers and ultimately into signals circulating at speeds and scales that defy human perception: too fast, too small. Picnoleptic lapses become, in the digital era, a fading not just of subjectivity but also of objectivity. Moreover, by eradicating the effect of distance through their

immense acceleration of perception, media-instigated picnolepsia has eradicated the distance (the 'horizon') between subject and object, the constitutive difference that allowed one to perceive the other. 'How can we but
fear now', Virilio asks, 'a profound sense of being shut up in an environment
deprived of both horizon and *optical density*?'(Virilio 1997: 41).

The governing theme of this discourse is clearly one of loss, elegantly
summarised as 'the more speed increases, the faster freedom decreases'
(Virilio 1986: 142), and in a paraphrase of Kipling: 'the concept of reality is
always the first victim of war' (Virilio 1989a: 33). The implication is that
freedom and reality were mutually dependent on the difference between
subject and object in perception, and that with their dissolution, the
possibility of free choice has disappeared. Not surprisingly then Virilio
occupies an exclusively critical stance towards the technologies of transport
and transmission, which have, in his analysis, reformulated what it means to
be human. In this way, as Kellner (1998) has proposed, he follows in the
phenomenological footsteps of Martin Heidegger (1977) and Jacques Ellul
(1964) in offering an account of mass media as totalitarian, adding a specific
spin concerning the loss of the local. As he expresses it to Oliveira,
'Globalization – and don't we have a paradox here? – also means the end of
one entire world: the world of the particular and of the localized' (Oliveira
1996). The human scale of perception is inundated by the sheer speed of
communication, and in its place there arrives a fierce, inhuman gaze whose
motive is assault and destruction, and whose mechanical delivery systems
not only carry into daily life the imperatives of warfare but, by demolishing
the human scale of face-to-face perception, also deprive us of the basis from
which we might resist its domination. We cannot even blame some warrior
class for this state of affairs. The position is summed up in an essay dating
from the mid-1980s:

> The will-to-power of those industrial nations who, at the turn of the century,
> practised the techniques of total war, has now been replaced by the theoretical
> operations of a totally involuntary war, on the part of post-industrial nations
> investing increasingly in informatics, automation, and cybernetics. In these
> societies, the use of human labor-force and the direct responsibility of people has
> been displaced by the powers of 'anticipated' and 'deferred' substitution, the
> power of the system of auto-directed armaments, self-programmed detection
> networks, and automatic respondents who lead humanity to the confinement of a
> hopeless waiting. (Virilio 1991b: 136)

The invention of total war was a deliberate, willed act, but once set in
motion, the war machine has its own logic, its own evolutionary momentum,
regardless of poltical will. In the new post-industrial information economies,
self-programmed, fully automated systems – both factories and early warning systems, for example – have taken the power of decision away from
human agents. A military decision in the age of cybernetics cannot wait for
human reaction times: automatic alarms must set off automatic weapons. All
human beings can do is wait to find out what happens: they are no longer
participants in their own history. This invasion of the social by the ethos of

the military Virilo calls 'endo-colonisation' (the prefix 'endo-' indicating an attention to the internal state of a system; its opposite, 'exo-', concerns external relations with other systems): our societies have been colonised by their own war machines: peace is only hibernation, the period of preparation of the next conflict.

The Gulf War, as we shall see in Chapter 6, was to some extent a conflict between two historical epochs. The Iraqis fought for a territory in which they still believed; but for the information warrior, territory has no meaning. It has been assimilated into the datastreams of the battle computer and has become immaterial. So the extreme form of the warrior's ancient demand for mobility is, ironically, the extreme immobility of the bomber pilot watching not the target but the electronic image of the target generated not by a camera but by a three-dimensional computer simulation of the desert below his wings. Both cinema and the typical civilian transport of our time, the automobile, likewise produce an immobile spectator rather than a mobile participant. From the first cinematic pan-shot of the 1890s to the broadcasting technologies of the post-war period, Virilio argues in an essay on 'The Last Vehicle', travelling has been diminished, losing first the idea of a journey due to the acceleration of trains, cars and now planes, then losing the concept of departure, since new media allow us to travel without ever leaving home (as in a sense we are 'at home' in our cars). In the end we are left with 'the primacy of arrival (which is momentary)' (Virilio 1989b: 118).

With the diminution of journeys, there arrives the possibility of the elimination of space. Global electronic information and transmission systems now provide the technological infrastructure not only for the end of geography, but also for its replacement with the 'time of light', the instantaneous transmission of data at the limit speed of the universal constant. But while Virilio, rather inaccurately describing transmission rates as 'instantaneous', argues for the triumph of time (speed) over space, he is also able to offer an insight into the changing nature of time. 'Today', he notes in *The Vision Machine*, ' "extensive" time has given way to "intensive" time. This deepens the infinitely small of duration, of microscopic time, the final figure of eternity rediscovered outside the imaginary of the extensive eternity of bygone centuries' (Virilio 1994a: 72). The old Christian sense of eternity as an endless extension of time has given to the time of machine decisions: a time of the infinitely small. For Virilio, technology and science are indistinguishable, just as political theory and political actuality are for Baudrillard. The advanced dematerialisation Virilio sees in quantum physics, as indeed in the emergent mathematics of fractals, is intrinsic to the opto-electronic technologies which are busily substituting for first-hand experience. Equally clearly, he goes against the flow of Anglo-Saxon postmodernism, with its emphasis on spatialisation and relative lack of interest in temporality (for example, Harvey 1989; Jameson 1992; Wilson and Dissanayake 1996). Instead, he sees the lure of inhabiting ever smaller fractional moments as the end of historical experience, an experience which had been premised on spatial and especially local awareness. The picnoleptic moment is no longer simply the innocent inattention that permits the illusion of cinema, and instead has become the goal of new datastreaming technologies whose speed exceeds that of perception, and which therefore promote a permanent state of unawareness, of null experience, with all activity delivered over to the optical machine, and all passivity delivered to the passenger immobilised aboard Concorde or immersed in virtual reality.

'The thing described takes over from the real thing' (Virilio 1995a: 43) in the politics of disinformation, indeed the 'essential culture of disinformation' (Virilio 1995a: 61). This substitution or 'commutation' of virtual for physical proximity reduces to zero that distance which, for Virilio, is constitutive of human identity: the distance between observer and observed, subject and object. Disinformation is then the creation of a fiction in which the world is no longer object over against the subject, but simply a concatenation of malleable and consumable entities, almost like Heidegger's 'standing-reserve', the world reduced to the status of raw material by the technological mindset (Heidegger 1977). When, as Virilio believes, representation ceases to evoke a real world of immediate perception, the representational media also curtail the possibility of democratic representation, not least because of the degree to which democracy is a system which allows for and even encourages the sudden arrival of unforeseen events. In *The Vision Machine*, Virilio addresses the intersection of militarisation and representation in terms of 'the logistics of perception':

> It is a war of images and sounds, rather than objects and things, in which winning is simply a matter of not losing sight of the opposition. The will to see all, to know all, at every moment, everywhere, the will to universalized illumination: a scientific permutation on the eye of God which would forever rule out the surprise, the accident, the irruption of the unforeseen. (Virilio 1994a: 70)

War has changed, in the era of stealth bombers and smart weapons, by a process of absolute acceleration, from the face-to-face struggle for occupation of physical space to a thoroughly mediated struggle for absolute surveillance. This absolute surveillance and its counter, camouflage and deception, are extended to the politics of the militarised state. In the meantime, visual media accelerated to the point of instantaneity have altered the terms of perception, through the ambition to emulate God, in the erasure of the contingent, of that quality of chance which always helps us recognise the perception of reality, and the reality of our perceptions: only reality can truly surprise us, since artificial worlds are always too perfect, too planned in advance and too controlled.

This brings us to one of Virilio's key terms, 'accident', a word with two meanings. One of these meanings derives from mediaeval philosophy. Virilio argues that mediation first eradicates the 'substance', the immutable essence of objects, and later, in a second movement from mechanical to electronic media, obliterates even the 'accidence', the material form in which substance presents itself to perception. The reality of an object's image is thus displacing the virtuality of its presence (Virilio 1994a: 64); that is, in transmission, even the materiality of the image is substituted in a process of virtualisation which is in some way the offspring of camouflage and military dissimulation. We are then faced with the 'fusion of the object with its equivalent image' (Virilio 1994a: 68) tending towards 'an artificial reality involving digital simulation that would oppose the "natural reality" of classical experience' (Virilio 1994a: 76). At such a juncture, '*Vision, once substantial, becomes accidental*' (Virilio 1994a: 13). This means, not that vision becomes random, but that it loses sight of the substantive essence of things, their ideal forms, and sees only the inessential material shape they take up in physical reality, especially the microscopic, atomic or molecular properties which contemporary scientific technologies can investigate. We observe not being but seeming. If the substance is the truth of the object, then the truth lost in digital representations is that ideal form that precedes and exceeds the limits of the mundane, while accidence, which is all that can be captured in photo-mechanical or opto-electronic media, is the merely ephemeral and worldly.

For Virilio, the triumph of ephemeral appearance is a sign of the abolition of the weight, mass, bulk and depth of truth. The truth of objects lies in their obdurate otherness, a position relative to subjects that they have lost in the instantaneity of transmission. Without that relative position, accident takes on its second meaning, of catastrophe. Stripped of the density of their essential substance, objects are no longer governed now by truth. Instead, they are subjected to the rules of digital hypermedia, which administer themselves not according to the truth of human scales but according to the laws of quantum mechanics that govern the miniscule spaces of electrons. And quantum mechanics is the domain of the undecidable and the uncertainty principle, a space in which even science abandons pursuit of pure truth. These appearances, no longer hindered by the weight of truth, circulating at unheard-of speeds, bring us to the brink of info-war and data-crash. Such is Virilio's account of the 1989 Black Friday stock market crash, which he reads as a function of the uncontrolled acceleration of machine-driven trading in derealised stocks and shares. As with our loss of control over the military machine, our devices first disassociate money from reality, and then accelerate its circulation to speeds which only machines can handle. Human beings no longer have a chance to guide or manipulate the global economy, which has become an autonomous machine whose ultimate goal is to produce disaster. Likewise hacker hits on power supplies and databanks appear to him as the disaster which is always invented at the same moment as the vehicle, in the same way that derailments and wrecks are the necessary accompaniment of trains and cars. The 'general accident' (Virilio 1997: 132) will prove Virilio right in the moment that it makes all statements of truth or probability impossible. The insubstantial will, in that moment of wreckage, ruin the substance of the world, homogenising all differences previously guaranteed by the distance between objects and subjects.

To clarify Virilio's arguments, I want to develop an analysis of the car. For Greens, the private automobile is without doubt the single most deleterious innovation of the last century, even more so than the military technologies deployed in wars too often begun to secure supplies of fuel for it. Motorists are careless of the ecological effect of the noxious fumes expelled by their vehicles, despite the fact that their own children suffer from the respiratory diseases they cause, just as they claim innocence for the oil spills attendant on the trade in petrol. The car instils in its driver and passengers that sense of right and invulnerability that is responsible for so many deaths. It inscribes in the motorist the expectation of surveillance. It travels far faster than the human sensorium can cope with. Few people would batter an animal to death in cold blood, but roadkill is considered an acceptable by-product of the right to speed, as indeed is the statistical record of human deaths. The car is a device which isolates the driver from the world, transforming bodies into pure trajectory and removing all but the most rudimentary communication with others, consisting solely of signals concerning direction and velocity. The motorway is the scene of picnolepsia, the suspended consciousness of driving on auto-pilot. The non-space of the car's interior, underwritten by its isolating soundtrack of radio and recorded music, abstracts us from the randomness of the weather and other people. Inscribed in discourses as various as advertising campaigns and Chuck Berry songs as the individualist icon of freedom and mastery, the motor is in fact quite the opposite: a device for immobilisation and subjection. Its reality is neither the open road nor even the moment of arrival but the horizonless no-man's-land of the traffic jam.

In Virilio's vision, it scarcely matters whether you are bowling along the open road or stationary in gridlock. In either case, the driver is immobilised inside his or her vehicle, a prisoner of its restricted horizons, the world beyond framed in the artificial rectangle of the screen. In traffic, the only direction is through, the only speed relative, and the vaunted freedom of the road is restricted by every law of the highway code, a code which is ingrained in every motorist, a second nature, a harness worn in so deeply we no longer realise we are wearing it. Near and far, here and there are collapsed into the actions of getting into and out of the vehicle. The architecture of the freeway is no longer that of gatehouses, staging posts, nor even of hills and valleys, since the car ignores the effort a pedestrian, rider or cyclist puts into traversing the terrain. Instead it is the empty, purely functional architecture of airports, there not to detain your interest but to speed you through. Meanwhile, back on the road, the environment is smeared across the windscreen, devoid of detail, no longer a world of objects but a landscape flattened into a perpetual and undifferentiated present. Only signs remain, traffic signs that tell us where we are or, in the more remote routes of North America, remind you that you are still travelling across a landscape rendered featureless by speed. We drive on roads which are more intensively policed than our homes, more heavily surveyed, and which, at any point of crisis, can be taken away from us for the military uses for which they were first designed.

But the main attraction of Virilio's writing for simulation theory is not his account of transport, fascinating though that is, but his analysis of the media. Central to this is the 'lost dimension' of time. Instantaneous transmission of miniaturised data in quantities baffling to human reason is the beginning of a new mode of time. The philosophy of time is among the most demanding and the most uncertain; surprisingly, since time is such a universal human experience (for a scientist's view, see Davies 1995; for a philosopher's, see Osborne 1995). The great French historian Fernand Braudel defines three scales of time: *histoire événementielle*, the scale of day-to-day events and ordinary experience; biographical time, the timescale of poitical events that can occur over someone's lifetime; and the *longue durée*, the large time-scales over which empires rise and fall, climates and trade routes evolve, or media formations come and go (Braudel 1972: I, 20–1). But for Virilio, 'Chronological and historical time, time that passes, is replaced by a time that exposes itself instantaneously. On the computer screen', he explains, 'a time period becomes the "support-surface" of inscription' (Virilo 1991b: 14). To understand this new form of time, Virilio's books argue, we have to understand the nature of the militarisation of space. Digital time is simply the outcome of a longer history of warfare, in which

> The erection of the hillock, then of the donjon, is another answer to the problem of mastery over dimension, the latter becoming perspective, geometry of the gaze from an omniscient fixed point – and no longer, as it was before, from the synoptic route of the horseman. (Virilio 1986: 72)

To the rider, the landscape reveals itself in the stages of the journey, and seeing and travelling occupy the same time The point of the castle as viewpoint, by contrast, is that it allows you to see without travelling. This it gives a literally commanding gaze over the space that surrounds it – the more usual English translation for 'donjon', the central tower in a mediaeval castle, is the revealing word 'keep'. But Virilio's point is more fundamental than that: he argues here that this commanding gaze is the beginning of the geometricisation of vision as perspective in the Renaissance, an abstraction of vision from which commences the tendency towards seeing all space from a single point. This command tower is then the origin of a mastery not only over space but over 'dimension', including the dimension of time, since it does not depend, as the horseman does, on the time of travelling to see the territory. This move from nomadic to fortified warfare, which, as we shall see, is also a major theme of Deleuze and Guattari's work on miltary history, is then one which begins the process of delocalisation, of abstracting the process of command and control from the specificity of the terrain: we confront here something like the process Baudrillard evokes with his story of the map the same size as the territory.

The figure of the donjon as control over space through the loss of time leads directly to the art of the siege, and in the phrase 'state of siege' we can already hear the echo of Virilio's thesis of endo-colonisation of civil society by the military ethos. But with the arrival of nuclear deterrence and strategic computers, we have moved *'from the state of siege* of wars of space to *the state of emergency* of the war of time'* (Virilio 1986: 140). Victory today is won not by controlling space but by the speed of attack and response, the infinitesimal time of computer strategy. The politics of deterrence is then an agreement between the powers to share the world under threat of destroying it: deterrence denies the difference between supposed enemies. But it also promotes a state of crisis which spreads throughout society on either side of the battle lines to deny freedom and enforce submission to the miniaturised, automated will of strategic machines, which now control not only the army but manufacturing, supermarket supplies and the global financial markets.

The state of siege moved us from the age of the statesman to the age of the state; the state of emergency moves us into an age of global corporations, which no longer respond to the will of an individual or a class, but operate as autonomous automata. In an essay for *Le Monde Diplomatique* in 1995, Virilio argues that cyberspace (which no longer has a single centre, since every node of the net functions as a centre) has produced a new perspective. This perspective is global, deploying a global time which supplants both local times (and their histories) and local space. Information technologies promoting real-time interaction and instantaneous response are effectively a new type of bomb, an electronic bomb to replace the atomic one, whose disintegration 'will not merely affect the particles of matter, but also the very people of which our societies consist' (Virilio 1995b). That implosion of the human is promised by the latest technological developments, implants, stereo laser goggles that write their images directly onto the retina, artifical memories hard-wired into the cerebral cortex (this latter as yet a science fiction idea, but one seriously touted by contemporary roboticists like Hans Moravec [1988]). The human body itself is becoming an exposed territory within which the accelerating technologies of miniaturisation and automation are being installed.

No wonder then that there is no space left to mark the differences between us; only the automated datastreams of a thoroughly militarised state of global emergency. Perhaps the invention of the ship was also the invention of the shipwreck, but at least the shipwreck, the train wreck, the traffic accident were local events. In the global networks of cybernetic society, the accident will be global: like the stock market crash of 1989, or like the Mutually Assured Destruction of nuclear holocaust. Virilio's thought is in some ways even bleaker than Baudrillard's, for the only alternative he can see to the 'code' is the total destruction of the planet, and even that will come about without tragedy or glory, since it will not be one of us who sets it off, but the ordinary workings of the machines to which we have entrusted ourselves, and to whom, as a result, we have become enslaved.

(iv) Umberto Eco: irony and hyperreality

> Imagine a family of four grown men, one in bed with a sore throat, one
> with fresh plaster dust on his pants, one who played baseball all last
> summer and one holding the basin.
>
> (William Carlos Williams, *The Descent into Winter*)

Slavery, of course, is not the only relation we can have with our machines.
But, sometimes positive, sometimes negative, the belief that machines have
come to dominance over human beings is one of the most deeply seated
truisms of contemporary culture. The theme goes at least as far back as
Charlie Chaplin's satirical vision of workers swallowed by machinery in
Modern Times (1936) and the writings of the Italian Marxist Antonio
Gramsci (1891–1937) on Fordism and Taylorism, in which he argued that
the then novel organisation of factory work was the precursor to socialism,
in which individual desires would be subordinated to social needs (Gramsci
1971). While the humanist line of thought defied and decried mechanisation,
more technologically inclined writers would continue to promote modernisa-
tion as synonymous with mechanisation, and more recently with computerisation. An important strand of the work of the Italian writer Umberto Eco
(b. 1932) has been to point out the dependence of both of these arguments on
a single, shared faith in the efficacy of machines and the way we presume, in
popular culture and in the academy, that they change us, rather than that we
change them.

Professor of Semiotics at the University of Bologna, a major scholar of
mediaeval literature and thought, an influential editor with the publishing
house Bompiani, a widely read newspaper columnist, Umberto Eco is
nowadays even better known as the novelist of *The Name of the Rose*
(1983), *Foucault's Pendulum* (1989) and *The Island of the Day Before*
(1995). Starting from a professional career in television in the 1950s, Eco
has been an influential commentator on popular culture as well as receiving
international acclaim for his work on topics as diverse as the aesthetics of
the great mediaeval theologian St Thomas Aquinas, comic-strip super-heroes
and James Joyce and other avant-garde writers and artists, and for his
pioneering semiotics, assimilating concepts from information theory into the
analysis of sign-systems.

For our purposes, however, the most important aspect of Eco's work is a
series of essays ranging back into the mid-1960s which use the literary and
rhetorical skills of semiotics on the seemingly banal topics of comic books,
pop songs and political speechifying. In an early exegesis of the state of play
in studies of pop culture first published in 1964 (Eco 1994: 17–35), Eco
distinguished between two types of commentator. The 'apocalyptic' critic
sees in every novel turn of culture a new reason to bemoan the loss of the
old values. But the real hallmark of the apocalyptics, he argues, is that they
do not blame specific films, comics or programmes but whole technologies.
Eco accuses structuralist thinkers, especially Roland Barthes and Michel
Foucault, of an even more extreme variant on this process of blaming. Like

their influential predecessor Jacques Ellul (Ellul 1964), they believe that language itself is a machine, and one which, bent to the purposes of what Ellul called technique, is capable of controlling and directing our very thoughts. For Eco this belief is a tragi-comic travesty of our complex negotiations in and with culture. Though it precedes the earliest writings of Debord, Baudrillard and Virilio by several years, Eco's critique can very easily be extended to their apocalyptic versions of simulation theory.

Opposing the apocalyptics are the 'integrated' critics, for whom the new is by definition better than the old, and every novelty is a sign of progress towards an ultimate goal. It is clear from other essays (notably 'Cogito Interruptus' in Eco 1986: 221–38) that Marshall McLuhan falls into this category. While much of Eco's spleen is directed at the totalising fears of the apocalyptics, not least because they formed the direct opposition to his own attempts to establish popular culture as an object of serious academic discussion, he is equally distrustful of the naïve utopianism of integrated commentators. Indeed, he sees both as the two sides of the same coin, for both have wildly overestimated the powers of the media, for good or for evil.

In their place, he argued, in *The Role of the Reader*, a book which had an important impact on cultural studies in the English-speaking world, that 'The unity of a text lies in its destination, not its origin' (Eco 1981: 8). Any text, even the most humble, is capable of carrying many types and levels of meaning, and can be read from any one of a number of points of view. We can read something as evidence of its author's state of mind, as a historical document, as symptomatic of a particular religious world-view, as a formal exercise in the use of a language, and so on. What unifies these facets of the work is not its writing, its manufacture or its publication (remember Eco knows these aspects of culture from his days in the television and publishing industries), but the moment at which it is read. Only then does a text achieve unity (the word 'text', for Eco as for all semioticians, means anything that has a meaning, from a novel to a lawnmower). In fact, in the same book, Eco makes a strong case for the power of readers over texts: our ability to take the most banal TV panel game and invest it with deep significance, or the most profound novel and read it in the most trivial way. Texts, from highway signs to art-house movies, only have a meaning for us, and we are partners in the construction of that meaning.

All of which seems quite acceptable and even consoling. Except that Eco is rarely satisfied with the obvious conclusion. The problems begin with his attempts to understand the relationships between signification and reality. As we will see in Chapter 4, Eco is very involved in thinking about the transition we make between perceiving things and thinking about them. In general, he is content to accept that we belong to communities of speakers who share a general idea about how the world is, and who use that shared idea as the basis for communication. But what happens when the bases on which a community builds its shared assumptions are no longer exactly real? This is the problem which he confronts in what is, in many respects, a simple and straightforward piece of travel writing, the 1975 essay, 'Travels in Hyperreality' (Eco 1986: 3–58). In this essay, the three concerns we have already noted in his work – with the falsity of faith in technology, with the powers of readers to remake and reinterpret texts, and with the implications of information theory for semiotic interpretation – come into contact with the impressive weirdness of the North American leisure industry. Eco's essay, unlike the works that have occupied us so far, scarcely needs a gloss. It is lucid, entertaining and at times very funny. But it does require some elucidation, if only in order to clarify what marks out Eco's concept of hyperreality from Debord's spectacle, Baudrillard's simulation and the 'transappearance' of Virilio's technologised world.

Eco starts from the ideal position of the cultural analyst: the journey to a foreign culture. This is where cultural studies began: in aristocratic expeditions into peasant folklore and anthropological investigations of civilisations alien to European perspectives. Eco in the USA presents us with the spectacle of kitsch, as the old anthropologists showed us the spectacle of strange customs and beliefs. But he also shows us, quite deliberately, the spectacle of a European intellectual aghast at the sheer scale and depth of the kitsch he unearths from Florida to San Diego. Surrounded by a consumer capitalism which equates prosperity with waste and whose slogan is 'more', he argues, 'the American imagination demands the real thing and, to attain it, must fabricate the absolute fake; where . . . falsehood is enjoyed in a situation of "fullness", of *horror vacui*' (Eco 1986: 8). The dream of prosperity has become a fear of emptiness, so that, in order to cover over the possibility of a real void, US culture creates a fantastic, lurid and entirely false world of kitsch and imitation. Elsewhere he refers to the same phenomenon, especially in California, as 'an obligatory model of "happiness" ' (Eco 1986: 101). We recognise already the inspiration of Debord: the shock of compulsory consumption.

When ex-President Lyndon B. Johnson builds an ultra-precise replica of the Oval Office in his personal museum in Texas; when Forest Lawn cemeteries offer an undamaged Last Supper, brighter, newer and cleaner than the old and battered one Leonardo left in Italy; when a waxworks museum presents not just fake canvases but full-size three-dimensional mock-ups of the peasant bedroom painted by van Gogh *in the style of van Gogh*, the Italian professor's jaw drops. And, as professors will, he offers us some possible explanations. The US's 'ravenous consumption of the present' (Eco 1986: 9) results in an 'alternate process of futuristic planning and nostalgic remorse' (Eco 1988: 10), which would account for the apparent incompatibility between the visionary USA of Frank Lloyd Wright's architecture, the machine aesthetic and the rigorous abstract art of Jackson Pollock, on the one hand, and the kitsch world of Ripley's Believe It Or Not and Las Vegas honeymoon hotels, on the other.

As an alternative explanation, Eco suggests that perhaps the heterogeneous mishmash of styles in Randolph Hearst's immense San Simeon mansion (the model for Citizen Kane's funerary palace in Orson Welles'

1941 film) is a way of speaking to the future: 'These eclectic reconstructions are governed by a great remorse for the wealth that was acquired by methods less noble than the architecture that crowns them, a great will to expiatory sacrifice, a desire for posterity's absolution' (Eco 1986: 27–8). Here, as in the fake Michelangelos that proliferate across Eco's journey, 'The eternity of art becomes a metaphor for the eternity of the soul' (Eco 1986: 56), and we intuit that the root cause of the *horror vacui* is in fact a fear of death.

A third possibility is that the most egregious examples of kitsch seem to arise in those areas of the country where there is nothing else: nothing but nature. In order to tame the plains and forests, they have had to be cleared, and with them all memory of the past, all history. Instead of a history that has been made in the local arena (such as still persists, says Eco, in New Orleans), the US is condemned to build an imitation of history. In Europe, the awareness of history is so strong that it stops us falling for the hyperreal, but in its absence, brought on by the furious consumption of the present demanded by the world's strongest economy, North America falls prey to the hyperreal: 'the frantic desire for the Almost Real arises only as a neurotic reaction to the vacuum of memories; the Absolute fake is offspring of the unhappy awareness of a present without depth' (Eco 1986: 30–1). It is worth noting here, since Eco elsewhere condemns apparently similar metaphysical belief in the loss of the real, that this 'present without depth' is specific to North American consumer capitalism, and especially to its understanding of whatever is present as raw material for producing and reproducing more and more commodities, a process which destroys the sense of history as well as its monuments.

And finally, we consume these hyperrealities for the entirely circular reason that they confirm our status as consumers. Finding yourself in the General Store of a reconstructed ghost town, you participate in the illusion by buying the mementos on offer, so securing the only relation that matters, that of buying and selling. The illusion is completed in the trade, and your participation is authenticated by the fact that you have paid for the privilege. As Eco puts it, 'What is falsified is our will to buy, which we take as real, and in this sense Disneyland is really the quintessence of consumer ideology' (Eco 1986: 43). The 'will' to buy, itself already a social and cultural construct, is further falsified by its assimilation into the play-world of Disneyland, so removing us even further from any 'natural' desires. Moreover, as Eco points out in his essay pinpointing Marshall McLuhan as the major exemplar of integrated thought, this falsification is typical of mass entertainment, in which 'the confusion of collateral information serves only to make appetizing a central structure that is unrelentingly redundant, so that the reader will receive always and only what he has already known (or understood)' (Eco 1986: 236). Thus circularity – inhabiting a culture that only tells you what you already know – is implicit in the self-reproducing world of the hyperreal.

This theme is taken up five years before 'Travels in Hyperreality' in an essay in which Eco addresses trade fairs and the 'sociology of objects' which marked Baudrillard's first steps towards the theory of simulation (Baudrillard 1968). Eco identifies two orders of objects: attractive consumer goods like motor boats and easy chairs, and 'ugly' objects like lathes and presses not aimed at the consumer market. Imagining a visitor who decides he wants the consumer goods, not the machine tools, he argues that

> In reality he has not chosen; he has only accepted his role as consumer of consumer goods since he cannot be a proprietor of means of production. . . . He will work at the lathe, which is not his because (the fair has told him) he doesn't want it. (Eco 1988: 185)

Clearly there is a political aspect to Eco's reading at this earlier point. It is possible to see, however, in the development of Eco's thought a gradual drift away from this Marxist vocabulary, similar (but by no means identical) to the anti-Marxist turn in French thought after 1968. In Eco's case, this would appear to be a result not simply of the failed revolutions of '68, also very important in Italy, but also of the bizarre episode of the Red Brigades. During the mid-1970s, a group of ultra-leftists in Italy set about a series of guerrilla attacks on central institutions and individuals in Italy, culminating in the kidnapping and eventual murder of the Prime Minister, Aldo Moro. In an essay twice translated into English (Eco 1986: 113–18; Eco 1994: 177–81), Eco considers the Red Brigade's claim to be 'striking at the heart of the state'. Like most contemporary political commentators, he discovers that there is no such thing. We do not inhabit a hierarchical, feudal structure in which the death of the king, as in chess, signals the end of the game; rather we inhabit a system, closer to those analysed by Norbert Wiener than those outlined by Marx. This essay, first published in 1978, contains several points that remind the reader forcefully of Baudrillard. For example, 'when you live in a universe where a system of productive interests exploits the atomic stalemate to impose a peace useful to all sides . . . national revolution can no longer be waged; everything is decided elsewhere' (Eco 1986: 115). Moreover, despite the belief of the Red Brigades that Moro held some kind of conspiratorial data on strategies for defeating the working class, 'the great systems have no secrets' (Eco 1986: 116) – a thesis extremely close to Baudrillard's 'obscenity', the radical transparency of contemporary societies that leaves them without depth.

Like his fellow simulationists, Eco goes on to argue that 'Terrorism is not the enemy of the great systems; on the contrary, it is their natural counterweight, accepted, programmed' (Eco 1986: 116), since it licenses the state to apply similarly terroristic tactics to suppress the terrorists. And, because 'everybody has something to lose in a situation of generalized terrorism', the attempt to use terror as a way of mobilising the masses is doomed, as they will inevitably 'stand firm against terrorism' where it threatens their daily lives (Eco 1986: 117). As he remarks in another essay, also published in 1978, far from decapitating the state, assassination 'doesn't weaken the system, but rather recreates the consensus around the symbolic ghost of its "heart", wounded and outraged' (Eco 1986: 175). Only by encouraging attacks on its absent heart can the system persuade us that it really possesses one. In other words, the terrorists are part of the system's own reproductive cycle, helping to reinforce the symbolic logic of the Code, to use Baudrillard's expression, at the very moment in which they believe they are attacking it.

What then are the limits of the hyperreal? Is there a real outside its rule? To answer this question, Eco invites us to ponder another: what is a mass medium today? His example is a sports shirt. The firm advertises the shirt, people wear it (and display its logo), TV actors wear the shirt to evoke the lifestyle of the people who wear it: we are confronted with a circuit of images which no longer has a single authority behind it. Like the Red Brigades, older theories of ideology saw it as the product of some kind of plan, but 'there is no longer any telling where the "plan" comes from. Because there is, of course, a plan, but it is no longer intentional' (Eco 1986: 149). There is no originating power here, only the permeation of everyday life by the imagery of consumption. A system without a heart.

In yet another essay, where Eco owns up to his rather inventive and active dislike of sport, this circulation is attached to a specific linguistic function, phasis. The phatic mode of speech is exemplified in those meaningless but socially binding phrases we use every day: phrases like 'Hello', 'How are you?', 'What's happening?'. Such phrases don't communicate content; they establish a channel for communication. The butt of Eco's analysis this time is the chatter of sports presenters on TV. Here we have the necessity of talking, without there necessarily being anything to talk about. Any kind of chatter, he argues, is phatic rather than communicative; indeed, at its purest, it is purely phatic (Eco 1986: 165). But where idle talk serves the purpose of binding a community together, TV sports chatter has no such goal, even though it tries to pass itself off as creating a community of sports fans. The significance of sport on TV is that it takes the already wasteful expenditure of energy in games, then raises the waste-value by removing the physical involvement of the athlete or even the fan who goes to the ground to watch. Thus, just as he had spoken of 'media squared' in the case of the sports shirt, so

> Born as the raising to the nth power of that initial (and rational) waste that is sports recreation, sports chatter is the glorification of Waste, and therefore the maximum point of Consumption. On it and in it the consumer civilization man consumes himself (and every possibility of thematizing and judging the enforced consumption to which he is invited and subjected). (Eco 1986: 165)

By the same process through which 'In an exposition we show not the objects but the exposition itself' (Eco 1986: 299), in sports commentaries we deal no longer with sport but with the mediated spectacle of sport as a pure communication without content. And insofar as that purity equates with the purity of exchange-value divorced from use, sports chatter confronts us with the most intense mode of consumerism, a mode which even erases the possibility of understanding that that is what is happening.

In earlier writings, Eco had been a champion of the power of readers. In certain ways, this thesis derived from the events of 1968, which altered so many of the old hierarchies. Asking the question, 'Does the Audience Have Bad Effects on Television?', he remarked once that 'If the apocalyptic theorists of mass communications, with their pretensions to an aristocratic Marxism of Nietzschean origins, their diffidence towards praxis and distaste for the masses, had been right', the generation of '68, immersed as never before in mass media, should have been 'church-going wage slaves' (Eco 1994: 88). As it turned out, they were growing their hair, exploring alternative beliefs and throwing Molotov cocktails at the police. But as the euphoria of the historic moment faded, we find him arguing that 'If Mallarmé once said "le monde est fait pour aboutir à un livre [the world exists to culminate in a book]", the filming of the Royal Wedding said that the British Empire was built in order to produce splendid television' (Eco 1994: 106). Now the question is less one concerning the ways audiences shape television, and more how television preconstructs reality in order to film it. So criticism has to shift its attention to the systematic re-creation of reality by the media in pursuit of televisual *mises-en-scène*,

> to the masking of reality directly realized using what we call reality (bodies, buildings, roads), and away from the interpretive stage which we once considered the moment when looking became ideological. Now ideology moves back a step in the process. The television critic must look less at the screen, not just at the screen, and always behind the screen – interpreting images as signs of other signs. (Eco 1994: 107)

In this way Eco comes round to the notion of a hyperreal: the use of real things – for example, the staging of events especially for the media, from summit meetings of world leaders to World Cup finals – to produce spectacular TV and media. The TV image is thus a second order of sign, a sign referring not to the real world but to a world that, though it was real once upon a time, is now rendered unreal by being preprocessed by television in preparation for its conversion into a further order of electronic signals and screen images.

The idea is clearer still in an essay on 'Neo-TV' published in English in 1984. Here Eco gives his account of the aesthetic changes which overcame Italian television in the 'savage deregulation' (Mattelart et al. 1984: 30–1) which took it from two state-run channels to a mass of privately owned commercial channels. 'Paleo-television' is Eco's name for the old-fashioned, government-owned and clearly ideological aesthetic which, unlike the British 'public service' ethos, actively supported the cause of the political party in power. 'Neo-TV' describes the entertainment aesthetic of the deregulated televisual market-place associated with the media entrepreneur Silvio Berlusconi. One of Eco's examples is of the shift from invisible cameras to visible ones. In paleo-television, cameras were always off-screen. But in neo-TV, they appear all the time. Their purpose, however, is not to demystify the production process, but to present us with the spectacle of television itself, and, moreover, to legitimate TV's claims to realistic portrayal of the world, a world which now also includes television. However, 'the disquieting fact is that if you see a TV camera on television it is certain not to be the one that is filming. . . . Hence, every time the TV camera appears, it is telling a lie' (Eco 1984: 21). At this point, Eco himself becomes something of an apocalyptic. He analyses teletext, for instance, in terms that would not be out of place in Virilio's critique of computer-mediated communication: 'The screen will give information on an outside world where no one will go any more. . . . The body becomes useless, and the eyes are all you need' (Eco 1984: 26). Revisiting this essay some years later, he opines that the apparent liberation of the channel-surfing viewer is based on neo-TV's characteristic narcissism:

> Each programme talks about itself and addresses an audience that is part of the programme: the message, obsessively repeated, is not 'This is how the world is', but, 'I am here, do you see me? This is the only reality that you will recognise from now on'. (Eco 1994: 110)

At moments like this, for all his protestations that he is not to be counted among the apocalyptics, Eco allows himself the luxury of accusing a whole medium of adopting strategies and techniques – what I have been calling an aesthetic – which destroy older, humanistic values, older and more direct perceptions. Even the ideological broadcasts of paleo-television were more trustworthy, because all the reader had to do was apply a filter to understand the spin applied to current affairs reporting. But neo-TV brings in a falsification of reality such that it will conform not to a known ideology with roots in the real world, but only to the fictionalisations inherent in the medium. The only truth of the media is that they stage reality to fit their requirements.

However, as Eco matures, his writing loses some of its satiric anger, and instead takes up irony as its key strategy. At times this irony is outrageously funny: the description of the Madonna Inn in 'Travels in Hyperreality' (Eco 1986: 24) had this reader laughing out loud. What allows him this more cheerful outlook is his firm belief in common sense, for irony depends on norms shared by author and reader with which to compare the absurd and the overblown. In his technical writings, especially in the 1990s, Eco has developed a meticulous defence of the community of shared values, on which he bases his refusal of the more pessimistic attitudes of other simulationists. He refuses the nihilistic trend which, arising from Nietzsche and Heidegger, produces a kind of secular mysticism, where the role of an originating God has been replaced with the concept of an originating nothingness, a void at the heart of the universe. In a 1979 essay, he accuses neo-Marxists and neo-liberals alike of adopting the kind of negative politics which we have seen in particular voiced by Baudrillard, seeing in them the threat of a 'new Middle Ages . . . a time of secular mystics, more inclined to monastic withdrawal than to civic participation' (Eco 1986: 94). Here participation is the norm, and withdrawal is absurd, not because Eco has proved it is so, but because he can allow himself to presume that this is a belief he shares with all his readers.

Though there may be some universal elements to common sense, the beliefs shared in real communities are more often very specific. There can be little doubt that 'Travels in Hyperreality' evokes a European common sense in opposition to that of North America. But this does not mean that Europe will have everything its own way in Eco's thought. So he argues that the museums of North America seek to preserve the European heritage from Europe's decay, but only because it was the triumph of North American capitalism that drove Europe into decline. The US is the home of an 'imperialistic efficiency' required for preservation. But efficiency is only needed because that very efficiency caused the crises that left Europe's old grandeur in ruins. At the same time, he asks, hasn't the European tourist in Europe an equivalent, fetishistic relation to the great landmarks of European art? Do we see Michelangelo's *David* or Leonardo's *Mona Lisa* through eyes any less clouded by our own hyperrealisms than the US visitor to Forest Lawn or the Getty Museum?

The theme is taken up in other essays on the popularity of mediaeval themes in contemporary film, television and fiction, but also in Eco's second novel, *Foucault's Pendulum*, in which a small clique of occultists become more and more deeply embroiled in an increasingly fantastical dream of arcane and ancient wisdom and metaphysical and apocalyptic disaster. The novel is full of references to mystical traditions of the Old World. For example, the team's computer is nicknamed Abulafia, which turns out to be the name of a thirteenth-century Jewish mystic, inventor of the 'ecstatic kabbala'. Kabbala is a traditional interpretative scholarship of the sacred texts of Judaism, and as a tradition of the Book it had in general maintained its respect for the letters of the ancient texts. Abraham Abulafia, however, devised a vast, quasi-mathematical system for rewriting the kabbala in such a way that it would reveal the secret wisdom of God and grant its adepts magic powers: 'For the ecstatic kabbala, language was a self-contained universe in which the structure of language represented the structure of reality itself' (Eco 1997: 31). The modern bearers of these hermetic traditions 'convince their adepts that everything is the same as anything else and that the whole world is born to convey, in any of its aspects and events, the same Message' (Eco 1986: 71). Like the millennial expectations which we have inherited from the mediaeval mystics, the involuted and interminable quest for hidden truths in the interpretation of both sacred texts and 'the book of nature' lead to a peculiar kind of madness.

And it is this delirium of interpretation which, in later technical works, has attracted much of Eco's expertise. On the one hand, as we shall see in Chapter 4, this leads to a dispute over the nature of perception and cognition and their relation to signification. On the other, it asks us to consider very carefully what, in a debate with the philosopher Richard Rorty, Eco refers to as the 'intention of the text' (Eco 1992: 25). Eco's problem here is to find a middle way between the idea of endless interpretation which he ascribes to Rorty and the older and, he argues, impossible reference to 'the author's intention'. At its heart, Eco's argument is that there exists neither a single correct interpretation, nor a completely free universe of possible interpretations, but a vast field of possibilities constrained by the text itself. If

Rorty is right, then so is Abulafia, in the sense that his pursuit of the lost Message of God's word is no more and no less valid than any other reading of the Talmud. Rorty and other deconstructionist critics are then in effect neo-mediaevals, pursuing a mystical belief in the endless interpretability of their texts regardless of the evidence of the texts themselves. Eco, however, argues for a way of reading texts that recognises their limitations: that a tune by the Spice Girls cannot be interpreted as a repair manual for a Land Rover. We can interpret the song in a thousand different ways, but only within the constraints of a common sense which gives us a general idea of what the text does and does not want to communicate.

In fact, the illusion of freedom to interpret as we will, according to our own decisions, is part and parcel of Eco's vision of the hyperreal produced by contemporary mass media. He is able to argue this case because he reserves the right to interpret the media according to the qualities which they possess and their difference from other, older media forms. Thus he does not claim that there is any pure and unmediated communication, but rather that the mode of communication, especially, as we have seen, televisual communication, can, under particular circumstances, limit the range of interpretations possible. In the case of neo-TV, the limitation concerns the structuring of reception in accordance with the precepts of consumer capitalism. Neo-TV teaches us how and why we should consume, by offering us the illusion of free choice among goods precisely designed and marketed to be chosen, by offering us the illusion of community through the empty phatic chatter of compulsory speech, and by engaging us in the aimless game of recycling images according to a plan without hierarchy or origin.

In this instance, Eco's hyperreal looks very like Baudrillard's simulation, or Debord's spectacle, and has certain affinities with Virilio's more specific critique of technology. At the same time, however, Eco sees in the political practices of '68 the germs of another practice, one that is not tied, like terrorism, to the dominant against which it seeks to rebel. This novel form of critique he calls 'semiotic guerrilla warfare', and it is based in the idea of interpretation. Certainly, we seem to have been given (but by whom and for what purposes?) the capacity for endless reinterpretation of the media. Indeed, he argues, 'variability of interpretation is the constant law of mass communications' (Eco 1986: 141). However, 'The problem of mass communication is that until now this variability of interpretation has been random' (Eco 1986: 141). While Debord, Baudrillard and Virilio argue with the sources of broadcast media, Eco asserts that 'The battle for the survival of man as a responsible being in the Communications Era is not to be won where the communication originates, but where it arrives' (Eco 1986: 142). What this will require is 'an action to urge the audience to control the message' (Eco 1986: 143), even though this means engaging in mass media forms which, by the same logic, can never be assumed to carry their messages unambiguously to their audiences. But while Baudrillard especially is a political fatalist and argues that the shared resource of mass media will always win out against the attempt to build mass movements based on any premise other than the simulacral circuit of images, Eco constantly demands that we respect the common sense of the ordinary communities to which academics and broadcasters, workers and peasants, cosmopolitans and marginalised, all of us belong. At the heart of this is a profoundly held belief in the power of reason.

Like the mediaeval philosophers who are so important to the foundations of Eco's thought, for Eco himself humanity is recognisable through such time-honoured attributions as 'the featherless biped' who possesses those unique characteristics laughter and rationality. This is a second function for Eco's infectious sense of humour: it belongs with what is properly human. He invites us constantly to share his sense of whimsy, his crazy chains of analogy, his donnish jokes and his journalistic comedy, not just to persuade, but to encourage us to participate in a dialogue which exemplifies what it argues for: wit, as an unalienable human characteristic. Similarly, he introduces into even his most comedic articles a sense of the structured argumentation of logic, the supreme model of rationality. The Latin tags that pepper his prose refer us over and over to the mediaeval logicians and their formulas for ascertaining, if not the truth, then the provable or falsifiable nature of statements. *Post hoc ergo propter hoc*, after this therefore because of this, he reminds us, doesn't necessarily prove that because computers were invented after ploughs they were caused by them. But it does disallow the statement that ploughs were caused by computers. Such fundamental rules of rational argument form the basis for Eco's claim that there is a way out of the vertiginous spiral into hyperreality.

Even if revolutions are only 'the catastrophes of the slow movements of reform' (Eco 1986: 255), still there is no general crisis of reason: 'If somebody comes and tells us he has a direct view of the Absolute and tries to impose it on us, we kick him. But don't call it crisis of reason. It's that man's crisis' (Eco 1986: 128). As the euphoria of '68 dies away, Eco, never one to ride in any triumphalist party chariot, still does not lose his sense of human proportion, underpinned by reason and expressed in laughter. With logic in one fist and mockery in the other, he invites us to the spectacle of neo-television's absurdity. Unlike Baudrillard, he can ground his vision of that monstrous, meaningless perpetration of unreality in the solid ground of rationality. But at the same time, as the hopes for alternative presses and alternative radio diminish in his horizons, and the long, slow task of education settles over his shoulders as the burden of the intellectual in the age of mass communications, his readers begin to ferret out a sense of Eco's own monastic retreat into the fortress of reason. You begin to sense that his jibes are – as he often suggests himself – the tactics of weakness, like a bullied child turning to sarcasm as her only remaining weapon. At the same time that the sense of community becomes more and more vital to his arguments, his claim on our sympathy with his wit becomes more and more dependent on a logic which can no longer be presumed to hold sway in everybody's hearts. The irony with which he treats the hyperreality of Las

Vegas or Los Angeles seems more and more the product of his own elitist presumption. If Nietzsche was the populariser of moral and aesthetic aristocracy, Eco is the populariser of scholarly and historicist aristocracy. With this significant difference: where Nietzsche felt himself above the world, Eco feels himself apart from it, not alone on the mountain top, but in some remote and ideal city of exile where reason rules, and from which the community of the just can watch with Olympian amusement the foibles of the masters of the poor. Ironically, then, it is Eco's irony, the charm of his invitation to share in a reasonable, common culture, which throws him open to the same charges of snobbery and utopianism which he levelled at the apocalyptic and integrated intellectuals.

(iv) The televisualisation of the world

> For the agora, the general community, has gone. . . . There is no place left where people can discuss the realities which concern them, because they can never lastingly free themselves from the crushing presence of media discourse.
>
> (Debord 1990: 19)

Where once trade unions, clubs and town squares gave societies the physical meeting places that allowed for a genuinely shared and negotiated common culture, we have television. All of the authors reviewed in this chapter see TV as a crucial, central device of simulation, whether as its cause or its supreme metaphor. In concluding the chapter, I would like to look at some recent statements on television by Virilio, Eco and Baudrillard that may help distinguish between their conceptions of simulation.

In an essay on problems of representation, Eco offers to consider television 'in its purest state, which would be a *closed-circuit* apparatus' (Eco 1999: 372). Installed in a bathroom, there is no reason why we should not replace mirrors with CCTV monitors (with the image reversed to resemble a mirror image). Similarly, it is possible to imagine replacing remote closed-circuit systems with a carefully positioned chain of mirrors bringing the image from A to B. In other words, allowing for the small-scale and poor resolution of TV images compared to mirrors, the only difference between a mirror and a closed-circuit system is that we can't see more of the image by shifting our angle of view (though even this might have a technical solution). So, Eco argues, this 'pure state' of television is only an as-yet more clumsy variant on any other way of looking through glass: through windows, mirrors, telescopes and microscopes. In each case, we accept the mediation of glass or electronic signal unconsciously, because we are assured that what we see is equivalent to a direct perception through air: 'We do not distrust TV, because . . . in the first instance it provides us not with signs but with perceptual stimuli' (Eco 1999: 375). The distinction he then draws is between television and photography or cinema, which 'freeze' the endless flow of the remote camera, preserving it in time, but also converting the perceptual stimulus into an image, a sign. So, for Eco, the television

image, like the mirror image, is not a sign but something prior to signification, a kind of object waiting to be perceived. Because, in this pure state, it
is not a sign, it cannot take part in the codes and conventions on which
hyperreality depends. The hyperreal is not a stimulus but a surrogate
stimulus. Unlike the mirror or CCTV, hyperreality is always a phenomenon
of signification. But it takes its particular quality from the use of reality itself
as a sign, replacing the real material that can be perceived as a stimulus with
signs masquerading as stimuli, masking the real with a sign of the real which
tries to hide the fact that it is not real but a sign. The hyperreal is an abuse
of common sense, since it confuses the orders of signs and realities.

For Baudrillard, this diagnosis is only half true. 'Illusion', he argues, 'is
not the opposite of reality; it is a more subtle reality which enwraps the
primary one in the sign of its disappearance' (Baudrillard 1996a: 85). Where
Eco's hyperreal can be challenged through the ironic appeal to common
sense, Baudrillard's simulation marks the place at which reality disappears
under the pressure of signification. Eco sees television as the pinnacle of a
technological movement which begins with the mirror, developing via the
microscope and telescope, and taking a brief detour through the recording
media of photography and cinema. Television without recording is merely
an extension of vision. But for Baudrillard, photography differs from film
and television only in its silence: 'Whatever the violence, speed or noise
which surrounds it, it gives the object back its immobility and silence'
(Baudrillard 1996a: 86). But that stillness is only 'the moment of the
negative . . . that slight time-lag which allows the image to exist before the
world – or the object – disappears into the image . . . the photo preserves the
moment of disappearance and thus the charm of the real' (Baudrillard 1996a:
86).

In the mature metaphysical system offered by Baudrillard in *The Perfect
Crime*, 'Reality exists, then, only within a certain time-frame' (Baudrillard
1996a: 45). 'Modern' societies are accelerating to the point where they are
leaving reality and its slower speeds behind. The older technology of
photography still allows us to capture reality at the moment of disappearance: in the more recent technologies, like television and computer
media, 'the real has already disappeared' (Baudrillard 1996a: 86). If there is
any irony, it no longer arises from common sense, from a shared agreement
that the stimuli we all encounter belong to a primal relationship with reality.
Irony 'is no longer a function of the subject; it is an objective function, that
of the artificial, object world which surrounds us, in which the absence and
transparency of the subject is reflected' (Baudrillard 1996a: 73). The critical
or artistic use of irony – in Surrealistic juxtapositions, or through the
dialectics of montage – no longer confronts reality with its absurd disjunc-
tion from reason. Instead, objects, designed and packaged as emblems of
themselves, mediated via advertising and lifestyle media, are already
divorced from both their uses and their meanings. So while Eco's theory of
hyperreality drives towards a return to the solid grounds of common sense,
and in doing so towards a re-instatement of a common set of ordinary beliefs

in reality, Baudrillard's simulation theory proposes 'the opposite hypothesis that there is nothing rather than something' (Baudrillard 1996a: 98). Eco mourns the commercial masking of reality in terms that Debord would have recognised, and, like Debord – though in a less revolutionary way – seeks a social strategy to get back to it. Baudrillard, on the other hand, comes around, in the mid-1990s, to the belief that reality was a brief construction of a social history that has now gone beyond it. The purpose of radical thought is to expose the nothingness at the heart of everything.

Baudrillard tends to overlook technological differences in favour of a fairly linear vision of history, even if it is one that neither arrives at a recognisable destination, nor disappears over the horizon of the future, but simply peters out in the desert of the present. Virilio, as we have seen, distinguishes passive optics from active. Unlike Eco, he groups together the telescope, microscope and camera lens as passive, and television and computer media as active. He is alert to the technical developments in astronomy when he describes the critical difference between the two:

> On the one hand, the speed of electrons and photons indirectly lights up what remains distant, thanks to video reception of the broadcast appearances (video-scopy being a great improvement on classical telescopy). On the other hand, the speed of electronic pixel calculation accelerates the definition or clarity of the picture, over-shadowing the optical quality even of the soft lenses of the new telescopes. Thus, it is less light than speed which helps us to see, to measure and therefore to conceive the reality of appearances. (Virilio 2000: 56)

Here Virilio begins by accepting that electronic telescopes, such as the photon counter aboard the Hubble Space Telescope, are more powerful than any optical machine. But, he argues, the definition of the image has less to do with the gathering of light than with the manipulation of data, the electronic circuitry that converts the faintest of interstellar illuminations into a definite and clearly visible entity in the telescope's viewfinder. The 'soft lenses' of the largest optical telescopes use tiny motors to bend the mirrors in order to achieve the best possible view. Similarly but with even more intensity, the electronic components of active optics can subtly distort the image far faster than the eye can perceive (indeed there has been some controversy over the possibility that some of Hubble's observations may be the result of computer distortions rather than astronomical events).

For Virilio the central point is that electronically assisted vision is no longer unmediated. Even transmitted instantaneously, like Eco's CCTV system, the intervention of light-speed electronic circuitry means that what we observe no longer has the geometry of the mirror or the lens, a geometry of separation, of time and space. Instead of an image, we confront the sheer speed of transmission. We no longer see the thing, or the relationship between us and the object, but the sole fact that we perceive it instantaneously. Virilio observes here that speed 'is not a phenomenon but *a relationship between phenomena*' (Virilio 2000: 56): in the semiotic terminology used by both Eco and Baudrillard, speed is a *sign*; not a thing, but a relation between things. In Virilio's own terminology, this quality of speed, and especially the replacement of the older linear geometry of natural perception, is central to the phenomenon of transappearance, his equivalent to Eco's hyperreality and Baudrillard's simulation. In active optics, human and machine share the same mode of perception and become interchangeable. What is more, subject and object also become interchangeable in a real-time geometry where, as in quantum physics, the act of observation alters the reality that it observes. For Virilio, the threat is not simply the disappearance of reality, as it is for Baudrillard, but the impact of that disappearance on subjectivity. Immobilised by the speed of our new perceptual tools, we become overinflated egos caught up in illusions of godhead while really disabled by our own prostheses.

4

MAKING SENSE OF SIMULATION

These then are the disparate findings of a reading of the four major figures in the theory of simulation. The questions which Chapter 3 leaves in dispute are:

- Is there such a thing (any more) as reality?
- Was there ever a reality, or has it disappeared or been destroyed?
- What is responsible for the loss of reality?
- Can reality ever be regained?

As we have seen, our authors differ between themselves, and even, in the case of Baudrillard, have altered their beliefs significantly over their careers. Eco believes reality has been masked by an impoverished culture; Debord that it has been stolen by commodification; Virilio that it has disappeared under the impact of technology; and Baudrillard, in the end, that it was always an illusion. Eco believes that common sense can triumph; Debord that it will take a revolution to restore reality; Virilio seems to see no end to its perpetual disappearance; and Baudrillard wants us to confront the void of nothingness. But simulation is not only a theory, nor is it only our four authors who have confronted it. In this chapter, we look at how some cultural practices seem to have embraced simulation; how simulation relates to other major theories of contemporary culture and society; and at the limits to simulation as theory and practice in the context of an increasingly global society. The purpose of this chapter is not so much to find a resolution to the differences between the four authors, but to hammer together a working definition of simulation which we can carry forward to Chapter 5, where we can test it on three case studies that have been at the heart of simulation theory.

(i) Hyperrealism: the art and practice of simulation

In a film widely touted as the first movie of the new millennium, Neo (Keanu Reeves) keeps his illicit computer disks in a hollowed-out copy of Baudrillard's *Simulation and Simulacra*. It is one of those in-jokes that delight postmodern movie buffs, evidence of an intertextual game of quotation that seems to prove that all the culture we make, in our crowded present, is a mosaic constructed out of the broken pieces of older cultural artefacts. *The Matrix* (1999), whose title echoes both the language of simulation theory and the discourse of the internet, proposes a world very like that envisaged in the darkest of Virilio's nightmares. Slaves of the machines they created, humans are swaddled in amniotic immobility, plugged into a virtual world which seems entirely real. The most interesting character for us is the treacherous Cypher, who decides that unreality is better than the miserable existence he has been leading aboard the resistance craft. His decision strikes at the heart of the ambivalence which the film creates in its viewers. On the one hand, we are rooting for Neo and the cause of waking up from the clutches of an alien, machine-run universe. But, on the other, the big box-office attraction was the film's state of the art special effects: we came to enjoy the illusion. Given the choice, a fair number of us would prefer to inhabit the glamorous world of cinema rather than the humdrum banalities of everyday life.

This particular allure of the cinema we can trace back at least as far as the heyday of the star system during the 1930s. The star is a simulacrum. The star is not the real person – Marilyn Monroe is not Norma Jean Baker. Nor are stars actors, identifiable simply by the work they do: many act, but few become stars, and some of them clearly not as a result of their acting ability. Stars exist not only on screen but in what Richard Dyer (1979) calls the 'secondary circulation' of fan magazines, shop windows, product endorsements, gossip and fantasy. Indeed, the quality we call glamour or charisma can be described as that kind of personality, constructed in films, magazines and other media, that becomes an object for fantasy. To become part of our daydreams, the star relies on a particular effect of media, his or her ability to create the illusion of presence. At the same time that illusion of presence depends on the absence of the real. The illusion provided by a close-up of Clark Gable depends on the real Clark Gable being somewhere else. If the real person is there, the unusual, unstable relationship between presence and absence that invites our fantasy cannot happen: real people follow their own desires, objects of fantasy obey ours – but only at the price of being unreal.

This peculiar dialectic of presence and absence has been taken even further. The founding act of contemporary art occurred in 1912, when Marcel Duchamp took a porcelain urinal, laid it on its back, signed it 'R. Mutt', and exhibited it, on a plinth, at an art exhibition under the title *Fountain*. How are we to take this? Did Duchamp mean that art is no more important than a toilet? Or that even plumbing can be art? Like the glamour of the Hollywood stars, Duchamp's *Fountain* got its still considerable influence from the way in which it answers both questions in the affirmative. Yes, all art is rubbish, and yes, everything is art; yes, art is the highest and the lowest, and yes, art is a social fiction masking absolutely nothing of value to anyone. At one and the same time, Duchamp's *Fountain* can be exactly what it is – a piece of shop-bought, machine-tooled ceramic – and something that, by all rights, it cannot be – an entirely conceptual conundrum. Thus the *Fountain* both is and is not art. But more even than that, if it is an artwork, then it is no longer what it is: a urinal. Thus Duchamp's little

Figure 1

joke turns out to be remarkably profound. Where the Hollywood star is both
present and absent, the urinal both is and is not.

This problem doesn't arise with reality. As Wittgenstein notes, 'One
doesn't "*take*" what one knows as the cutlery at a meal *for* cutlery'
(Wittgenstein 1968: 195): it simply is itself, and we see it and use it as such.
But with certain signs, this isn't necessarily the case, as happens with the
famous duck–rabbit (Figure 1).

In Wittgenstein's example, we can simple see the cutlery, but we have to
see the picture *as* – either as a duck, or as a rabbit. The distinction between
'seeing' and 'seeing as' may help clarify the complexity of Duchamp's
urinal. What we see there depends not on sight as such, but on *seeing as*. On
the one hand, if we see it as a urinal, then we must also see the absurdity of
generations of artists and critics thinking of it as an exemplary, even the
exemplary, work of modern art. On the other, if we see it as art, then we
must also accept that becoming art has meant ceasing to be a urinal, losing
its reality, becoming a sign so powerful that the reality of the urinal is no
longer visible beneath it. Yet both views can be held, if not simultaneously,
then at least in rapid succession, just as the duck–rabbit can be seen as a
duck or a rabbit, or both in succession. What simulation theory can add to
this oscillation between one aspect and another is the observation that, by
becoming part of this flip-flopping double vision, the reality of the urinal has
become a token of itself. By this I mean that even if we insist that the urinal
is a urinal, not an artwork, we are taking the reality of the urinal as a sign, or
more specifically as a signifier, something that now takes its place not
among other real objects in the real world, but as a signifier in a system of
signification. Its reality itself has become a sign.

Andy Warhol's silk-screens of Marilyn Monroe derived from newspaper
images of Monroe, rather than from photographs, and certainly not from
photos he might have taken himself. His images played on the grain of
newsprint, emphasising them by magnification, and by the additional grain
added in the serigraphic process. Not content with this remove from reality,

in the most powerful of the series, he adds only three colours, cornfield yellow for the hair, crimson for the lips, and blue for the eyes, so emphasising the contradictory cultural codes of racial purity, artifice and infantile innocence which underlay the image of female beauty in the 1950s. Everything about the image tells us that what is being depicted is not the real woman, not Norma Jean Baker, but the culturally encoded signifier, duplicated by the million in newspapers and magazines, that she had become. When, in 1987, the English video artist George Barber made a tape called *1001 Colours Andy Never Thought Of*, a work which flashes electronically varied colour versions of Warhol's Marilyn, there is no allusion, no reference, to the real Monroe left in the work. Instead, Barber's video is a commentary on the Warhol version, which is now not only a famous bit of art history, but one of the major images we use in ordinary culture when we want to talk about modern art. The film star returns to the silver screen once more as a projected image, but now without the residual promise of presence. Only the absence is left. Not only has reality been abandoned, now we are forced to confront the emptiness of the sign as well.

The reason for emphasising these art practices is to show that, despite the pessimism of most of our sources, cultural practitioners have been able to discover all sorts of inspiration for new work in the idea of simulation. We should not forget that Debord was a member of the Situationist avant-garde arts group and made several films; Baudrillard is an exhibiting photographer; Virilio is an architect; and Eco a novelist. Even when they are deeply pessimistic, they are also involved in creative practices. We need to be careful here, though, if we are not to sentimentalise the idea of creativity, and imagine that it will give us an instantaneous escape from the closed-down worlds of simulation and simulacra. We might, instead, take the hard line, and argue that stars fulfil only those desires which they have been manufactured in order to evoke; that Duchamp's *Fountain* is a symptom of the death of art; and that Barber's video finally demonstrates the impossibility of the attempt Warhol made to make art popular again. Alternatively, it is possible to argue that in his art Andy Warhol, for example, criticised commodity fetishism and the spectacle, but at the same time provided, in the artworks, further examples of the power of spectacle and simulation.

Reviewing the New York art scene between 1960 and the mid 1990s, Hal Foster describes one particular trend in post-pop art as 'the art of cynical reason' (Foster 1996: 99–124). When, for instance, Jeff Koons exhibits two high-tech vacuum cleaners in an immaculate glass case, he argues, the critical relation with reality that allows Duchamp's ready-made urinal to act on its own reality is snuffed out by the simplicity of exhibiting not something ordinary and even abject, but something shiny and desirable. Duchamp asks profound questions about art; Koons makes us notice only that artworks are just more commodity objects, and like vacuum cleaners they sell on their brand names – notably Koons' own, as he became one of the most expensive artists of the 1980s. So Koons dryly mocks a system from which, regardless, he continues to extract a healthy living: this is the cynicism of which Foster accuses him. His reference is to Peter Sloterdijk's massive *Critique of Cynical Reason* (1988), which offers, as a definition of modern cynicism, the oxymoron 'enlightened false consciousness' (Sloterdijk 1988: 5). The phrase, as Sloterdijk points out, is an oxymoron because one meaning of the philosophical tradition of Enlightenment is disillusion, seeing through false consciousness. Modern cynicism begins in the Enlightenment's sceptical frame of mind, which Hegel had already referred to as the 'unhappy consciousness', forever incapable of bringing together its certainty of reason and the uncertainty of facts (Hegel 1977: ¶ 205, 126). Cynical reason both accepts the truths of Enlightenment reason and ignores them in favour of getting by. It is the everyday unhappy consciousness of knowing what's right but doing what's wrong. But it is also the attitude that looks at any other way of living with sneering irony.

The proverbial definition of the cynic is someone who knows the price of everything and the value of nothing. In a philosophical sense, Sloterdijk argues, that is what has happened to contemporary culture: we recognise the exchange-value of commodities, but our value systems are based on the presence of absence, the void underneath all our realities. For this cynical perspective, which I believe gives an accurate statement of the philosophical nihilism which Baudrillard has adopted as his own, signification is everything, so much so that it no longer even requires or produces meaning. But if this is the case, what is the real? It is, as it was for Lacan, what lies beyond signification and therefore beyond knowledge or comprehension: it is the end of signification. Or, to look at it differently, if the real exists at all for us, it must be as a signifier, but a signifier that signifies nothing. So, like Duchamp's urinal, the real object functions no longer as pure presence but as its opposite: pure absence.

The problem is that this sheer absence, which provides the powerhouse for so much of simulation theory, is in the end an effect of the signifying system. The ultimate void, which structures twentieth-century thought from Heidegger's being-towards-death to Lacan's Real, is only another social and historical artefact, no more profound than the trivial absence of the real person from the star's image. Death, the ultimate and melancholy arbiter of the master–slave dialectic in Hegel, the gift in Bataille, symbolic exchange in Baudrillard, the divine in Virilio, is only death, not a universal cataclysm. We only die. And then, either something happens, or it doesn't, which we can't know about. Either way, the world doesn't stop when one of its creatures dies. To pretend otherwise, to claim death as the terminus of all meaning, is to demand that the universe throws itself onto my funeral pyre. Cynical reason has put its own unreasonable fear of death into the position of philosophical absolute, and built its pessimistic diagnosis of the world on that basis.

Eco of course can take a jaundiced look at funerary arrangements in the more lunatic North American cemeteries, and show us the absurdity of philosophical nihilism (Eco 1986: 37–8). But though he wants to be able to claim that communities of sense fill up the gaps in contemporary society, there are signs that the void is still alive and well. Take for instance the familiar TV quiz show format in which contestants have to name 'something you would take on holiday'. They win if their guess matches the most popular response in a random poll asking the same question. The prize is awarded to the most average. Not the fastest, the cleverest, the one with the best aim or the best memory for trivia, not even the one who, asked to name a bird with a long neck, answered Naomi Campbell (to understand this mistake, you have to know that 'bird' is British slang for a woman, and Campbell is a famous model). Television is the cult of the ordinary, using the extraordinary only as a way of emphasising the importance of being normal. What it prizes most, what it awards prizes for, is not nothingness but nullity.

It is this sense of the null that makes so much commercial culture seem so full, even so excessive and wasteful. It is crammed, as Eco argues, with 'more', more of the same. In his critical history of recorded music, Michael Chanan (1995) makes the point that recording studios and technologies, together with the choice of 'authentic' scores and 'original' instruments, converge on an entirely artificial construction of an entirely ideal perform-ance. It is that null imitation of an impossible authenticity which is produced in batches of thousands, and played and replayed again on thousands of record players. The null point of endless imitation of a non-existent original is at the heart of what Hillel Schwartz, in an extraordinary book covering everything from shop-window mannequins to cloning, photocopiers to camouflage, calls the culture of the copy (Schwartz 1996). Far from there being nothing rather than something, contemporary culture strikes us as overstuffed, leaving no room for anything but conformity. To describe this culture as 'vacuous' is a loose use of metaphor. In fact, it is not a vacuum but a plenum, as full as an egg. This is why Virilio can make the mistake of calling electronic transmissions instantaneous: because messages from one part of a full field to another only restate what is already known, since there is no room for anything new, only for 'more'.

Even those areas of culture where we could legitimately hope for something genuinely new end up disappointing us. More than to any other field of endeavour, and certainly more so than to art, we turn to science for a breath of the unheard-of, the never-seen-before, the unthinkably new. But, as Virilio argues, what we are offered is 'a cosmological optical illusion' (Virilio 2000: 43) according to which each discovery and every theory of contemporary science is either so unimaginably complex, so subject to the distortions of scale, or so tied up in bizarre mathematical conceptions that it cannot be visualised. In place of the passionate visions once offered to the amateur by microscopes and telescopes, we have the End-of-the-Millennium special issue of *Scientific American* devoted to 'What Science Will Know in 2050'. Over sixty-three pages, 'Today's top scientific authorities speculate on the great questions that further research will answer within the next five decades' (*Scientific American* 1999: 2). Even when, introducing the issue with due modesty, John Maddox notes the scale of our ignorance, it is clear that whatever it is that is proposed or discovered, *Scientific American* expects to be there to monitor and administer the arrival of the new. In other words, no matter how radical scientific culture may become, it will achieve its social function if it continues to provide a steady stream of novelty. That novelty, like fashion or food fads, can then be treated not as the kind of shock that threatened Catholicism with Galileo or Christianity with Darwin, but as the flag-bearer for the perpetually innovated sameness of the contemporary. However authentic and dangerous the activities of the athlete, his or her prowess is always only the material for more of Eco's endless sports chatter. No matter how staggering the achievements of future scientists, they will only ever generate more of the endless chatter of popularisation in best-sellers like Hawking's *Brief History of Time*, magazines and TV documentaries. Their function is not to innovate, not to challenge our most fundamental beliefs, but to provide an endlessly renewable spectacle of innovation.

The pursuit of science is certainly one of the highest callings in the modern world. Yet it too becomes, willy nilly, another hyperrealism. The deeper it plunges into reality, the more unreal its findings become, or rather, the less real they appear to the layperson and in many instances to the professional. To this extent, as public spectacle, science is as much a simulation as *The Guinness Book of Records*. Whatever the internal pupposes of science, its *social* purpose is to make us say 'Wow!' In the null fullness of contemporary culture, having our most fundamental beliefs challenged is just another entertainment, an effect like getting vertigo on a fairground ride. Until, of course, we have to confront an event every bit as much a part of popular culture as the TV quiz show or the magazine stand, an event like the N30 demonstrations which in late 1999, most famously in Seattle, challenged the World Trade Organisation with the riotous sounds of a generation of college kids acquiring a political education.

(ii) Mediation: democracy and the politics of interpretation

> oh, for such saying as never the things themselves
>   hoped so intensely to be . . .
> *Here* is the time for the Tellable, *here* is its home.
> Speak and proclaim. More than ever
>   things we can live with are falling away, for that
>   which is oustingly taking their place is an imageless act.

(from Rilke's Ninth Duino Elegy)

Is it possible that contemporary culture leaves us no room for real innovation because we are simply too crowded? 'Criticism is a matter of correct distancing. It was at home in a world where perspectives and prospects counted and where it was still possible to take a standpoint. Now things press too closely on human society.' So wrote Walter Benjamin, the tragic philosopher, in an epigram devoted to 'the most real, the mercantile gaze into the heart of things', advertising (Benjamin 1979: 89). Written sometime between August 1926 and September 1927, this fragment suggests that the contemporary was, to some extent, already in place by the time of the Wall Street Crash, at least in the hothouse of Weimar Germany. It is characterised by an awareness not only that things have become too close for comfort, but that, as a result, we can no longer inhabit the Renaissance geometry of the point-of-view whose passing Virilio laments so often. For both thinkers, critique, rational inquiry into the foundations of a belief, requires a distance based on 'the anthropic principle, which regards the existence of any observer as inseparable from the existence of rationally observed phenomena' (Virilio 2000: 51). The object of critique requires a subject, and their mutual separation is critical. Benjamin notes that the sheer proximity of things, and especially commodities, debars us from taking the necessary step back. But it is intriguing that he should refer us not only to 'prospects', the architectural principle of creating a view by framing it with buildings or trees, but also to perspective, the great technique of illusion.

Some traditions in painting, such as the Chinese, make a direct address to the viewer, showing not just the scene but the fact that they are showing it. The art historian Norman Bryson refers to this as deixis, the linguistic term for those expressions that tell us about the conditions of communication. For example, using the present tense in speech gives us information about the situation the speaker and listener are in, as when we say 'I'm telling you, that's how it is.' But, argues Bryson, perspectival painting, which begins with a deictic contract ('Stand just there, where I stood to paint, and you will see the scene exactly as I saw it'), rapidly sheds this demonstration of the scene to a specifically placed viewer's body and becomes instead a disembodied form of vision. Drawing on Saussure's distinction between the synchronic and diachronic (see Chapter 1.ii), Bryson argues that the new illusionism of Renaissance perspective replaces the time-based looking of deixis with the timelessness of the Gaze:

> Elimination of the diachronic movement of deixis creates, or at least seeks, a synchronic instant of viewing that will eclipse the body, and the glance, in an infinitely extended Gaze of the image as pure idea: the image as *eidolon*. (Bryson 1983: 94)

A painting by Titian which captures a fleeting moment of chaotic movement in the story of Bacchus and Ariadne, for instance, Bryson takes as an example of how, in this new form of illusion, 'the action is over as it happens: the viewpoint is that of an all-knowing eternity'. In other words, 'it represents discontinuity so extreme that the origin of the image (this is its fascination) in fact becomes irrational' (Bryson 1983: 95). Important for our argument is Bryson's term *eidolon*, the Greek word coined by Socrates in the earliest statement of simulation theory. Bryson argues that the painter's freezing of the action destroys its credibility as a depiction in favour of presenting the spectator with a spectacle. Like Plato's painting of a bed, Titian's *Bacchus and Ariadne* has no origin: it is a simulation.

But if Bryson is right, how are we to make sense of Virilio's claim that Renaissance geometry was the basis for all subject–object relations, and therefore of all critical thought and ultimately all human values? Has modernity been simulational ever since the Renaissance five hundred years ago? The first thing to note is that Bryson is only doing art history, while Virilio is using perspectival geometry as the unique model of correct thinking. Cultural historian Martin Jay argues that vision has provided the model for a great deal of Western thought, and that ideas about illusion, (loss of) perspective and forgery have been central to what he calls 'the denigration of vision', especially in twentieth-century French ideas (Jay 1993). The core concepts of simulation theory – spectacle, simulacrum, transappearance, hyperreality – are all clearly part of this visual rhetoric of thought. The North American philosopher Richard Rorty notices that one of our words for deep, philosophical thought is 'reflection'. Tracing the history of philosophy from the roots of Enlightenment thought in Descartes, Locke and Kant, Rorty argues that philosophy professionalised itself by offering to clarify the foundations of truth. Central to this pursuit was a visual metaphor which involved separating mental from physical, so 'inventing' a separate category of Mind. Once invented, the mind could then be asked to do certain things, notably to know the physical world. In order to do so, it would have to represent. And that, of course, is where simulation comes in.

The branch of philosophy dealing with the problems of representation and knowledge is called epistemology. Rorty complains that epistemology is based on the visual metaphor of the mind as a mirror, reflecting more or less accurately a physical world apart from itself. When epistemology deals with the foundations of all knowledge and all representations, it is seeking some form of absolute, universal and eternal system for establishing whether or not a representation is accurate. Rorty describes this as 'the end-product of an original wish to substitute *confrontation* for *conversation* as the determinant of our belief' (Rorty 1980: 163). The confrontation is not just the argufying of professional philosophers: it is the confrontation between the world and the mind's mirroring of it. In place of epistemological confrontation, Rorty argues for a conception of truth as 'justified belief', 'something continuous with common sense instead of something which might be as remote from common sense as the Mind of God' (Rorty 1980: 308). This 'common sense' is rather specific. Obviously it is different from the idea of Absolute Truth or the concept of a foundational philosophy for all truths. Less clearly, it is distinguishable from the kind of 'ideological' schemes of belief shared only by specific communities. 'Common' in this context refers to things that pretty much every language-using creature would agree to: water is wet; a son is always younger than his mother; if I go to Washington, my nose goes with me. When it comes to common sense about things that can't be perceived immediately, like where babies come from, or whether the Earth is round, we need conversation in order to achieve agreement. By proposing this conversational mode of truth, Rorty escapes from the problem of knowledge as representation, and at least in the first instance offers us a way of thinking that doesn't end up in the dead-end street of pessimistic simulation theory, for which there can be no such thing as an accurate representation, and therefore no such thing as knowledge.

In Rorty's thinking, language, indeed all our communications, is not a mirror but a tool. Without the ideal foundations which Enlightenment philosophy sought for it, there can be no 'strong' theory of truth, only a 'weak' one based on the *use* of ideas rather than their intrinsic and absolute merits. Only by using an idea – on the physical world or on other people – can we discover whether we are justified in believing it. This theory is then a profoundly sociable one. It depends on conversation between people, and even between people and things. Unlike critique, it relies not on the distance which Benjamin saw was necessary for strong truth-discourses, but on proximity, the give and take of social life. Of all our simulationists, it is Eco who comes closest to this democratic vision of truth. He also brings this tradition of shared interpretations of the world into contact with the problem of knowing how the world is.

Eco's analysis of critics and readers of popular culture is grounded in a version of the semiotic theories we looked at in Chapter 1.ii. The novelty of Eco's contributions comes from two sources: his reintroduction into the Saussurean tradition of the thought of the American philosopher and semiotician Charles Sanders Peirce (1839–1914), and his interest in the critical development of the vocabulary of information theory. From Peirce, Eco derives a set of as-yet unresolved questions concerning the American's thesis that semiotics proceeds by threes (rather than the binary twos of Saussure), and also a thesis concerning how we get ideas about the world. Firstness, the Dynamic Object, corresponds loosely with direct perception – the world as a mass of sensations touching our perceptual organs. Secondness, the Immediate Object, is the process by which we separate out what we perceive as objects as distinct from the rest of the flux of sensations we receive from the universe at large. Thirdness is the condition under which the Immediate Object becomes a sign, and more specifically acquires a meaning (see Ducrot and Todorov 1972: 113–15). As Eco notes, the act of changing primary perceptions, which are by definition individual, into secondary Immediate Objects 'to some extent . . . eludes the individuality of perception, because insofar as it is interpretable, it is already public and intersubjective' (Eco 1999: 65). Where much of the Saussurean tradition of semiotics has emphasised the problem of representation (how can a word or a picture or sound grasp an external object?), Eco uses Peirce as a road towards understanding language as primarily a social phenomenon. By emphasising language as a relation between people rather than its relation to things, Eco's linguistics throws itself open to change and to history, always a problem for structural linguistics, with its emphasis on homeostatic systems capable of maintaining themselves in equilibrium.

Meanwhile, Eco's address to information theory gives him a sharper definition of the key concept of code: a code is a shared set of rules for creating and deciphering messages (Eco 1979: 36–8). Where the code is not shared – either because one person doesn't know it properly, or because two people are using different codes to create and decipher the same message – the messages become open to interpretation; to argument, to reinterpretation and misinterpretation, and to blank incomprehension. At the same time, the mutual interdependence of Peirce's three modes of Firstness, Secondness and Thirdness implies that there are limits to interpretation, since interpretation is always anchored in both the limits of perception and the limits of the shared nature of codes, the basis of his particular notion of common sense (see Eco 1990, 1992) which we looked at in Chapter 4. Here Eco undertakes a quietly radical rewriting of the Saussurean tradition by substituting the encyclopaedia, which contains statements about things, for the dictionary, which defines words in terms of other words. Each of us has a sort of mental encyclopaedia, or perhaps several encyclopaedias. One we share with everyone who shares our culture: under 'Moon', for example, we have green cheese, howling dogs, phases, 'One small step for a man' and one giant leap for the cow that jumped over it. We may also carry specialist professional encyclopaedias that allow us to talk about the moon as astronomers, astrologers, mythologists or simulation theorists, specialist tomes whose contents might not be shared by a stranger we happened to fall into conversation with, and whose contents we might therefore have to argue over and prove or disprove. These mental encyclopaedias are then nothing like as schematic as dictionaries, but rather labyrinths of interconnected ideas always open to change.

But it is here that Rorty parts company with Eco. Rorty is wary of a distinction Eco makes between the interpretation of a text and a use of it, the former being a way of finding out what the text is about or what it could mean, the latter a way of reading the text as proof of something we already know or evidence of a thesis we are determined to prove. For Rorty, this distinction rests on a further distinction of which he also disapproves: 'there is no point at which we can draw a line between what we are talking about and what we are saying about it' (Rorty 1992: 98). Objects, says Rorty, can never be separated from what we say about them. So the assertions which fill our mental encyclopaedias

> are always at the mercy of being changed by fresh stimuli, but they are never capable of being checked against those stimuli, much less against the internal coherence of something outside the encyclopedia. . . . You cannot check a sentence against an object, although an object can cause you to stop asserting a sentence. You can only check a sentence against other sentences to which it is connected by various labyrinthine inferential relationships. (Rorty 1992: 100)

In other words, we inhabit language so thoroughly that only in conversation, only via communities of communication, can we check whether our beliefs are justified. Eco is unpersuaded in the debate that follows: 'When everybody is right, everybody is wrong, and I have the right to disregard everybody's point of view' (Eco 1992: 151).

Eco satirises this state of affairs, as he did also in *Foucault's Pendulum*, by parodying it in the guise of the theory of analogy, the mystical tradition which allows any similarity, however far-fetched, to form the basis of a metaphysical system. In analogical thinking, specificity and differences are overlooked in favour of similarities. If the reader is feeling a slight sense of déjà vu here, it may well be because of our discussion of Baudrillard in Chapter 4.ii, and especially of the understanding of the Code which emerges in *Symbolic Exchange and Death*. In his mature works, Eco wants to define codes (in the plural) as the labyrinths of connection that tie entries in our mental encyclopaedias to one another. Baudrillard, as we saw, describes the Code (in the singular) as the structural law of value which represses and denies the first difference, that between the original and the copy, and therefore destroys all other possible differences (Baudrillard 1993a: 71). Like Rorty, Baudrillard does not accept the existence of an 'outside' against which we can check the truth of our representations, but for him, this is a product of the Code, a Code which has so infected the social that the social itself becomes an indistinct, undifferentiated mass. Rorty, of course, does believe in the social, and specifically in the powers of conversation to edify us, and to bring new statements and new modes of truth. What separates the two is not an act of faith in society which Rorty makes and Baudrillard doesn't. For Baudrillard, one characteristic of the Code is its immediacy (Baudrillard 1983b: 102); it is clear from Rorty's writings, however, that for him, the social is implicitly mediated, and most of all mediated through language.

Mediation is the fabric of Rorty's conversation, a fabric which depends upon difference. Without mediation, as Baudrillard argues, there can be no difference. The point is crucial: Virilio's instantaneous media also erase difference, but only if they are instantaneous, that is, if they erase the materials and processes of mediation that make a difference. Both Eco and Rorty, despite their disagreements over the status of things outside language, emphasise the social process of sharing and debating truth and meaning. It is a faith shared by the N30 demonstrators, who sought to intervene in a dialogue which excluded them, but a faith denied by Baudrillard's thesis that any political action is always only the self-regulation of the Code, always only a mode of sameness. Any theory of simulation that can find a way out of this pessimism must demonstrate the necessity of social mediation as the actually existing place where difference exists.

Curiously enough, we can find a way of securing this happy result through a critique of Rorty written by the Italian philosopher Gianni Vattimo. Vattimo seizes on a suggestion of Rorty's that a crucial form of conversation, the conversation between disparate cultures, takes place in cultural anthropology. Vattimo's critique depends on an understanding of anthropology as a discipline which addresses 'other' cultures. But, he argues, the discipline actually constructs an ideal of 'primitivism' which it sets out at once to document and to protect from Westernisation. In bringing a strange culture into a familiar science and simultaneously asserting its strangeness, anthropology moves between two poles, otherness and sameness, both of which it constructs as absolute opposites, yet which actually stand in a circular relation to each other, rather like an intellectual duck–rabbit. When we understand them as aspects of the interpretative process of mediation, sameness is the moment when we think we understand, otherness the moment when we realise we have misunderstood. As things stand in the contemporary world of global Westernisation, there is no absolute other. But neither, Vattimo argues, is there an absolute 'Same': Westernisation takes many forms, incomplete, marginal, more contamination than domination. The kind of homogenisation envisaged by Baudrillard and Virilio, and which Vattimo believes is also present in Rorty's concept of anthropology, has resulted not in absolute sameness but in 'this sameness in a weakened and contaminated form; it possesses neither the iron-clad unity of the total organisation of the metaphysical and technological world, nor some sort of "authentic" unity which could be diametrically opposed to the former' (Vattimo 1988: 159).

Rorty and Eco had imagined what Vattimo refers to as a 'strong' subject: common-sensical individuals sufficiently differentiated to participate in dialogue or the interplay of dialogue and things. Baudrillard and Virilio had imagined a world in which individual differences have been erased under the sheer homogenising power of the Code or militarised technology. By concentrating on the material detail of cultural mediation, Vattimo offers us a less clear-cut but more persuasive answer: neither the undifferentiated mass nor the enlightened individual exists. There is only the 'weak' subject of 'weak' knowledge, without certainty, without purity, whose hallmarks are 'survival, marginality, and contamination' (Vattimo 1988: 162).

(iii) Residual realities: globalisation and the limits of postmodernisation

For Vattimo, these margins exist in their traces, their unfinished constructions, their contamination of and with Westernisation not only in the Third World but in the ghettos of the First. It has become very fashionable to glamourise these border zones, not least as a result of the global marketing of African-American hip-hop. It is easy enough to imagine Baudrillard answering Vattimo with the argument that the selling of rap music is a case not of the commercial theft of an authentic music, but of the commercialisation of authenticity: what we buy with every Public Enemy disc is the assimilation into the Code even of the opposition to the USA's urban apartheid. Vattimo's response would undoubtedly be that no matter how many wealthy white suburban boys are permitted the simulacrum of themselves as ganglords of Compton, the music does not therefore become inauthentic and indistinguishable. Contaminated and compromised, the musics of the African diaspora are nonetheless part of a global dialogue. Vattimo argues for the persistence of difference. Baudrillard, on the other hand, is adamant that all these differences are consumed in the production of a universal language.

Here is how Baudrillard defines that moment:

> The perfect crime is that of an unconditional realization of the world by the actualization of all data, the transformation of all our acts and all events into pure information: in short, the final solution, the resolution of the world ahead of time

by the cloning of reality and the extermination of the real by its double. (Baudrillard 1996a: 25)

We will look at this thesis in more detail in Chapter 7, but for the moment we need to recognise the main drift: information technologies, tracking our purchases and our journeys, the flows of electricity and water to our homes, schools and offices, the computer monitoring of the factory floor and the supermarket shelf, all double up reality by transmuting it into pure data – and then eradicating the 'real' original. Information constitutes a perfect language against the disorderly differences of natural languages.

> . . . we are condemned to the universal programming of language. Democratic fiction of language in which all languages would be reconciled under the umbrella of sense and good sense. Fiction of information, of a universal form of transcription which cancels out the original text. With virtual languages we are currently inventing anti-Babel, the universal language, the true Babylon, where all languages are confounded and prostituted one to another. (Baudrillard 1996a: 90–1)

From Baudrillard's point of view, it is meaning and communication that are disastrous: the ebullience of the natural languages derives from their mutual incomprehensibility. What he fears and despises is the prospect of mutual transparency, the possibility of a dialogue involving everyone regardless of their language, and therefore of the cultural differences that natural languages embody. Worst of all is the automatic writing of computers that reconciles all data into the single form of computerised information flows.

Baudrillard is not alone in fearing universal language. Eco has devoted a whole book to a scholarly investigation of the history of universal and perfect languages. At certain moments he comes close both to Baudrillard's angry denunciation and to Virilio's grief at the technological theft of the divine point of view. At one point he looks into the theory that Hebrew, being the language of the book of Genesis, must also have been the first and most perfect language. In its later forms, this belief

> was not to defend the contention that Adam spoke to God in Hebrew, but rather to defend the status of language itself as the vehicle of revelation. This can only be maintained so long as it is also admitted that language can directly express, without the mediation of any sort of social contract or adaptations due to material necessity, the relation between human beings and the sacred. (Eco 1997: 114)

The same thesis, he argues, also underlies the argument of a natural language of things, the language of analogy mentioned in Chapter 4.ii. But he also suggests obliquely that in certain semiotic understandings of the genetic code and in the scientific hypothesis of a 'language instinct' or a universal grammar common to all languages, the ghost of a primal language of nature at the origins of human speech still lingers on. The key terms in the critique appear in the quotation above: 'social' and 'adaptation'. But as we have seen, it is the social that differentiates Eco's alternative to universality from Baudrillard's championing of absolute untranslatability. For Baudrillard, there can be no adaptation, since all change is already assimilated into the Code. The only alternative to being spoken by the universal language is to refuse meaning, and to embrace the disordering of meaning and logic, the absolute singularity of languages that cannot be used for communication.

But data traffic is not the first attempt at a global language of communication. The dream of a universal language is a constant companion of modernity. We find it, for example, in D.W. Griffith's pursuit of a new kind of cinema that might speak across nations and ideologies to voice eternal verities: 'We have gone beyond Babel, beyond words. We have found a new universal language, a power that can make men brothers and end war forever' (cited in Gish 1969: 183) Film historian Miriam Hansen (1991: 173–98) describes Griffith's hybrid form as hieroglyphic, modelled on the ancient picture-writing he quotes in the intertitles to his masterpiece *Intolerance* (1916). The idea of cinema as a universal language would remain key to its ambitions throughout the silent period, and was lamented by Eisenstein, Pudovkin, Chaplin, Clair and others when the introduction of recorded dialogue ended the transnational appeal of silent film. Even today it is not unusual to hear the phrase bandied about at the more self-congratulatory Hollywood shindigs.

But it was not only cinema that raised the spectre of a universal tongue. The Enlightenment had proposed Fraternity as one of its key virtues. The holistic theme of universal brotherhood is extended to the fringes of contemporary science in the Gaia hypothesis, according to which the planetary ecology of the Earth is a self-healing intelligence (Lovelock 1979). The concept of all biological life sharing a single organic network of relationships, the concept of the biosphere, finds parallels in the 'noosphere', or ecology of minds, first described by the Catholic theologian Teilhard de Chardin, and deeply influential on Marshall McLuhan, and which returns explicitly in the age of digital media in the work of Joël de Rosnay (1986) and more recently Pierre Lévy (2000) as the trope of a global intelligence composed of human 'neurons' linked by telematics and information technologies to form a single giant mind. Within such a mind, of course, mediation is no longer necessary, since the only truly unmediated form of communication is telepathy, which is all a unified brain needs. Unlike Debord, Baudrillard and Virilio, these accounts of the noosphere are not horrified but utopian. For these writers the eradication of the difference of mediation is a step towards a global unity, a single thinking and willing entity, a common subject of history. We have already seen two problems with this utopian vision of universal language: it seeks a fullness without room for adaptation and change; and in its pursuit of absolute purity it imagines an impossibly complete language and an impossibly complete subject speaking it. A further problem arises from the specific social history of contemporary society, whose central tendency is towards globalisation.

Firstly, universal language operates by exclusion. Those who are not connected cannot form part of the planetary collective. In the punning language of cyberculture, as Olu Oguibe (1998) points out, they become

PONA, persons of no account. Ironically, it is the very people whose labour is so carefully hidden inside the hygienic white boxes on the desks of the wired world, the free-trade zone workers of Mexico's borderlands, the Vietnamese and Filipino women in offshore assembly plants, who will be left outside the world their work creates. In this way, the material conditions under which the machinery of contemporary communication is produced are erased under the sign of the universality of its language, its claim to speak for all and with every voice. Of course, the counter-claim is that the universal language of computer-mediated communications networks can speak on behalf of, in the place of: that they can be represented. But representation, in both the democratic and the semiotic senses, is the claim made by universal languages which simulation theory cannot accept.

Secondly, the universality of universal language is an imperial gesture, in the sense that it operates literally universally. The presumption of a universal language is that it can say everything, so that anything which it cannot speak cannot be spoken at all. But the universal language of information technologies, as Virilio argues so forcefully, alters what it speaks about, most of all altering the dimensions of space and time on which any language depends. Informatics have their own dimensions, and therefore, as universal language, cannot speak the material nature of existence, the phenomenological sensation of being in the world. As we have seen, the mathematical theory of information on which contemporary communication is founded denies the centrality of either meaning, reference or the medium of communication to the commerce in dataflows. Information theory addresses the statistical mathematics of order and disorder in a communication system, the ratio of ordered signal to disordered noise. In mathematical terms, both the message and the channel are potential sources of noise, since they are material and therefore not subject to the ordering of data on which communication is supposed to rest. The contingent, chance, random conditions of reality are suspended in information theory, or rather treated as interference in the naked task of transmission and reception.

If a language is perfectly universal, there can be nothing outside it: there can be no pre-discursive reality. This doesn't prove that there is no reality, but rather that reality is by definition that which escapes or eludes discourse. Just as Lacan argued that the Symbolic structured the unconscious by excluding it, so simulation theory argues that exclusion from the dominant discourse in any time constructs the specific terms under which the non-discursive – reality – can exist. As we have just seen, information theory, the mathematical ground of contemporary communications media, is meticulous in its exclusion of reality, just as its universal language excludes those who are not connected to information pathways. In this way we can argue that reality is that residual zone remaindered in the drive to universal digital communication: reality is the condition of those outside the loop of digital networks.

This little philosophical conundrum would remain an intellectual game were it not for another new condition of the world in the age of information:

the rise of finance capital. The nineteenth century was the period of industrial capital. The period since World War I was the boom-time of service capital. But, to take a more or less arbitrary date, since the conversion of the world's financial markets to 24-hour electronic trading in 1989, finance capital has become the dominant mode of the economy, and indeed the dominant form of communication at the turn of the millennium. From the end of the gold standard in 1925 to contemporary corporate raids that leave whole industries in ruin, we have witnessed a shift from material production of material goods to the circulation of financial data on a scale that, not so long ago, brought down the economies of Thailand and Malaysia, and wreaked immense damage even on Japan, till the late 1990s the world's single strongest economy. The processes of exclusion from the cycles of the information economy, by which I mean the now-central sources of wealth in electronic stock market trading, leaves whole continents at the margins of a communication system which is also now synonymous with the global economy. Africa between the Maghreb and the Limpopo, the Andean nations, Bangladesh and Central Asia have been eliminated from the core of the contemporary world economy. Their bitter reality stands marginalised in the drive to a global finance economy powered by the self-same communications technologies which provide Lévy and others with their utopian vision of a planetary mind.

This new universal language differs from that envisaged by Eco's visionary mystics, and from that dreamt of in the Enlightenment concept of fraternity, not because of its power, but because it is composed not of words but of numbers, and finally not of familiar arithmetic numbers, but of a system of absolute difference, the zeros and ones of binary machine code. Since all that is encoded in this language is the flow or blockage of electrical current, we can call this realisation of the dream of a universal language a universal currency. The electronic media have displaced the reality of production with the pure communication of difference, a circulation of having and not having, being and nothingness: an economy of data. This universal currency has driven out the real, to which it now refers only in the most marginal of terms, for example in the futures markets where global commodities can be bought and sold years before they are brought to harvest. Put differently, finance capital has usurped the place of material reality. Its last links with physical being lie in the geopolitics of exclusion, the power to deny a population the means of communication, to embargo those who dare confront the terrible potency of global capital, to exclude them from participation in the universal currency in which their exploitation and oppression is conducted. From the standpoint of this global capital, Africa, the Andes, the Caribbean, Central Asia and the dispossessed of every continent are immaterial because they are only real, unwired, outside the 'get real' financial reality which is now exclusively the electronic parsing of financial data.

This universal currency is universal by its own definition, a definition which denies its own materiality, driving the material out of the inner circuits of finance capital, into those marginalised and immiserated spaces excluded from the global communications economy. In Lacan's famous statement, 'the real is the impossible': where only universal currency is possible, we confront the impossible reality of the material. But the mere fact that, on the principles of information theory, financial networks ignore the material of the world cannot alter its continued existence. Simulation theory in its toughest forms is only true of those societies enclosed in the webs of a communications structure now synonymous with economic transaction. Only where money, in the increasingly immaterialised and mediated form of e-cash, is the dominant form of communication does simulation theory hold good. It is therefore a partial theory masquerading as a totality. Moreover, as the N30 demonstrators discovered, global financial flows are a form of communication and dialogue, even if the rich get to talk far louder than the poor.

To sift through this chapter's findings then, we have argued, firstly, that there is not nothing but something, a culture of fullness, so stuffed that it cannot permit anything other than itself: a culture of totality. But this total culture is only so within strict bounds, the boundaries of a self-defining universal language, which certain statements of simulation theory, far from criticising, as Debord foretold, have begun to support. At the same time, in the central section, we argued that there is no such thing as the perfectly 'same', or the purely other. I have used this slightly uncomfortable vocabulary for a specific reason. The French philosopher Emmanuel Levinas uses the opposition between the same and the other as a way of speaking about the problem of totality. 'The same' is his name for the self-identical subject. If the same is all there is, then the self can be free. But the same always confronts the other – a social interaction that begins with recognising the equal claims to reality and freedom of the person in front of you. The 'imperialism of the same is the whole essence of freedom', Levinas argues (Levinas 1969: 87). But neither the same nor the other exists independently: both are contaminated by each other, both are marginal to each other, both are the partial constructs of each other. Totality is only possible from a standpoint in which there is no other; that is why the total freedom of the same or self can only be purchased at the price of utterly ignoring or erasing the claims of the other. Totality can only exist at the expense of an other, without which, to return to the dialectical and contradictory language of Debord, totality is always incomplete. If this is so, then simulation theory, like any theory, has boundaries, and describes only a partial aspect of the world. Two consequences follow. Commodity culture, the spectacle and the simulation, the transapparent and the hyperreal, may be triumphant, but they cannot be total. And we must give up our claim to the total freedom promised by consumerism, because that is the only way we can come face to face with the other, with either the pre-discursive outside of simulation or the social difference on which dialogue depends. In this way we answer the questions with which we began this chapter: some reality remains, but it is structured by its exclusion and marginalisation from the spectacularly null totality of commodity culture. And we can regain it, in some form, but only by giving up our belief in the illusion of free will on which consumer culture depends. If we dare to step outside the matrix of totality, we confront not the endless void, but the painful poverty of reality and the extraordinary wealth of diversity.

SECTION 2

CASES

5

DISNEY WORLD CULTURE

You're a fake, John Doe, and I can prove it

(*Meet John Doe*, Frank Capra/Columbia, 1941)

How is it possible that simulation theory, which offers itself as the most radical theorisation of the social, can come to play a part in the processes through which the world loses its reality? Although simulation theory disallows the critique of ideology, Peter Sloterdijk's comments on it also seem to apply to simulation, notably when he suggests that it 'risks alienating the opponent more and more deeply; it reifies and diminishes the other's reality' (Sloterdijk 1988: 19). Marxism already risked this by suggesting that, as false consciousness, ideology was necessary. False consciousness was precisely the right consciousness for the functioning of the system. Marxists like Debord believed that there was at least the possibility of a true consciousness, Marxism itself. But as for post-Marxist thinkers like Baudrillard, who still use a systems analysis of society but without the possibility of truth, 'in alliance with neoconservative currents, they proclaim that useful members of human society have to internalize certain "correct illusions" once and for all, because without them nothing functions properly' (Sloterdijk 1988: 20). Theorising society as total illusion is, for Sloterdijk, a cynical ploy, leaving the critic with his 'truth', and the rest with their illusions.

Nowhere is the critique of total illusion and absolute simulation more concentrated than in the analysis of Disneyland. Since Dorfman and Mattelart's (1984) groundbreaking study of imperialist themes in Disney comics, Disney cartoons, theme parks and corporate practice have been accused of:

sexism, racism, conservatism, heterosexism, andro-centrism, imperialism (cultural), imperialism (economic), literary vandalism, jingoism, aberrant sexuality, censorship, propaganda, paranoia, homophobia, exploitation, ecological devastation, anti-union oppression, FBI collaboration, corporate raiding and stereotyping. (Byrne and McQuillan 1999: 1)

In this chapter, we look at how it has been analysed by Baudrillard and Eco among others, and whether a simulational analysis can avoid the accusation of cynicism. This comment from urban geographer and historian of Los Angeles Mike Davis is symptomatic of how Disneyland has come to stand as the epitome of simulation:

> . . . social fantasy is now embodied in 'tourist bubbles' – historical districts, entertainment precincts, malls, and other variations on theme parks – that are partitioned off from the rest of the city. As all the postmodern philosopher kings (Baudrillard, Eco, Jameson) constantly remind us, Los Angeles is the world capital of such 'hyperreality'. This distinction has deep historical roots. Southern California's pioneering theme parks of the 1930s and 1940s were primarily simulations of the movies and later of television shows. . . . Disneyland of course opened the gates to the Magic Kingdom of cartoon creatures familiar from both the movie screen and television set. . . . The consumers of this junk-food version of urbanity are generally homogeneous crowds of upscale shoppers and tourists. . . . Moreover, a largely invisible army of low-wage service workers, who themselves live in Bantustans like Santa Ana barrio, . . . keep the machinery of unreality running. (Davis 1998: 392–3)

Davis, here writing in a journalistic polemic rather than one of his scholarly works, draws on a vocabulary we have become accustomed to by now: simulation, hyperreality, the machinery of unreality. He adds some other crucial terms here: tourism for one, an industry which has grown in leaps and bounds in the years since the end of World War II left a surplus of planes and pilots, and a population accustomed by their war service to travelling long distances. As Dean MacCannell (1976) was one of the first to observe, tourism creates a curious contradiction: we want to travel to exotic destinations in order to have authentic experiences, but the experience we have is never one of being truly at home in the local culture. Because, as tourists, we are always uprooted, and always bring with us something of our home culture, we can never find that home away from home that we seek when we go looking for authenticity. What then do we find? Simulation: places that exist only in order to be photographed. Disneyland at Anaheim, California, and Disney World at Orlando, Florida, explicitly offer a second level of simulation, by providing their visitors with a staged reality that imitates the stereotypical architecture and food of distant countries, and by inviting them, through the provision of Kodak-sponsored 'Picture Spots', to get the perfect photo of the perfect staging of a perfect simulacrum. If tourism is already a simulation, why go all that distance, when you can get a perfect simulacrum right here?

This is of course the basis of Baudrillard's famous account of Disneyland in 'The Precession of Simulacra', possibly the most reprinted part of all his work (Baudrillard 1983a: 11–79; 1983c; 1988b: 166–84; 1994a: 1–42; Storey 1994: 361–68, this last an abbreviated extract). The passage on Disneyland is headed 'The Hyperreal and the Imaginary', scarcely occupying two and a half pages in the Glaser translation to which I will be referring. The passage begins by arguing that Disneyland – specifically the Anaheim park – 'is a perfect model of all the entangled orders of simulacra'

(Baudrillard 1994a: 12), that is, that it is not simply a simulacrum, but a knot composed of the three orders of simulation. Firstly, it comprises 'a play of illusions and phantasms' (Baudrillard 1994a: 12), corresponding to the phase in which the image 'masks and denatures a profound reality' (Baudrillard 1994a: 6). Secondly, the park lures the crowd with 'the social microcosm, the *religious*, miniaturized pleasure of real America' (Baudrillard 1994a: 12), corresponding to the image that 'masks the *absence* of a profound reality' (Baudrillard 1994a: 6), since, as we recall from Baudrillard's discussion of the iconoclasts, religion exists to mask the fatal truth, 'that deep down, God never existed . . . that even God himself was never anything but his own simulacrum' (Baudrillard 1994a: 4). At this stage, it is still possible, Baudrillard says, to perform an ideological analysis of Disneyland, like the one written by Louis Marin in 1973 (Marin 1984: especially 239–57): the park's celebration of America dissimulates the disappearance of American reality, a disappearance that can still be considered as in some sense a truth that has been concealed. In the third phase, where the image 'has no relation to any reality whatsoever: it is its own pure simulation', we discover that

> Disneyland exists in order to hide that it is the 'real' country, all of 'real' America that *is* Disneyland. . . . Disneyland is presented as imaginary in order to make us believe that the rest is real, whereas all of Los Angeles and the America that surrounds it are no longer real, but belong to the hyperreal order and to the order of simulacra. It is no longer a question of a false representation of reality (ideology) but of concealing the fact that the real is no longer real, and thus of saving the reality principle. (Baudrillard 1994a: 12–13)

In this third order of simulation, the purpose of the park is not to dissimulate the absence of reality but to re-create a simulation of it so that the idea of reality can continue to operate as a key social function. Paradoxically, Baudrillard argues, the fake world of Disneyland supplies, a constant supply of 'reality' flowing into the city of Los Angeles, which has become 'a network of unreal, incessant circulation', a word which in French also carries the sense of automobile traffic. The endless driving has demateri-alised the city's architecture, so that to the motorist it appears as 'a perpetual pan shot', to such an extent that it loses its dimensionality, to become merely an image of itself. Disneyland's function is to be a factory of unreality which, by pretending to be more unreal than the already unreal city, can persuade its visitors that the world beyond is still more real than the fantasy world inside the park gates.

Eco is similarly succinct, devoting six pages of the essay 'Travels in Hyperreality' to Disneyland (Eco 1986: 43–8). He too cites Marin approvingly, especially on the architecture of Main Street, with its use of scaling to exaggerate perspective and draw the visitor onward and inward toward the Magic Kingdom. Eco distinguishes Disneyland from waxworks museums which try to convince us that they are imitating reality. Disneyland, on the contrary, 'makes it clear that within its magic enclosure it is fantasy that is absolutely reproduced' (Eco 1986: 43). Here we are at Baudrillard's first level of simulation, and at the level Davis refers to as 'simulations of the movies'. Eco notes along Main Street, whose façades contain a plethora of shops, the loss of distinction between play and shopping, and between the fantasy of play and the reality of consumption, arguing, as we heard before in Chapter 4, that 'What is falsified is our will to buy, which we take as real, and in this sense Disneyland is really the quintessence of consumer ideology' (Eco 1986: 43). We are now travelling in a rather different direction to Baudrillard's argument, one that seems closer to Debord's conception of the spectacle. Eco suggests that visitors are invited not just to succumb to the illusion but 'to admire the perfection of the fake', in such a way that the illusion 'stimulate[s] desire for it' (Eco 1986: 44). Like Baudrillard (and indeed like almost all Europeans), Eco stops to look at the vast car parks surrounding the Anaheim Disneyland. Here is a crucial transition, he says, because 'for a Californian, leaving his car means leaving his own humanity, consigning himself to another power, abandoning his own will' (Eco 1986: 48). So we can say that Disneyland has a second agenda. On the one hand, it celebrates the fake as a route towards dissolving the distinction between play and spending, resulting in 'the conviction that imitation has reached its apex and afterwards reality will always be inferior to it' (Eco 1986: 46), and that 'technology can give us more reality than nature can' (Eco 1986: 44). Neither of these imply a loss of will-power; rather, they seem to give an ironic commentary on those gullible enough to lose sight of what seems to be an unchallenged truth in Eco's thought: that nature is always the prime and reliable source of reality. The word 'more' in the phrase 'more reality' is a clue: this is the 'more' of consumerism, the 'more' that implies more of the same, a 'more' which can ultimately be distinguished from the 'natural' reality which still exists away from the kitsch of hyperreal America. More worrying still, however, is the second agenda, first flagged when Eco suggests that the perfection of the fake that so impresses us is tied up with 'its obedience to the program' (Eco 1986: 44). The animatronic pirates and ghosts, highly photo-realistic three-dimensional robots which form part of the park's attractions, he argues, stun us not only with their life-likeness but also with their absolute reliance on routine, a routine which, as visitors to the parks all know, also governs the movement of people through the attractions. For Eco, these mechanical puppets 'transform the whole city into an immense robot' (Eco 1986: 47), whose visitors 'must agree to behave like robots' in 'a place of total passivity' (Eco 1986: 48). What disturbs Eco most is the extension of this principle to the much larger, more secluded and in many ways more ambitious Florida Disney World, where the robotic passivity of Anaheim is rendered as 'the model of an urban agglomerate of the future' (Eco 1986: 47).

We can see here that there are significant differences between the two accounts. Armed with the ironic weapon of common sense, Eco can contrast Disneyland with, on the one hand, nature as the repository of natural reality, and, on the other, a common faith in the proper model of urban living as one which involves active citizens participating in the life of the community. Baudrillard has no such armoury. For him nature itself is a construct, tamed by science, exploited by production and deprived of its reality by being turned into a signifier of an innocence that no longer exists. As Neil Smith has argued, our times are characterised by the way we flatter ourselves that we have achieved complete autonomy from the natural world (Smith 1996: 38), a tradition that stretches back to the Renaissance, brought to a head in the Enlightenment, enshrined in the Marxist theory of production and dismantled by simulation theorists who point towards the second nature of technology and nowadays of information networks. Simulation argues that even human nature has been irredeemably altered by consumerism, and feminists argue that where we still use the word 'nature', it is usually in order to promote an ideology of the 'natural' subjugation of women, animals and raw materials to the corporate desires of patriarchal capital. As we shall see, however, there are some additional tangles in the story of nature in relation to the Disney experience.

On the second of Eco's principles, Baudrillard is rather explicit. There is no active citizenship. The social has imploded, and we are left with the masses and their silence. That silence is not in itself a bad thing. Reflecting on his polemic with German poet and media critic Hans Magnus Enzensberger, Baudrillard says 'Today . . . I would no longer interpret in the same way the forced silence of the masses in the mass media. I would no longer see in it a sign of passivity and alienation, but to the contrary an original response in the form of a challenge' (Baudrillard 1988c: 208). In the earlier attack ('Requiem pour les medias' in Baudrillard 1972: 200–28), Baudrillard had argued that the nature of mass communication is such that it does not allow response: mass media are one-way conduits. In that argument, the audience appears as alienated from the source of their culture and silenced by it. But on further reflection, Baudrillard argues,

> We are no longer even alienated, because for that it is necessary for the subject to be divided in itself, confronted with the other, to be contradictory. Now, where there is no other, the scene of the other, like that of politics and of society, has disappeared. Each individual is forced despite himself or herself into the undivided consistency of statistics. (Baudrillard 1988c: 210)

The processes of homogenisation intrinsic to the culture of simulation ensure that there are no longer contradictions either internal to individuals or in societies. Deprived of communication by the mass media, we have lost our other, be it the unconscious or the ruling class. In this scenario, where political action has been subsumed into the statistical machinery of opinion polls, the apparent passivity and alienation of the masses is in fact a strategy of refusal, a kind of post-punk attitude of sullenness, boredom and indifference which is the last possible political act. With this argument, Baudrillard not only parts company with Eco's obvious dislike for passivity, revaluing the robotic as a strategy of resistance, but also destroys the grounds on which might be built the principle of common sense, for the only thing that is common is the mass media, and the one thing that mass media do not allow is participation. Therefore the sense that they produce is not 'common' in the sense of being produced by a community; it is simply the working-through of the Code's internal reproduction. Baudrillard sees this as a kind of irony, but it is very different to Eco's stance, which relies on a shared knowledge of what is right; for Baudrillard, the refusal to know, the decision to let others decide for us, is intrinsic to the last mode of politics available in the simulated world.

Nonetheless, both our thinkers agree on at least three things: Disneyland's visitors are passive; Disneyland is consistently successful in what it sets out to do; and Disneyland belongs to the order of the fake and the hyperreal. Our task in the remainder of this chapter is to discover whether they are right. In what follows, we will be concentrating not on the original Anaheim park, but on Walt Disney World outside Orlando, Florida, on the basis that Disney World, despite being deliberately more remote from city life, functions in identical ways to Disneyland. Moreover, the bulk of recent research concerns the newer, larger and more ambitious park there, a site which also includes extensive corporate buildings and important animation studios, several hotels and associated leisure facilities like golf clubs and marinas, and most recently real estate for domestic dwellings at the now famous Celebration model town. And as Baudrillard himself has observed, whereas the Anaheim park was still in the order of the spectacle, Disney World truly belongs to the order of simulation (Baudrillard 1996b).

To give an idea of the continuity of the two sites, it is worth recalling that the 1998 hit film *The Truman Show* was largely shot in the town of Celebration. In that film the hero, played by Jim Carrey, discovers that his idyllic life is broadcast twenty-four hours a day as a TV show, and that his every decision has been influenced less by his wishes than by the directorial decisions of the show's producer, and ultimately by the pressures of the ratings. In other words, Disney have allowed and promoted a film which portrays life in Celebration as governed by precisely that 'undivided consistency of statistics' which we have just heard Baudrillard describing. Even the Walt Disney Corporation, it seems, have assimilated the concept of simulation into their understanding of the Orlando Disney World and their public relations concerning it. In the film, the protagonist discovers the truth of his situation and decides to escape from the idyll, performing a last ideological role by proving that the instinct for freedom is more important than the desire for comfort. Of course, in Baudrillard's vision, there is no outside to escape to. The film of Celebration performs exactly the same function as Disneyland: to assert, despite everything, that there is a reality somewhere outside the Disney empire.

Jim Carrey offers a role model – Baudrillard would say a simulation – of active refusal. The theorists we have been investigating all imply the power of spectacle and simulation to induce passivity. But how true is it that visitors to Disneyland are passive? If we are to believe Baudrillard, even if they are, that is a form of resistance. For him, the hero of *The Truman Show* would have been more subversive of the simulated world had he opted to stay in it and do, ironically, exactly as he was told. We can perhaps deduce from the conclusion to Eco's essay that the escapee has nowhere to escape to, for what is 'outside' is urban sprawl, a massive and unruly space of conflict and threat compared to the charmed and protected world inside Celebration. How will Truman cope, never having experienced that scale or complexity of urban antagonism? In Eco's universe, Truman lacks the common sense which every city-dweller has. We have to imagine him, perhaps, as Peter Sellers' character in *Being There* (1979), an innocent used only to TV who embarks on life in Washington DC armed only with a remote control in a film whose comedy depends, once again, on the disjuncture between television and reality, or, in Eco's terms, hyperreality and common sense.

We return then to the question of passivity. My own visit to Disney World was rather unusual in that I spent a good deal of the time visiting attractions alone. It is very clear that Disney World is designed for families and couples. Although the new hotels also host a large number of conventions, delegates tend to visit the park, if at all, in groups. To be a single in Disney World is itself oddly alienating: one imagines both Baudrillard and Eco wandering through Anaheim in a similarly unusual state of dislocation brought on not just by their status as European intellectuals but by visiting on their own. Much of the time, visitors to Disney World are queuing. Most of the queues are reasonably short and fast-moving, and are cheered up with video screens and patter from cast members (the Corporation's name for workers who come into contact with the public). Nonetheless, a single is always that much less involved in one of the crucial functions of Disney World: to produce a shared experience. No matter how many people you may strike up acquaintances with in the line, the queue is properly a place where families and lovers can talk up the expectation, and begin the process of remembering what they have done so far. Without that purpose, the queue becomes a place for analytical reasoning, and, often enough, for starting to criticise a construction of your time that becomes far more obvious since you cannot use it for its intended purposes. This is by no means the only way in which a visitor can resist the passive role suggested by Eco and Baudrillard, but it is one shared by others I have spoken to and read about. Being the wrong kind of person is like being the smart-alec at a children's party: a certain way to ensure that the magic doesn't work.

On the other hand, I greatly enjoyed some of the rides, loved mooching about in the warm winter sunshine, especially when my partner could join me, and was fascinated by one attraction in particular, the backstage tour which takes you underneath one of the bigger rides to look through huge windows into the animation studios where some of the work for *Toy Story* (1995) had just been done, and where work on *The Hunchback of Notre Dame* (1997) was just beginning. The tour guide was surprisingly informative on animation techniques, in between the usual barrage of numbers, and the clips and glimpses of studio life were fascinating. Even more so because, a day or so later, I found myself on the other side of the glass with some friends editing a Disney TV documentary. Chatting away in the edit suite, we were peripherally aware that every fifteen minutes or so another party of backstage tourists would swing by, stand in a bunch and listen to a commentary we couldn't hear about what was going on in the room we were working in. The director of the documentary, during a lull while soundtracks were being processed, decided to liven things up by putting on a show for the next tour group. As they hove into view, he threw his cap onto the floor in a show of rage and danced up and down on it. Someone hurled empty styrofoam cups at the video decks. The director of photography pretended to strangle the producer. After a couple of minutes, the tour group moved on and we settled back down into logging the soundtrack.

Cast members at Disney World, which includes studio employees who might be observed by visitors, are a vital part of the organisation. Many are in character as Minnies and Mickeys, Chips and Dales, while others are waiting tables, cleaning, working in the stores, restaurants and hotels or handling security. All are well schooled in their roles, often enough taking courses at the Disney University in hospitality and leisure management, but most of all in the Disney 'philosophy'. Among their skills are patters and routines that they can deliver whenever needed for most foreseeable situations: scripts for illnesses and accidents, breakages and mischievous children. In the sense intended by Eco and Baudrillard, they are indistinguishable from the animatronic androids that repeat endlessly their repertoires of dialogue and gestures. Yet it is also true that cast members do bring with them, at least on the days when they feel up to it, a certain creativity like that I witnessed in the edit suites underneath the Indiana Jones ride. Several commentators observe the same thing: tour guides whose narratives begin to turn into something like stand-up comedy, shop assistants who strike up long and involved conversations with guests (Disney's name for park visitors as well as those staying in the hotels). A lot of this improvisation simply extends the scripted role, especially when cast members are in character. It is rare to hear of anything directly critical, or even chatter that would puncture the 'magic' in more innocent ways. Yet these creative interpretations of the Disney universe suggest that there is more to Disney World than the entirely preprogrammed experience that Eco and Baudrillard imagine. The three-week walkout in 1985 by two thousand Disneyland cast members adds more weight to the point: Disney reality is not without its moments when the Code breaks down.

Almost every visitor to Disney World has a story about disasters. Favourite tales include the seizing of small children by alligators native to the swamps that preceded the building of the park, beheadings on the more adventurous white-knuckle rides, muggings, rapes and murders. It is as if these tales, whether suppressed truths or urban folklore, are necessary parts of our understanding of Disney World, a necessary addition of risk to the saccharine security of the park. Those cast members who wear the heavy cartoon heads of Donald and Mickey are widely known to suffer from heat exhaustion, one of whose symptoms can be throwing up:

You're never to be seen in a costume without your head, *ever*. It was automatic dismissal. It's frightening because you can die on your own regurgitation when you can't keep out of it. I'll never forget Dumbo – it was coming out of the mouth during the parade. You have a little screen over the mouth. It was horrible. And I made $4.55 an hour. (Cast member quoted in The Project on Disney 1995: 136)

Like the stories of injuries and deaths sustained by guests, and indeed like the 1988 and 1990 lawsuits against Disney's pollution of the local ecology, the gossip among cast members and the meticulous ethnography conducted among them by the members of The Project on Disney suggest that there are very real problems of exploitation, health and safety infringements and draconian management, all summarised in the quotation above, that simulation theory does not seem capable of accounting for. At the same time, as Jane Kuenz of The Project on Disney argues,

Walt Disney World is *really* not what it seems to be, though the nature of its deceptiveness may not be what it seems either. Disney's conceit of theater marshals the creative and emotional energies of its workers and creates a situation in which they are always performing for the company. . . . It is also, however, the vehicle for whatever departures they make from it – the determinate structure that brings forth in spite of itself the indeterminate practices for which it nevertheless finds uses. (The Project on Disney 1995: 113)

As a workplace, Disney World is an advanced model for the new style of corporate management, recruiting the creativity and playfulness of its employees at the same time as it channels and structures its outcomes, promoting 'indeterminate' innovations which can then be rehearsed and built into future productions.

But are guests equally unable to rebel against the careful manipulations of Disney World? The park benefits from some innovations initiated at Disneyland and others developed in airports and shopping malls in the movement of large numbers of people. The meandering paths are there to stagger the arrival of guests at turnstiles. The architecture of Main Street, a feature common to all four Disney parks, has ground floors at seven-eighths and second floors at five-eighths normal scale, creating at once a sense of defamiliarisation and fantasy, and a receding perspective that encourages visitors to move along its axis towards the next attraction. People-movers, trams and monorails, presented as attractions in their own right, provide fully controlled transportation between areas of the park. But it is also true that in these entirely privatised commercial spaces, under the gaze of an apparently all-controlling eye, people do stop for picnics, run up the down escalator, fall asleep on the lawns and generally mess around. Although the overwhelming impression is one of serene surrender to the tempo which the park dictates, there are constant reminders that people are setting their own pace and creating their own sense of locality. This emphasis on active participation in the production of contemporary culture is a strong theme in cultural studies. There is indeed something profoundly utopian in the attempt, at Disney World, to produce a family idyll, a vacation from the pressures of the everyday world where relations between parents and children, and even between siblings, can be restored and renewed; where the past can be revisited and the future re-imagined. This utopianism can be seen in a very negative light. Henry Giroux, for example, argues that 'The pervasive symbol of ideological unification through which Disney defines its view of capitalism, gender, and national identity is the family' (Giroux 1994: 98), where the family is merely the most convenient unit of consumption. But it can also be argued that the bonds holding families together are genuinely utopian, even though, like sex and hunger, they have been reshaped and restructured by the consumerism of the society in which nowadays they find themselves. Families use Disney World just as much as Disney World uses them.

This utopian dimension can also be part of a visit to the park that goes against the park's own grain, creating personal spaces grafted onto but quite separate from the commercial domain of the park's public face. On the other hand, there are also counter-utopian and counter-Disney moments, especially when family rows flare up, often enough spurred by the very pressures which Disney World places on family members: to shop when a budget is limited, to enjoy on schedule despite tears and tantrums, to behave nicely on a hyperkinetic diet of sugar and caffeine. Though the considerable expense of a visit tends to keep out the more egregious crazies, it is far from unusual to find guests, especially children, engulfed in anti-social squalls of anger and misery. While these are certainly not utopian aspects of the life of the park, they are part of its reality, and testimony to the resistance of its visitors to the overwhelming control posited by Baudrillard and Eco. The N30 anti-capitalist demonstrators in Seattle in the last months of the twentieth century, after all, were children who grew up in Disney culture. Disney World may encourage passivity; it cannot guarantee it.

Likewise, it is essential to realise that Disney World is not universally successful. I have tried over the last few pages to indicate that there are limits to its 'success' in terms of producing a passive audience. I want to go on to show that Disney World is not a universally successful business venture either, and that rumours of the omnipotence of consumer capital are therefore somewhat exaggerated. One reason for insisting on this aspect of Disney World is because the various Disney companies can appear as models for the commercial power of getting into new technologies early. Disney's great break came with the Silly Symphonies of the late 1920s and early 1930s, shorts which pioneered the use of synchronised sound with animated action. Throughout the decade, the studio had a series of hit songs to add to their earnings, the first of them 'Who's Afraid of the Big Bad Wolf', which one of Disney's biographers calls 'the nation's unofficial depression era anthem' (Eliot 1995: 75), and the rights to which, like all subsequent new songs, remains the studio's property. The company pioneered the merchandising of its characters, from Mickey Mouse onwards. The studio's most significant hit, *Snow White and the Seven Dwarfs* (1937), was touted not only as the first animated feature film, but also as a pioneer in the use of technicolour. The deal that sealed the financing for Disneyland came from a contract to provide the ABC television network with a weekly show, initially also called *Disneyland*: while other studios reeled from the double impact of anti-trust action in the courts and the suburbanisation of leisure in the post-war USA, Disney joined forces with the new growth industry and used the power of the medium to cross-market its new theme park. The first park in particular is widely regarded as the original both of the boom industry in contemporary theme parks and of the huge number of heritage parks that now litter the globe. The association with innovation continues with films like *Toy Story* (1995), the world's first computer-generated feature film, as well as the expansion into the hotel business and the diversification into real estate at Celebration, sold on the appeal of instant community. Both the company itself and simulation theorists speak of the 'timeless' appeal of the Disney 'magic' (although perhaps meaning slightly different things) while at the same time extolling its 'enduring' popularity and its ability to stay on the cutting edge of entertainment technologies.

However, the story has not been all roses. The company nearly crashed in the 1940s, and would have done had it not been for a series of educational films made for the US government during and immediately after the war. The deal with ABC gave the company a vital cash flow; the unregulated promotion of the park through the TV show worked wonders for attendances, and there were some unexpected benefits. The TV show included a three-part dramatisation of the life of Davy Crockett. Because the first episode ran several minutes short, scriptwriter Tom Blackburn and house composer George Burns tacked on a title song, 'The Ballad of Davy Crockett', that would spend thirteen weeks in the hit parade (Hollis and Sibley 1988: 69). Meanwhile,

> Even before the first episode had aired, [Disney] quietly purchased thousands of raw racoon tail skins for 5 cents apiece from a manufacturer after a government embargo prevented him from selling them to mainland China. The day the first episode premiered, Walt launched a fully prepared merchandising campaign that resulted in the sale of more than ten million hastily sewn 'Davy Crockett coonskin caps'. (Eliot 1995: 228)

However, Disney never replicated the success of this early offering, and increasingly had to rely on the re-release of their classic animated features to maintain revenue streams outside Disneyland itself. In 1959, the disastrous release of *Sleeping Beauty* (the studio's most expensive animation till then, intriguingly described in the New York *Herald Tribune* as 'Disney imitating Disney' [Schickel 1968: 253], perhaps a preface to the simulations of Disney World) dropped the company into the red with losses of 1.3 million dollars over the year. From this low, the company clambered back up to be valued at one hundred million dollars and record twelve million dollars profit in 1966. Disney had turned themselves around, from a minor studio to a major theme park operator.

But the 1970s were lean years again: films flopped, the TV series was cancelled and attendances began to dip at the theme parks. The revival of Disney's fortunes is often ascribed to the 1984 arrival of Michael Eisner, still CEO at time of writing, but as Douglas Gomery argues in his astute and succinct history of the company's fortunes since its founding, Eisner and sidekick Frank Wells cannot be congratulated on pure business acumen: 'They took a company which was underperforming and began to fully exploit its rich assets during one of the greatest peacetime economic expansions on record' (Gomery 1994: 79). But once again in the 1990s profits began to decline. The failure of a number of TV ventures, the expensive launch and slow beginnings of the Disney Channel, the failure of Hollywood Records after hefty investment, the collapse of a planned merger with Jim Henson's Creature Shop and the demise of several real estate and theme park deals over environmental and other political issues all ate into a business which was forced to sell the family silver. For years, Disney had always been able to count on theatrical re-releases of classic films. Now they have all been sold as video, and the company is reliant on the fickle box office to generate new classics to market across merchandising and the parks, now far more expensive than in their heydays. The failure, despite massive investment, of EuroDisney, now known as Disneyland Paris or DLP, has not helped. Tokyo Disneyland is far the most successful park, but the need to attract partnership funding means that Disney see less than 50 per cent of revenues. Should DLP ever move into profit, Disney will only recoup a similar proportion there too.

It has never been true that Hollywood or anyone else is able to predict public response to cultural products. *Cleopatra*, *Ishtar*, *Heaven's Gate* and *Waterworld* all demonstrate the fallibility of the 'machinery of fantasy'. Disney paid twelve million dollars to sign Queen for their Hollywood Records label, but the album only sold a half million copies. They spent twenty million developing Port Disney, a marine theme park at Long Beach, only to lose their investment when the local community objected, having already been outmanoeuvred in the real estate negotiations to the tune of a hundred million dollars (Gomery 1994: 83). In the cultural industries, the majority of products are indeed created according to formulas that have proved successful in the past. But to some extent, since most products must also have something new about them to attract new audiences, every product is also to that extent a prototype. The winning formula of *Star Wars* did not help Disney when they lost an estimated twenty million dollars on their response, *The Black Hole*. More innovative projects run higher risks. It is still unclear whether the billions invested in the EPCOT Center at Disney World, showcase for the future, even with corporate sponsorship from General Motors, Exxon, Coca-Cola, American Express, AT&T, General Electric and others, has shown a profit to date. Plans for two new parks in the People's Republic of China will be tests for current corporate strategy. Entry into the new economies of South East Asia are widely seen as critical for global companies, but it is impossible to tell whether the Chinese will take to Disney's theme parks in sufficient number and with sufficient spending power to provide a new lease of life for the company. As Gomery has it, 'the Disney company is simply another capitalist enterprise' (Gomery

1994: 86). In an era in which major companies like Barings Bank, cultural entrepreneurs like Orion Pictures and whole industries like shipbuilding in the UK and the USA can collapse, it would be foolish to equate capitalist enterprise with foolproof guarantees of success. In the cultural industries, this means that there is no way of knowing with any degree of certainty what makes for success. As scriptwriter William Goldman has it in his account of the Hollywood industry, 'NOBODY KNOWS ANYTHING' (Goldman 1983: 39).

These discussions of the activity of Disney World visitors and of the economics of the industry are necessary to offset the tendency of simulation theorists towards presuming the power and success of consumer culture. Nonetheless, it is still possible to see ways in which their theorisations still apply. One can clearly imagine Baudrillard especially arguing that the rise and fall of specific companies has nothing to do with the rise and fall of consumer capitalism. Indeed, the appearance they give of tumultuous activity is itself a simulation, since beneath it precisely nothing is happening. A company folds, but all its executives move on to other companies, workforces are redeployed, even specific product lines are reintroduced with a new brand name and all the trauma of bankruptcy dissolves in the homogeneous soup of the self-replication of commodity capital. Equally, it can well be argued that innovation of the kind that, as we have seen, has constantly been ascribed to the Disney company can also be seen from a neighbouring perspective as a process of standardisation. As Alan Bryman argues in an important text on the Disney theme parks, however active or resistant audiences may be, they are active and resistant in relation to mass media conglomerates that are far more powerful than they are (Bryman 1995: 188). Moreover, as Bryman goes on to suggest, Disney World promotes not just Disney but all the other companies involved in it, from 'official airline' Delta (who appear to have paid forty million dollars for the privilege) to fast-food franchises. Its allegiance is not even to itself alone but, as cultural phenomenon, to a corporate culture shared by Disney, its partners and 'the white middle class who are its typical clientele' (Bryman 1995: 193). In this way, even were Disney to go bankrupt, the parks would continue; and even if theme parks ceased to amuse the public, the corporate culture would find other ways to replicate itself.

But this argument is still a little too uncompromising, a little too universal. Bryman also notes a curious contradiction in Disney World, concerning its obsessive remaking of a pristine and innocent past. If the past is so great, surely then there must be something wrong with the present? We could also ask another, similar question: how do visitors square the construction of nostalgia for Main Street USA and Frontierland with the progress-oriented constructions of the future in the EPCOT Center and Futureland? One possible answer is that they do not; that like slavery and the civil rights movement, these contradictions never occur to visitors because they belong to an entirely different discourse. But this argument either falls foul of the critique of common sense argued above, or it can be countered with an argument that precisely there is no commensurability between different discourses: one cannot be used to critique another, since all are equated in the general loss of difference that characterises the society of simulation.

Another response is suggested by an observation from the literary critic Fredric Jameson, commenting on a key text of postmodernism, Robert Venturi and Denise Scott-Brown's book *Learning from Las Vegas* (Venturi and Scott-Brown 1972). In their book, Venturi and Scott-Brown argue that architecture should learn from the comic, symbolic and allegorical commercial architecture of places like Las Vegas (and, we might add, Disney World, although Disney architecture has itself been profoundly influenced by postmodernism – see Shelton Waldrep's essay in The Project on Disney [1995: 199–229]). Burger joints shaped like burgers and casinos built like pyramids, they argue, can provide postmodern architects with a vernacular inspiration that can renew the geometric rigour of classical modernist skyscrapers and high-rise flats. Jameson observes that such postmodernisms 'have, in fact, been fascinated by this whole "degraded" landscape of schlock and kitsch . . . materials they no longer "quote" . . . but incorporate into their very substance' (Jameson 1991: 2–3). A perfect example is the Disney corporate headquarters in Burbank, a building whose ornate classical columns turn out, as you approach them, to be massive three-dimensional models of the seven dwarfs, and which is capped by a roof shaped like Mickey's hat in *The Sorcerer's Apprentice*.

We should make two observations here. The term 'kitsch' which Jameson uses has a distinctive history in cultural criticism, especially in a 1939 essay by the modernist art critic Clement Greenberg, who argues that kitsch is the popular and degraded art of industrial culture, neither folkloric nor cultivated but a marker of social class (middle-class taste, working-class kitsch). Arguing that the realist art promoted by both Hitler and Stalin in the 1930s is precisely kitsch, he propounds the theory that 'the encouragement of kitsch is merely another of the inexpensive ways in which totalitarian regimes seek to ingratiate themselves with their subjects' (Greenberg 1992: 539). At that stage, on the eve of world war and in the context of a defence of avant-garde art, Greenberg was able to make a clear distinction between 'degraded' and 'superior' art. Jameson's argument is that it is no longer possible to make that distinction. Curiously, the bulk of his examples, throughout a very long book, come from 'high' culture, demonstrating that it has indeed learnt from Las Vegas. What is less clear is that 'low' culture has learnt from the Louvre. In a sense, this is what Eco set out to uncover in 'Travels in Hyperreality', but there is little evidence of anything similar happening at Disney World. Disney World's history comes from schoolroom colouring books, and its future from science fiction, not from historians, museums or scientists.

But our second observation must be that Jameson (1991: 46) is correct in noting that simulation is a matter not of quotation, which establishes differences, but of assimilation, which erases them in a process which the sociologist Scott Lash summarises as 'dedifferentiation' (Lash 1990:

11–15). Bryman observes a series of ways in which Disney World dediffen-
tiates traditional distinctions between amusements and retailing, theme parks
and hotels, work and play (among cast members, a process confirmed by
The Project on Disney), entertainment and education. However, work and
play *are* differentiated in the demarcation of the park as a distinctive space
apart from the city and the humdrum world of the everyday (Bryman 1995:
165–8). On the other hand, such distinctions are eroded in the presence of
Disney paraphernalia and photos from visits back home, Disney shows on
cable, Disney stores in the mall. As Chris Rojek argues, 'the distinctions
between the "real" world and Disney World are not so much destroyed
as eroded' (Rojek 1993). Simulation theory has yet to erase the traces of
contradiction.

6

WAR IN THE PERSIAN GULF

In the long run, we're all dead

To celebrate his victory, so Baudrillard tells us, General Schwarzkopf, commander of the allied forces in the Gulf, organised a massive party at Disney World (Baudrillard 1996b). There can be few places where the naked contradictions of a global society should show themselves as readily as in warfare, yet this conjuncture of war and theme park suggests the opposite. War has proved one of the most fruitful – and controversial – of the topics addressed by simulation theory. If war is not the ultimate confrontation between opposites, what is it? In this chapter we will be concentrating on the Gulf War of 1991,[1] not least because both Baudrillard and Virilio have written books on it (Baudrillard 1995; Virilio 1991c). Both are composed of essays published during the conflict itself, the collections appearing respectively in May and September of 1991, a matter of months after the cessation of hostilities. We will begin by looking at what each has to say, before moving on to some criticisms of their positions. We conclude by looking at how analysis of contemporary war refines and develops simulation theory. Once again, we are pursuing the gaps in the theory, the residual place of reality in theory, and the difficulty of presenting any theory as total.

One of Virilio's concerns is to place the Gulf War in a history of warfare. This history falls into three major periods: 'the pre-historic *tactical* epoch typified by contained tumults; then the historical and properly political *strategic* epoch; and finally the contemporary *logistical* epoch, where science and industry play determining roles' (Virilio 1991c: 79). Each period has its characteristic weaponry – respectively weapons of obstruction (ramparts, forts), destruction (bows, cannons) and communication (watch towers, signalling); and each promotes a particular type of battle – siege warfare, warfare by battlefield manoeuvring, and blitzkrieg (Virilio 1991c: 79–80). Moreover, each corresponds to a social organisation of warfare. In tactical war, decisions were ultimately made by citizen soldiers. In the strategic era, power was delegated increasingly to the officer class. But in the automated world of contemporary logistical warfare, the decision to use weapons of ultimate destruction comes to reside 'in one man, the Head of State, who in turn delegates its execution to a machine' (Virilio 1991c: 72).

---

1. There is some debate as to the proper name for this conflict. Chris Hables Gray suggests 'The War to Restore the Rightful Dictator of Kuwait' (Gray 1997: 265), which catches the essence of the matter.

The sheer speed of contemporary war exceeds that of human decision-making: at the limit, we have given our early warning systems the capability to launch 'defensive' or 'preventative' strikes with no human intervention whatsoever. Automated war is war in real time, lacking the time for decision-making.

Moreover, CNN's live coverage of the conflict, also transmitted, until late in the hostilities, in real time, extends this militarisation process to the worldwide television spectators of the war through a 'strategic occupation of the screen' (Virilio 1991c: 37) by news coverage heavily controlled by the Pentagon's news pool (from which even slightly dissenting voices like Agence France Presse were excluded). Virilio's second concern then is to establish the links between the innovative conduct of warfare in the Gulf and the changes in civilian life that he perceived in the first eighteen months of the 1990s. One aspect of this is the relation he feels is constructed for TV viewers by the television's coverage of the war. Interviewed for French TV in mid-January, on the eve of the first bombing raids on Baghdad, he argued:

> Since 2 August we've been living inside the theatre of operations, spectators of a staged event [*mise-en-scène*]. We have been living in an integral fiction. Faced with war, it's not enough to be a conscientious objector: you have to object to war's objectivity. You mustn't believe your eyes, not any more.

By June this fear has settled into something like a doctrine:

> [There has been a] *sudden militarisation of mass information* of which, for six months, we have been the innocent victims, and a likewise obsessional attention brought by Pentagon officials, via CNN, to the *subjective perception* of the passive consumers of images that we have become. (Virilio 1991c: 186–7)

Armed with the criticism of reading audiences as passive dupes presented in the previous chapter, we can perhaps ask how Virilio himself is capable of being such an astute and radical critic, especially as, it appears, he spent almost two months doing nothing but following CNN on TV. More importantly, we can ask why he opts for this pessimistic and totalitarian position. His answer is spread throughout the first two sections of the book, 'Desert Shield' and 'Desert Storm', but is neatly summarised in the concluding section, written a few months later, 'Desert Screen'.

Here Virilio summarises arguments developed throughout this and his other books on contemporary warfare, according to which the 'pure war' instigated in World War II has been accelerated by the shift from the air strikes of the blitz (whose German meaning is 'lightning') to information warfare. Air power was still used in the 1940s to secure the real space of geographical conquests, whereas the principles of C3I (command, control, communication, intelligence) which govern contemporary wars are concerned with the administration of 'real time', as in the inertial guidance systems used by cruise missiles, or the real time of anti-missile missiles like Patriot, used to intercept the Iraqi Scuds. Real-time warfare is not about attacking or defending territory, but centrally about knowing where the enemy are and disabling them. Thus it has less to do with the traditional land, sea and air battle-fronts, and more to do with control over information.

> Here then is the great metamorphosis of this 'postmodern' war: it denies both offence and defence in favour of control and interdiction on the battlefield, regardless of its scale. The *instantaneous electronic information front* (the fourth front) takes over from the front lines of land armies in the last two world wars, the aerial front only ever having served to prefigure what would become, after the historical importance of *maritime power*, the future *orbital power*.
> *The third dimension* of atmospheric (First World War) and stratospheric (Second World War) volume are losing, little by little, their strategic importance to the the extra-terrestrial or 'exospheric', which can be reduced simply to control of the *fourth dimension*, a purely temporal dimension of the *real time* of ubiquity and instantaneity. A dimension less physical than microphysical, which sums up in itself alone, more or less, the fourth front comprising the supremacy of communication armaments. (Virilio 1991c: 177–8)

The use of satellite technologies removes decision-making and strategy beyond even the stratosphere where World War II's superfortress bombers flew. Moreover, they shift the key space of war from the physical field of battle to the electromagnetic spectrum of satellite surveillance, jamming and radar. This godlike ability to see everything and everywhere at every moment constitutes a wholly new dimension in war.

Virilio then goes on to his crucial arguments. Firstly, the combination of omniscient communications warfare and media manipulation of public opinion combine to form a single communications armoury aimed not only at the 'enemy' but also at the folks back home. What is the difference, we might ask, between introducing a virus into the Iraqi air defence computers (see Patton 1995: 5) and introducing a lie into news coverage of the war? And secondly, these technologies evoke 'troubling analogies between marketing methods and the organisation of industrial production, on the one hand, and, on the other, the centralised management of the electronic battlefield' (Virilio 1991c: 186). This results specifically, Virilio argues, in three rules: constant listening to the market, analogous to advance warning techniques; on-demand manufacture based on the same globalisation of telecommunications that permits the kind of war witnessed in the Gulf; and permanent innovation, a rule of business that allows Virilio to see the Gulf War as an arms fair, in which advertising new weapons is as important a goal as winning the conflict. These three rules shared by business and the military are indications of the militarisation of everyday life which the Gulf War has only speeded along its way. Virilio concludes by asking 'how can we share power now that the time in which it is exercised escapes us?' (Virilio 1991c: 191), and again '*can we democratise ubiquity and instantaneity, the all-seeing and omnipresent, which are the qualities of divinity or, in other words, of autocracy?*' (Virilio 1991c: 192).

This is not to say that Virilio is blind to the effects of the war on the population and even the soldiers of Iraq. There is a great tenderness to his article of 11 February, in which he describes the mismatch between the territorial war fought by the frontline troops in Iraq and the information war waged on them by the UN.

> By no means victims of counter-propaganda, lacking neither spiritual conviction not hatred, these soldiers of another age will die like their forebears, to accomplish a goal of which they know nothing. No-one demands anything else of them. Television will provide the rest. (Virilio 1991c: 117)

Virilio is also highly alert to the consequences of war for refugees, and for the changing nature of social relations in Europe and the USA when the allies in the war against Iraq find themselves refusing entry to the populations displaced in this and every other conflict of the last fifty years. He writes with passion and anger about the misleading media, the cynical use of the Desert Shield standoff period before hostilities began to build reconnaissance knowledge of Iraq, and the savage reality of death in the battlefield and in civilian bombings. Likewise, he is under no illusions about the abrupt ending of outright war: open warfare is increasingly being replaced with what the Western media now universally refer to as 'policing', a large-scale version of the same surveillance and containment that characterise inner-city law and order throughout the North Atlantic alliance. It is a question for Virilio then not of the disappearance of reality but of control over it, a control effected through technologies that are not exclusive to the military or even the police, but which have entered into every particle of contemporary life, destroying the possibility of true communication, true democracy and even natural perception. We saw in Chapter 3.iii that there are problems with Virilio's concepts of 'truth' and 'nature'. Nonetheless, they serve here as the fulcrum for a powerful indictment of the conduct of the war in the Persian Gulf.

Baudrillard's account was if anything even more provocative. In three essays published in the French daily paper *Libération* called 'The Gulf War Will Not Take Place', 'The Gulf War: Is It Really Taking Place?' and 'The Gulf War Did Not take Place', he goes well beyond Rudyard Kipling's motto, a favourite of Virilio's: 'The first casualty of war is truth.' In fact, the title of the first essay is a direct echo of a well-known play first staged in 1935 by the French dramatist Jean Giraudoux called *The Trojan War Will Not Take Place*, whose last lines are 'Troy's poet is dead . . . the last word goes to the poet of the Greeks' (Giraudoux 1958). Giraudoux's play, written during the Popular Front period which followed Hitler's rise to power in 1933, asks whether war is ever inevitable, and centres on the tragic Cassandra, who is blessed with the gift of prophecy and fated never to be believed, so that the future war of Troy exists perpetually not as destiny but in a uncertainly flickering state between possibility and impossibility. Baudrillard's case is similar, right down to the media's constant recourse to describing Hussein as 'Hitler'. His first essay, written during the Desert Shield period, concerns a change in the nature of war, a shift from face-to-face combat to 'non-war' (Baudrillard 1995: 24). The Cold War's politics of deterrence resulted in the equilibrium of the 'balance of terror', allowing the superpowers to not-fight. But this strategy of non-war did not come to an end with the demolition of the Berlin Wall in 1989. Hussein, according to Baudrillard, continues the same strategy in 'that degenerate form of war which includes hostage manipulation and negotiation' (Baudrillard 1995: 24). At this stage of events, Baudrillard observes the reluctance to start the war, 'as though the irruption or the event of war had become obscene and insupportable' (Baudrillard 1995: 27). In place of real war, there is only a virtual war of diplomacy, threats and hostage taking, all deployed in order to ward off the actual event of battle, an effect he describes as 'the deterrence of the real by the virtual' (Baudrillard 1995: 27). It is as if, in a climate of mass media jingoism, Baudrillard sees himself as Cassandra, prophesying not the possibility but the illusion of war.

The second essay, parts of which were published in *Libération* during the fighting, introduces the idea that non-war, in a pastiche of Clausewitz's famous definition, is *'the absence of politics pursued by other means'* (Baudrillard 1995: 30), a theme that comes to dominate the third essay. Like Virilio, Baudrillard believes that the two sides are fighting wars from different epochs and so operate in different forms of time. The Iraqis attempt to negotiate, a process which, like haggling in bazaars, demands communication and most of all a recognition of the other person (actually Baudrillard, in a rather ugly bit of stereotyping of his own, describes the Iraqi as 'a rug salesman' [Baudrillard 1995: 65]). But the Americans, convinced that their power and their virtue are synonymous, cannot understand or confront this otherness. Indeed, 'What they make war upon is the alterity of the other' (Baudrillard 1995: 37); that is, it is the very difference of Hussein's Iraq, and especially of Islam, which the American war effort aims to destroy. While Iraq, fresh from a ten-year long war of geographical attrition as the USA's surrogate force against Iran, still expected to fight as if in World War II, the US/UN forces were engaged in another form of conflict:

> Electronic war no longer has any political objective strictly speaking: it functions as a preventative electroshock against any future conflict. Just as in modern communication there is no longer any interlocutor, so in this electronic war there is no longer any enemy, there is only a refractory element which must be neutralised and consensualised. (Baudrillard 1995: 84)

With the metaphor of electrocution, linking the electronics of smart weapons, battlefield data decoys and intelligence, censorship and disinformation, Baudrillard introduces the image of electro-convulsive therapy, the administration of powerful electric pulses used to control threatening mental patients, to reduce them to passivity, and to abolish as far as possible their difference from the shared norms of those around them. This is the goal of electronic warfare: to produce consensus by eradicating or containing difference. And the same weaponry of electronic transmission is used, he argues, in CNN and the other mass media: there is no enemy because the same weapons are trained on the UN's own troops and their own populations indifferently. When the US military planted false information on CNN about troop movements to fool the Iraqis, they also duped their own citizens: 'TV plays out fully its role of social control by stupefaction' (Baudrillard 1995: 52). Here of course we see once again the myth of television's 'fabulous powers' (Connell 1984).

Like Virilio, again, Baudrillard goes on to argue that one effect of this undifferentiated electronic assault is that the US gradually come to believe in their military activity as 'global policing'. But 'if they want to be the police of the world and the New World Order, they must lose all political authority in favour of their operational capacity' (Baudrillard 1995: 53): even the generals will no longer be able to decide – the model of efficient and total surveillance and control will make those decisions for them. The war in this sense is an only slightly extended activity of the model or Code of civilian life. In streets deserted for fear of bombs or by people rushing to their TVs, 'the war erases the guerrilla warfare of everyday life' (Baudrillard 1995: 52). Since it was reported that the US losses were lower than the statistical likelihood of the number of traffic accidents that would have occurred to the same number of people over the same timespan if they had stayed at home, Baudrillard can ask ironically, 'Should we consider multiplying clean wars in order to reduce the murderous death toll of peacetime?' (Baudrillard 1995: 69). As has happened again in Chechnya, where the Russian government is deeply concerned to disguise and minimise the death-toll especially among their own forces, war is painted no longer in terms of the final sacrifice that brings glory, but as a bloodless, 'surgical' excision of recalcitrant evil. Either or both of the conduct of electronic war, that is, war at a distance thoroughly mediated in all its phases, and the manipulation of information about it, work to produce contemporary war as non-war, a war that does not take place.

But Baudrillard reserves his strongest and most damning argument for his third essay, the retrospective view after the cessation of bombardment and the withdrawal of UN forces from Iraq. At this stage, rather than push on and eliminate the Ba'ath government in Baghdad, the US appealed to the principle of non-intervention in a sovereign state's internal affairs (rather hypocritically, after their invasions of Grenada and Panama and the bombing of Iraq) and left Hussein in office. For Baudrillard, this amounts to an acceptance of a simulated defeat and a simulated victory.

> This ignominious remounting of Saddam, replacing him in the saddle after his clown act at the head of holy war, clearly shows that on all sides the war is considered not to have taken place. Even the last phase of this armed mystification will have changed nothing, for the 100,000 Iraqi dead will only have been the final decoy that Saddam will have sacrificed . . . in order to conserve his power. What is worse is that these dead still serve as an alibi for those who do not want to have been excited for nothing: at least the dead would prove that this war was indeed a war and not a shameful and painful hoax. (Baudrillard 1995: 71–2)

Perhaps the US government really believed its own stories, that the people of Iraq needed only this defeat to rise up and demand their liberation from tyranny. But they didn't, in Baudrillard's view because the myth of liberation has proved itself a lie in the conduct of war by 'electrocution'.

Nothing has changed, and that was what the war was fought for. Most shamefully, even those thousands who died on the Basra Road and in the desert were never intended to live: they were simply a mass of symbols, designated even before they marched out as 'martyrs'. Deprived of their honour by this anonymous mass extinction in the interests of Hussein's propaganda, their corpses are doubly dishonoured by those television viewers and opinion makers who see in them the incontrovertible proof that there was anything 'real' about this war which was its own simulation. Not even these deaths retain reality, stripped of it once in the political decision to let them die, and again in the recycling of the images of their cadavers as further grist to the information media. Like the media feasting on the death, mourning for and funeral of Princess Diana, our media 'will continue with the involution and encrustation of the event in and by information' (Baudrillard 1995: 48). Deaths can no longer be real deaths, self-sacrifice for a cause, because they are so endlessly painted over with coat after coat of data, interpretation and opinion that the reality simply evaporates under the accumulation of chatter. Eco might have observed that the television war was conducted like television sport: the event de-materialised and substituted for by interminable commentary.

Rather unusually, there are two moments at which Baudrillard seems to find some hope for a change or a rift in the apparently seamless self-replication of this undifferentiated universe of simulation. We can hope, he says, 'that some event or other should overwhelm the information instead of the information inventing the event and commenting artificially upon it' (Baudrillard 1995: 48), though he admits that this is unlikely, and would require a redefinition of what society means by information. Perhaps something like this happened on the day of Princess Di's death, when UK radio stations devoted themselves to mournful music as, though they are notoriously prepared for the sudden demise of other, older public figures, there were no prepared programmes ready to drop into the schedules for the young Princess. On the other hand, even in that instance, the substitution of gloom for informed opinion also served to produce a mass upwelling of grief for a person who had only ever existed for the masses as a televised simulacrum. Perhaps more in tune with simulation theory is the possibility of a non-event occurring when the media expect something especially dramatic. This happened in the summer of 1999, when the British media talked up the cosmic and mystical significance of the only total eclipse of the sun visible in the UK in most people's lifetimes. The day was overcast. Though a handful of television interviewees dutifully claimed to have undergone transcendent change, by and large the media were underwhelmed by an event that pretty much failed to occur. But as we will see, this failure to occur, like the phony war period of Desert Shield, can become the permanent state of warfare.

His second hopeful moment comes in the conclusion to the book. Iraq had played the role of mercenary in the USA's earlier surrogate war with Iran, serving the West not by winning but by nullifying Islam's most radical challenge to Western hegemony. After the Gulf War, still not defeated, Iraq continues to serve the West by becoming itself the nullified threat of radical Islam. Meanwhile Islam as a whole remains, radically other, unrecognisable to the consensual politics of simulation, and therefore still the greatest threat to it. The new non-war is played out not only on the non-enemy but on the non-ally and the non-citizen. Since the threat is apprehended and constructed not only as substantial (by proximity to the West's oil supplies) but also, as terrorism, pervasive, it legitimates the increasing militarisation and virtualisation of Western societies. Here, however, Baudrillard sees the glimmer of a chance for a different future: 'the more the hegemony of the global consensus is reinforced, the greater the risk, or the chances, of its collapse' (Baudrillard 1995: 87). This appeal to something Baudrillard earlier seemed to have dismissed as a Marxist hangover in Debord, the internal contradictions of contemporary society, is a remarkable change in position, a rare flicker of optimism, though one which could all too easily be snuffed out on the grounds of historical evidence that misery tends to make people more, not less conservative. And indeed, on grounds of inconsistency. In the middle of the second essay, Baudrillard has already argued that 'The Apocalypse itself, understood as the arrival of catastrophe, is unlikely. It falls prey to the prophetic illusion. The world is not sufficiently coherent to lead to the Apocalypse' (Baudrillard 1995: 49).

The passage comes in a discussion of Baudrillard's differences with Virilio. There are a number of points at which Baudrillard's analysis swings very close to Virilio's. Both discuss the impact of real time and its distinction from the political time of debate, discussion and decision-making. Both recognise a distinct shift in the mode of warfare towards stealth, camouflage and disinformation. Both comment on the propinquity between electronic warfare and the informational nature of the contemporary global marketplace. Baudrillard distances himself initially from Virilio, whom he sees as an apocalyptic for whom the acceleration of technological time leads to the 'general accident', the eradication of space and with it of humanity. Of his own position, he stresses the theory of deterrence as 'the indefinite virtuality of war' (Baudrillard 1995: 49). But then he notes a curious phenomenon: that the war, still in progress at this stage, seems to be at once intensifying and dissipating, escalating in intensity and yet moving towards the undifferentiated stand-off of deterrence. 'The war and the non-war take place at the same time' (Baudrillard 1995: 49–50). This he takes not as a contradiction but as evidence of 'undecidability', a state proper to the mathematics of chaos theory in descriptions, for example, of chemical reactions that flip-flop between two possible outcomes.

However, in an interview originally given in 1998, he is a little more decided. Accusing Virilio of a realism which he cannot share, he tells journalist Phillippe Petit:

The coming of the virtual is itself our apocalypse, and it deprives us of the real event of the apocalypse. Such is our paradoxical situation, but we have to push the paradox to the limit. And Virilio himself does this, while reserving a fallback argument for himself. (Baudrillard 1998: 23)

While Virilio's Christianity allows him the right to take a position outside the trajectory towards catastrophe, Baudrillard himself argues that the duty of the thinker is not, as Virilio believes, to resist the end, but to hasten it. In line with the theory of apathy as resistance, Baudrillard promotes the idea of assisting the logic of simulation by anticipating its ultimate form. Virilio's fatalistic realism allows him nonetheless the distance, derived from a belief in a 'real' human nature, at which critique and resistance are still possible. Without that distance, Baudrillard can only chronicle and predict the processes of assimilation that bring all differences under the universal simulation of the same. This is the strategy that he is trying to defend in the final lines of *The Gulf War Did Not Take Place*, promoting the internal collapse of the global consensus. But it seems clear from *The Perfect Crime*, first published four years later in 1995, that the contradictions will be entirely philosophical, and the collapse not a 'real' event, since there is no reality to which we can return, but an entirely metaphysical one. Baudrillard's brief optimism turns out to be nihilism: what follows the collapse of simulation will be exactly nothing, the nothing that both reality and simulation had tried, throughout human history, to camouflage.

Virilio also had occasion to reflect once more on the war in a 1996 interview with the same journalist, Phillippe Petit. 'The war certainly did take place, contrary to what Jean Baudrillard affirms,' he says. Although this was the first miniaturised world war, and also the first to take place in real time, he reports, 'I see two events: the beginning of the war and the end of the war. First the firing of cruise missiles from the battleship *Missouri* and, later, the surrender of the Iraqi soldiers' (Virilio 1998a: 96). The contrast between these events is interesting: one remote from the place and the people that it is aimed at, the other a confrontation face to face in a specific place – the desert. We could perhaps contrast them as disembodied and embodied, especially if we bear in mind this statement from a 1998 interview:

. . . to me, the body is fundamental. The body, and the territory of course, for there cannot be an animal body without a territorial body: three bodies are grafted over each other: the territorial body – the planet, the social body – the couple, and the animal body – you and me. And technology splits this unity, leaving us without a sense of where we are. This, too, is de-realization. (Virilio 1998b)

The war begins in the creation of a de-realised non-territory, but it ends with the admission, after all the trickery and deception, that after all victor and vanquished must meet in the land over which they have fought. In his book of reportages on the war, Virilio makes a great deal of the use of the environment as a hostage: the coral reefs destroyed by oil slicks, the burning of the Kuwaiti oil fields. After the war, the desert returns as environment. The interview with Petit ends with even more clearly ecological considerations on physical landscapes, during the course of which Virilio says of the desert: 'It gives the feeling of our presence on a planet. I love a landscape where you feel the planet, where the territorial body of planet Earth can be perceived in a small scale' (Virilio 1998a: 108). It seems that Virilio literally grounds his ability to criticise the conduct of real-time information war on the 'real place' which it seeks to eradicate from consciousness.

One widely shown videotape 'smuggled' out of Kuwait purporting to show Iraqi troops dragging babies out of incubators turned out to be a fake staged by the daughter of the Kuwaiti ambassador to the USA. Likewise, the still circulating image of seabirds struggling to shore coated in 'Saddam's oil slick' were at least thirty miles and perhaps continents away, since the slick had not touched the coast at the time it was first transmitted. Just as similar fake footage of a nonexistent mass grave at Timisoara in Romania was hypocritically justified on the basis of 'human rights', so environmental fallout from the Gulf War has become the hypocritical and even hyperreal legitimation for the full panoply of non-war, as Baudrillard sees it, or real-time war in Virilio's analysis. What distinguishes them is that, for Baudrillard, nature has been eliminated in all the constructions – picturesque or sublime landscape, rural idyll, ecology – that we have made of it, while for Virilio, it is still possible to enter into a relationship with the natural, God-given world. The continuing possibility of this communion with the planetary body means, for Virilio, that the catastrophic defeat of reality has yet to happen, while for Baudrillard it already has. Virilio therefore inhabits a time where it is still possible, if not to make decisions, at least to resist them. For Baudrillard, as we have seen, this is neither possible nor desirable.

This turn of a nihilistic philosophy into what appeared as political acquiescence spurred one of Baudrillard's most acute critics, literary philosopher Christopher Norris, into a 1992 attack on the first Gulf War essay. Norris had already written scathingly of the postmodernist abandonment of truth, an argument he repeats in this critique. But he also and especially criticises 'the depth of ideological *complicity* that exists between such forms of extreme anti-rationalist or irrationalist doctrine and the crisis of moral and political nerve among those whose voices should have been raised against the [military] actions committed in their name' (Norris 1992: 27). Norris argues along similar lines to Sloterdijk, whom he quotes, that a theory which is not committed to ethical change is complicit with the processes it pretends to analyse. Although he raises serious questions about the theoretical premises of Baudrillard's arguments, Norris goes on to say: 'Of course I am not suggesting that the best thing to do in these present bad times is to sit around endlessly debating such specialized matters of truth, language and representation' (Norris 1992: 29). But this is precisely the case that Baudrillard and Virilio make: that it is especially at these 'bad times' that the issue of the suppression and possibly the destruction of truth must be debated; for Virilio, because they are in certain senses what is being fought over, while for Baudrillard the loss of truth has already polluted the very fact of death. The 'of course' in the last quotation is important too: from the standpoint of simulation theory it is an acknowledgement that the issue of truth should not be debated during a generalised state of emergency. But this neglect is exactly what the creation of war as spectacle seeks to promote. Whether reality is about to become the first victim of militarisation, or whether it has already been destroyed, as Virilio and Baudrillard argue respectively, are issues of prime importance.

Nor were they alone. Throughout the war, TV stations around the world carried digital images from cameras not just carried by reporters or military personnel but mounted in pilotless weapons and 'smart' bombs, images that, in their resemblance to console games, earned the conflict the nickname 'Nintendo war'. Timothy Druckrey comments on the way in which the uncanny accuracy of the images was made both to mask the apocalyptic 'collateral' civilian casualties of the bombing raids and at the same time to implicate the viewer into the point of view of the weapon itself. 'At the moment of their highest military effectiveness', he notes, the smart bombs 'ceased to perform, that is they ceased to be visual. Yet the real impact of the bombs exists not prior to detonation but in the moment in which the signal ends. Noise equals success' (Druckrey 1991: 21). Noise, the informational term for the absence of a message, becomes the central moment of the message. The fatal technologies of information war not only destroy things; they destroy communication. Marita Sturken talks of the same phenomenon as an erasure of embodiment, of the real bodies of real people that dominated the coverage of earlier wars, but which were eerily absent from coverage of this one. Writing a few years after the events, she also notes that the popular memory of the war is not, as even the Vietnam War had been, a memory of sacrifice, suffering and loss, but one of sitting in front of the TV screen. 'For the imagined community of the nation,' she writes, 'it is impossible to separate the "real" war in the Persian Gulf from the television war we experienced' (Sturken 1995: 146). Again, the possibility of a moral stand is preempted by the impossibility of an experience on which it could be based. British cultural critic Kevin Robins notes the loss of reality among soldiers watching video replays of the slaughter of an Iraqi platoon by their helicopter gunships: 'As sadism turns into voyeurism it somehow neutralises itself; in each case it screens out the actual reality of the killing, as it distances the killers from moral engagement' (Robins 1996: 78). Against Norris, who believes that a moral stance and political commitment should be prior to discussions about the nature of reality, Robins' example suggests that the loss of reality happens too suddenly, almost too mechanically, for there to be time for ethical response, resulting in a kind of moral schizo-phrenia in which those soldiers are part overwhelmed by the violence of war over which they have no control and part completely disengaged from it through the technologisation of vision.

Nonetheless, Norris's criticism of Baudrillard's political quietism, the reluctance to take a stand, is a powerful one, and echoes an earlier critique by the North American cultural critic Douglas Kellner, who wrote prior to the Gulf War debates that such views 'may be comforting to a "critical critic" in his Paris apartment who no longer wants to go out and do battle in the public sphere' (Kellner 1989: 113) but have no relevance to the victims of oppression, apartheid and armed diplomacy. On the other hand, at the larger scale of history to which both Baudrillard and Virilio want to alert us, the Gulf War was only a skirmish in a conflict that began with the Cold War forty-five years earlier. Norris's concerns are tactical; Virilio and Baudrillard's are strategic. Questioning the possibility of truth in conditions of war, and the repercussions of military technologies on civilian life in and out of wartime, is a vital task.

But Norris is quite correct to insist that there is a case to answer in the simulationists' belief in the absolute efficacy of militarised media. To some extent it is in the nature of war that combatants lie to one another and to their populace. It is certain that in the Pentagon's sycophantic pool of friendly press agencies, who never questioned the absence of policy-makers from news briefings, let alone the policies they announced, and among the battlefield reporters who ended up watching CNN to gain some intelligence about what was going on, 'Journalism failed in the Gulf' (Druckrey 1995: 27). At the same time, there were journalists doing what the best journalists have always done: telling the stories of individuals caught up in shattering events, and giving their readers lessons in political history. Such was Robert Fisk, who had done the same in the Lebanon (Fisk 1992), and whose informed, moving and angry columns appeared in the London *Independent*. Then there was Kenneth Jarecke's terrifying photograph of a charred Iraqi corpse on the Basra Road published in the London *Observer* on 3 March 1991 (reproduced in Walker 1995: 247) under the headline 'The real face of war', a photograph which was condemned by UK authorities as 'tasteless' and which was almost completely absent from the news media in the USA. Here was an image that escaped the general rule that the more we see of atrocity, the less we care. Since the coverage of the Gulf War was so sanitised, this one photo stood for all the horror that we somehow knew lay behind the careful hygiene of images enacted by the censors. Even in the 'quality' press – where, indeed, both Baudrillard and Virilio were themselves publishing – there were resisting voices. The media machine was not so totally monolithic, and therefore their readers should not have been so totally duped.

There are two possible reasons, and both have a grain of truth. There was, as there so often is, a strain of wilful ignorance. Some ignorance can be blamed on others, but some must be blamed on laziness. There was no shortage of materials for understanding that journalists and audiences (and intellectuals and politicians) didn't seek out, materials that, for example, the British columnist Christopher Hitchens (1991) marshalled for an essay on the political background to Western intervention published during the last days of the war in a journal, whose production schedules are usually far slower than those of the news media. But if we want to argue that people simply didn't want to know, then we must accept that at least some of the arguments raised by simulation theory are correct, and that the appetite for truth, if not truth itself, has faded from the forefront of public life.

A second possibility is that my examples of journalism written against the grain of the propaganda machine all come from print, while virtually all those mentioned by Virilio and Baudrillard come from the electronic media. As we saw in Chapter 3.iv, where we looked at Eco's particular dislike of television, it is the electronic media which conform most closely to the prognostications of simulation theory. Even though one chapter of Virilio's book on the war is a transcript of an interview on French TV a few days before hostilities began, he remains convinced, as does Baudrillard, that television has preempted the role of total medium for the masses, while presumably the intelligentsia, along with the politicians and others who need to keep a more active eye on things, rely on the written word. Interviewed by James Der Derian, Virilio warns that:

> The written work is threatened by the screen, not by the image. . . . No, it is the evocative power of the screen, and in particular the live screen. It is real time that threatens writing. Writing is always, always, in a deferred time, always delayed. Once the image is live, there is a conflict between deferred time and real time, and in this there is a serious threat to writing and the author. (Der Derian n.d.)

This would suggest that the antique, premodern medium of writing is the last resort of the postmodern intellectual, and that its appeal is precisely that it does not work at the same time as the events to which it refers. If so, the recourse to the written cannot and should not be a political action, since action requires responding to events at the time they take place. The fact that both theorists did intervene publicly during the war itself would appear then to be a contradiction, unless we accept the fatalistic belief that criticism and analysis must always come after the event and can never therefore be the source of action. One wonders then about the massive quantities of paper-work generated in the political and military conduct of a war. The privilege granted to writing seems odd too in the context of a theory which largely denies the possibility of a true face-to-face confrontation with the other, that even older form of communication. Vision, it appears, is a weapon, and one that has annihilated the constitutive difference that once made war a real event. Yet mysteriously a writing deprived of efficacy nonetheless survives.

There is one further criticism that needs to be made of simulationist accounts of the Gulf War. Both our theorists suggest that the war was the first of a new kind of war. Yet in the decade since it was fought, it appears increasingly as the last of the spectacular wars. In place of the staging of a show of strength in massed confrontation, showpieces of might and show-rooms of armaments, the wars that have followed, including the continuing actions on the ground and in the air over Iraq, have been far less impressive affairs. In the former Yugoslavia, in East Timor, in Chechnya and in proxy wars from the Congo to Burma, it is the process of non-war that has been the common experience. These non-wars are characterised not by swift and decisive action, but by their endlessness. This modern style of operation, characterised by a shift from the will to win to the decision to contain conflict, seems to have been tried out first by the British in Malaya in 1948, when 'it recognised that a Communist-inspired rising that broke out . . . could be suppressed only if the population was promised self-government as the condition for supporting the counter-insurgency campaign' (Keegan 1993: 379). This war fought in order to maintain the status quo became dogma during the war in the North of Ireland, which has dragged itself painfully into armed peace more than thirty years after it began. Like the war in Eritrea, such conflicts have few spectacular set-pieces, and when they do, like the ghastly genocide in Rwanda or Turkey's war of attrition against its Kurdish population, they are committed away from the cameras. When Baudrillard says of the Gulf War, 'Since it never began, this war is therefore interminable' (Baudrillard 1995: 26), he is closer to the truth. As Chris Hables Gray argues, the typical war at the turn of the millennium is 'High Tech, Low Intensity Deadly Conflict' (Gray 1997: 27).

The new war, the war of 'policing operations', uses the principles of C3I not for TV-friendly firefights and instant victory but in order to stabilise. Conferences between warring parties aim not at peace but at 'normalising relations'. Standoffs can last a decade, as they have in the West's conflict with Libya, or longer, as with the USA's continuing trade embargoes on Vietnam after thirty and Cuba after forty years. In these latter cases, the ancient principles of the siege still obtain, but they are aimed at punishing rather than defeating, and the prize is access to markets, not possession of territory. Perhaps we should understand the Gulf War better as a struggle to safeguard the West's oil-supply, a strategy of containment, policing, normal-isation and stabilisation that has kept the region at war since the rise of mass motoring. And both the intellectuals and the masses are the willing dupes of this endless war not because of television but because they do not wish to know that the price of their mobility has anything to do with oil slicks, blazing oil fields, unseen corpses or savage dictatorships.

7

WORKING WITH COMPUTERS

The whole of the strategic Persian Gulf region had been under intense satellite surveillance for several years before the Gulf War. So much so that the landscapes of the Iraqi desert, rendered as three-dimensional computer models, were used extensively in training by the US military. These were the same three-dimensional maps that were installed in the memories of cruise missiles, with which they compared their own video observations of the ground they hugged on their way to their targets. The proximity between war games and war reality can only add to the feeling that simulation is part of the new warfare. There is a widespread belief that video and computer games prepare young people for the affectless life of the military (for example, Provenzo 1991: 132–5), which, though often overstated in the hectoring language of moral panic, seems to indicate a strong relationship between the military and the games industry. Indeed, Atari were only one of the companies involved in supplying simulation software for military training, and several games are believed to be based on software originally developed for army and air force training. Perhaps, rather than thinking of games in terms of a naïve effects theory (see Cassell and Jenkins 1998), we should think of them in the terms suggested by Kevin Robins, cited in the last chapter, arguing that the video replay produces a doubling of consciousness, one fated to be caught up in the action, the other utterly removed from it.

For Paul Virilio, this distancing from emotional relationships with the other is a process shared in the development of the city. As professor of urbanism, one of Virilio's main concerns is with the past and present changes in city life. Playing on the biblical injunction to 'Love thy neighbour' in a book of interviews chillingly titled *Cyberworld: The Politics of the Worst*, he argues that the expansion of digital communication has resulted in a very similar effect in urban society:

> If tomorrow we love only at a distance without being conscious that we hate our neighbour because he is present, because he smells, because he's noisy, because he annoys me and because he talks to me, as opposed to a distant person who I can zap. . . . If, then, tomorrow we come round to preferring faraway people to the detriment of our neighbours, we will destroy the city. (Virilio 1998a: 42)

The same abolition of otherness that characterises the simulation of non-war has entered urban life as well, with the preference we are beginning to show for our internet likes rather than our local unlikes. The ghettoisation that has been so strong a feature of cities in the USA has now begun to affect

London, Paris, Naples, Berlin: cities where economic and political migrants have been forced into the bottom of the labour market, the worst housing, the poorest health and education, the highest imprisonment rates and the highest levels of surveillance. Moreover, what we hate is being forced to confront the other. In cyberspace, we never have to – the connection can always be cut with a video-game-inspired zap of the mouse. Perhaps there is also an equivalent in Western society's willing acceptance of road deaths. We need cars to get to work because we no longer want to live near the inner city, and looking through the windscreen is just like looking through a console: the people outside have lost some of their reality. They become targets, to avoid – or to zap. For Virilio this is by no means a matter of the supposed 'influence' of video games. It is instead a function of the militarisation of everyday technologies. C3I has invaded the whole of society.

Computer technology is central to contemporary warfare. Most responsible histories of digital machinery and computer-mediated communication also stress the role of the military in their development (for example, Abbate 1999; Asprey 1990; Edwards 1996; Hodges 1985). Analysts of contemporary warfare have stressed the cyborg nature of the contemporary battlefield, its hybrid of cybernetic devices with human organisms (Gray 1997; Levidow and Robins 1989), fictionalised in characters like Robocop, who magically escapes the C3I role he was designed for. One of the most celebrated accounts of the cyberneticisation of war and its impacts is that of Manuel de Landa (1991), who writes a history of the war-machine drawing on the 'philosophy of desire' propounded jointly by the French philosopher Gilles Deleuze and the psychoanalyst Félix Guattari, especially their concept of nomadic and sedentary warfare. Deleuze and Guattari distinguish between the geographically static cultures of farmers and city dwellers and the spatial freedom of nomads. Committed to defending a physical place, the sedentary are always going to be beaten by the placeless manoeuvre of nomadic warfare (Deleuze and Guattari 1987: 380). It is this placelessness of the great Tartar hordes that is emulated with increasing efficiency in increasingly technologised armies, using their speed, their lack of encumbrance, their reconnaissance and their ability to disappear into the landscape as the model for blitzkrieg and eventually the remote operation of war by distance technologies.

Though Deleuze and Guattari offer this as a model for radical thought and radical politics, the members of the Critical Art Ensemble point out that their nomadic strategy has already been assimilated by the opposition (Critical Art Ensemble 1994: 11–30). The new transnational corporations are themselves placeless creatures. In Deleuze and Guattari's language, they are 'rhizomes', a term deriving from the matted, interlaced root systems of grasses and fungi, shared and networked, as opposed to the roots of, for example, a tree, where one tree has one tap root specific to itself that anchors it in the place where it lives. The old companies were sedentary and rooted to a specific spot. But we can no longer picket or occupy the typical new company's headquarters, because there is none: only the shifting, headless rhizome of connections between its executives and their employees. The electronic workplace is a place only in name. It cannot be attacked geographically or located legally. In the terms of management science, firms have to keep their manoeuvrability. Wherever you try to make contact with them, they are always somewhere else. Increasingly, as we go to work with computers, we are entering this kind of non-space. This is the less inviting aspect of the culture we call cyberspace. Much of the literature on cyberspace has come from cultural studies traditions that, for very good reasons, opted to focus on home life and leisure time. But if we are to test the theory of simulation, we must take the analysis beyond the hyperreal of time off, and engage with the emergent culture of digital work.

The technologisation of work has a rich and complex history, one that accelerated especially in the eighteenth- and nineteenth-century Industrial Revolution, and has taken new forms in the present era. The introduction of robot labour in engineering and of containerisation in shipping have had immense effects on employment on a global scale. Computerised management of orders and stock control in the 'just-in-time' system of manufacturing, which allows customers to order complex variations on the basic product, have achieved a Holy Grail of commodity capitalism: the standardisation of diversity. In what follows, however, I want to concentrate on the office and retail trades, which have undergone massive expansion as well as radical transformation. Retailing was, not so long ago, a respected field of employment. Short-order cooks earned the respect of their patrons before McDonaldisation of the food industry, like assistants in shops with a detailed knowledge of stock and highly developed arithmetic skills before the bar-code reader and automated stock control. Automated retailing has undergone what Harry Braverman (1974) identified surprisingly early as 'proletarianisation'. This process, in which face-to-face contact and highly specialised personal skills are replaced by boring, faceless and repetitive labour for far lower wages in far larger networked corporations, has also impacted on the office. The skilled clerk of the nineteenth century, male, highly numerate, needing elegant copper-plate script and a sound knowledge of double-entry bookkeeping, filing and interpersonal skills, began to be replaced with the invention of the typewriter and the adding machine. These allowed employers to bring in unskilled and female labour, notoriously more difficult to unionise because of the double demands of work and home. The computerisation of the office would extend the proletarianisation of the office even further.

More utopian visions of cyberculture stress its freedom from the linear structures of storytelling (for example, Landow 1992; Lanham 1993; Murray 1997) and image-making (for example, Mitchell 1992; Ritchin 1990; Wood 1998). Maltby defines narrative as 'a fundamental way of organising data' (Maltby 1996: 324). Note that it is 'a way', not 'the way'. Narrative and disruptions to narrative, like perspective and disruptions to perspective, are frequently held to be central qualities of hypermedia (for example, by Bolter and Grusin 1999; Holtzman 1997). But there are other crucial ways of organising data, notably those associated with the instrumental techniques of representing economics (double-entry bookkeeping and the spreadsheet), geography (cartography and geographic information systems) and libraries (files, catalogues, indexes and search engines). To eyes accustomed to linear storytelling and illusionistic picturing, these can seem to be subversive or resistant. But from the point of view of account clerks, postal workers, secretaries and librarians, they are the ordinary tools of work. Computer media did not arise from entertainment, and though they may have originated in warfare, they have evolved most of all in the workplace (see Ceruzzi 1999).

The discourse of the computer industry has a name for a software program that not only sells well itself, but establishes the type of computer it runs on as a significant kind of machine: it is called a 'killer app', short for application. If personal computers had only been able to provide enhanced typing, or had been limited to specialist design programmes devoted to image manipulation and publishing, perhaps they would still be relatively unfamiliar. The killer app that brought about the PC revolution was Lotus 1–2–3, a spreadsheet program used for running business accounts. There is considerable evidence that many computer programs actually diminish business efficiency, as people fritter away their time making elaborate presentations, or chatting on e-mail. But transferring accounts to computer meant faster and more accurate accounting that could be handled without dependence on expensively trained staff. Ceruzzi quotes a financial analyst describing Lotus 1–2–3's forerunner, VisiCalc, as 'the software tail that wags the hardware dog', and reports customers asking for the program first and the hardware to run it on second (Ceruzzi 1999: 267–8). Using the idea explored in Chapter 2 that Nietzsche was the populariser of aristocracy, we could say that Lotus was the populariser of the 'bottom line' of accountancy. As everyone knows, the aim of double-entry bookkeeping is to balance the books: to get a series of figures that add up to zero. This is one way in which the computer hastens the process of simulation: by accelerating and democratising the idea that the goal of any process is equilibrium, the nullness of a zero sum.

There are other ways in which office computers expand on the processes of simulation. They solve four vital management problems: efficiency, employment, oversight and speed. The computer was more accurate than most human calculations, it could be used by fewer and less skilled operators, rates of work could be monitored in real time, and it was fast. Speed is a key factor in corporate mobility. The contemporary 'office' is no longer tied to a desk. Laptop computers and mobile phones, two technologies in the process of merging, eliminate the difference between work and leisure. Equally, they now interpose themselves during the one time that divided the two, the travel time that emerged in the process of suburbanisation during the post-war period. Commercial use of internet and value-added telecommunications services such as teleconferencing have allowed the expansion of office tasks on a planetary scale: as is well known, much data inputting for very large undertakings like censuses and international hotel chain bookings is now handled in Third World countries where wages can be as low as a tenth of those paid in the industrial West. But what makes these developments even more unusual is that internet connections and cellular phones are also the leading edge of the global consumer market in the first years of the twenty-first century. We are not only adopting the militarised technologies of a nomadic capitalism, but we are also paying for the privilege.

Moreover, we are paying twice, firstly as customers, secondly as audience. The services to which we subscribe electronically not only keep us in a limbo which is neither job nor travel nor leisure, but they also monitor and catalogue what use we make of them. Both the military surveillance to which we, as political societies, have succumbed in the name of protection against the faceless 'terrorist' of the new deterrence, and the specialist corporations operating in the business-to-business market who sell on data profiles of service users to advertisers address us citizens in a new way: as 'spectral bodies', in Virilio's phrase (Virilio 1998a: 49). This sale of data profiles in the interests of target marketing and targeted advertising is a sociological commonplace of cybercultural studies. On the positive side, Esther Dyson recommends common-sense commercial decisions: my data are my property, and I will allow others to use them only if I am recompensed in a way I am ready to accept, for example in exchange for free services (Dyson 1997). More radically, Mark Poster suggests that the 'additional self' produced in data profiles can become 'a reconfiguration of the self-constitution process' (Poster 1990: 118): once we learn how our spectral selves are constellated in interactions with the electronic media, we can begin to use new skills to configure a new kind of self. The anonymity of the net is not constrained by the reality principle or by the principle of identity.

Many others have provided similar arguments (for example, Plant 1996; Stone 1995), the most familiar being that the anonymity of online communities permits the adoption and creation of multiple, unidentifiable identities without fixed gender, race, geography, age or other marks of who or what you are. Such arguments frequently cite the influential 'Manifesto for Cyborgs' by biologist and cultural commentator Donna Haraway. Turning the pessimism of simulation theory on its head, a favourite rhetorical and conceptual move in cybercultural discourse and one that Haraway inaugurated, she argues that identity is socially constructed, and specifically constructed in the interests of control over women and oppressed ethnic, religious and otherwise 'different' groups. The virtual nature of digital media, however, provides the opportunity to turn the tables. Instead of being constructed, with digital media we can construct our own identities, our own genders, even our own species (Haraway 1985). In the context of our discussion of the work environment, there are two problems here. Firstly, anonymity does not appear to alter the power relations inherent in large-scale corporate structures, notably those using internet technologies for outworking (sending raw data to offshore and telecottage industries for processing): there is no evidence that workers in the NAFTA free trade zones along the Mexican–US border or the data processors of Kenya and South India benefit from telematic non-identity. On the contrary, the typical experience of electronic workers, in call centres for example, is of constant monitoring, constant surveillance, constant loss of authority over themselves, their identities and their work. Secondly, the playful manipulation of identity, the creative game of remaking the self in a new guise, is not only part of the art of camouflage and deception practised in war since Sun Tzu in the fourth century. It is also the preferred mode of personnel management in the creative industries, where food fights, beer bashes, softball and five-a-side games form part of the team-building strategy and the exploitation of creativity on which contemporary corporations depend. In the age of simulation, we can no longer distinguish play and work.

Play is also important to Baudrillard. The so-called 'natural languages', the everyday languages like English and French, are inefficient: their poetic beauty gets in the way of effortless communication. This poetic function

> no longer exists in virtual or digital languages, where the equivalence is total, the interaction as well-regulated as in closed question-and-answer circuits and the energy is as immediately decodable as a heat-source's energy is decodable by water in a pan. These languages are no more languages than the computer-generated image is an image. (Baudrillard 1996a: 53)

Unlike natural languages, computer languages transfer data as smoothly as heat moves into boiling water, without reflection and interpretation, bringing about the immediate equation of the two poles of the communication, since each now possesses exactly the same data. This 'universal programming of language' (Baudrillard 1996a: 90) can only be resisted through play, specifically through games, whose rules, being arbitrary, force everyone to obey them equally (unlike the law) (Baudrillard 1996a: 93). Since Baudrillard had already argued that production had ceased to have any function other than to provide the illusion that something was still being made, it is hard to see how he believes that gaming can provide anything but further simulation of enjoyment or meaning or even democracy. Curiously enough, Baudrillard's seizure on gambling as the essence of democracy chimes distressingly well with the ideology of the free market espoused by the World Trade Organisation (WTO), with the sole difference that the corporations who underwrite it believe in playing to win, while Baudrillard seems content to lose. Moreover, the WTO also recognise that today gaming is undertaken in the massive computer networks of the global financial markets in a 'free play' that has nothing to do with equality.

Play and games also have a major role in computer simulation as a major tool of business planning. To avoid confusion, I will call this kind of application 'modelling', but even this term shows that there are links between the computerised world of the information economy and the theory of the Code or the self-replicating 'model' that grounds Baudrillard's work.

Once again developed for war games, the purpose of computer modelling in business is to establish a map of a particular scenario – a battlefield and its armies, the structure of a particular industry – and get the computer to establish what would happen if certain variables are changed (for a fuller critical account see Curry 1998). The maps used in such models are multi-dimensional in the sense that they include data of every sort that might be relevant. Epidemics, weather, stock market fluctuations, crop failures can all be built in, based on data gathered electronically, and each of these factors can be varied to see what results they might have on the conduct of a campaign or the price of beans. The goal of computer modelling is to predict outcomes and to build in stability. It may be highly unlikely that a hurricane will strike the South Coast of England, but it is possible to use computer modelling to develop contingency plans.

In the case of public emergency planning, this seems quite innocent; in the case of transnational corporations, a little more sinister. Although early versions of modelling, such as the well-known Limits To Growth model, were concerned to demonstrate the long-term effects of industrial growth on the ecology of a crowded planet, and so had a public interest element, more recent versions are designed for corporate purposes. The profit motive is not the only one driving corporate strategy. Large companies will often bear even a few years of losses if it will strengthen them in other ways, such as their share of a market, which might be achieved by underpricing their products, or their long-term stability. It is this issue of stability which requires our attention in simulation theory. Computer models are used to predict: to look into the future. Of course nothing is certain (except, as Benjamin Franklin said, death and taxes), but companies can plan for all eventualities, and do so with more certainty of surviving if their predictive apparatus can be seen to provide accurate forecasts of market and other relevant trends during its lifetime. From the companies' point of view, the purpose is clearly to manage change: to be able to respond to events with carefully prepared plans of action. But from the standpoint of simulation theory, this is a machine for controlling the future. In Baudrillard's terms, the purpose of managing change and planning for stability is to replicate the present and to end history. 'Maybe after all the year 2000 will never occur, as I speculated long ago,' he writes, citing his 1986 essay, 'for the simple reason that the curve of History will have become so accentuated as to create a reverse trajectory' (Baudrillard 1993b: 99). Like those asymptotic graphs that swoop down towards zero and then swing away upwards again, Baudrillard imagines, History reaches a certain point at which it is no longer the narrative of human endeavour, and becomes something wholly different, under a different control, and no longer heading towards human goals. While this is not the same as Virilio's nightmare of real time superseding natural chronology, it shares the sense that time as we know it has been undone. This seems a telling interpretation of the colonisation of the future in computer modelling. The cost of the corporations' ability to manoeuvre nomadically across the planet is that they have eradicated time.

In a move that would horrify Virilio, many of these modelling programs now use the technology of artificial life, programs which require no input from human programmers other than their initial data. At this juncture, not even the transnational's chief executives are in control of the future which their devices are planning for them. Instead, computing begins to serve the 'viral' model of communication (or perhaps we should say non-communication) which Baudrillard has explored in several writings of the 1990s. A virus has no DNA of its own, only a smaller RNA, which is why it requires a host to reproduce. Like cancer, which Baudrillard describes, possibly inaccurately, as a virus, it enters a host system and turns its normal biological processes awry in order to secure its own goal. Cancer progresses by replicating its own code, producing massive quantities of identical cells at the expense of the cellular biology of the host. 'Cancer', he writes, 'is the *form* of the virulence of the code: aggravated redundancy of the same signals – aggravated redundancy of the same cells' (Baudrillard 1993b: 120). The code's virulence (from the root word 'virus') can be read as the eradication of all difference through the uncontrollable replication of the same. This is the viral nature of computer modelling in the service of corporate capital: to remodel the future as the clone of the present.

At this juncture, computer-literate readers will object that artificial life is employed in these and many other circumstances not because of its predictability but for exactly the opposite reason: to provide unpredictable results. Indeed, there are many projects which operate in the realm of pure research employing artificial life programs without constraints in order to model, for example, evolution. The difference in the use of artificial life in the business world is that it is used instead of human programmers, in a move resembling the use of typewriters and word-processors to make the old handwritten skills redundant. For example, artificial life is used extensively in the specialist software industry, where immense programs costing millions of dollars are required for managing aircraft routing or chemical plants and similarly one-off uses. Effectively, artificial life software-writing automates the creativity of human programmers, a creativity which, incidentally, Baudrillard, as we have seen, does not believe is possible, but which is a major current in the literature on computing (see, for example, Gelernter 1998; Turkle and Papert 1990). Every artificial life program requires a 'reaper' function: something that weeds out the expanding fragments of code that make them up. In biological systems, this function is carried out by mortality. Purely experimental programs may use a variety of criteria in order to work out, for example, what happens when cooperation is better rewarded than competition. In commercial applications, the reaper function is tailored to the desired result, not the unforeseen one. In software design, this will be an element of the program that seems to solve a specific problem. In large-scale modelling of the global economy, the criterion will be corporate survival and growth.

This is why Baudrillard's and others' recourse to chaos theory at this point is misleading. Chaos theory, or complexity theory as it is more formally known, is a development from the information theory that we looked at in Chapter 2.ii. One of its most persuasive and challenging arguments, highly influential in cybercultural circles, is the concept of emergence. As we noted in 2.ii, information has a theory of entropy based on the idea that energy and order tend to run down over time. Complexity theory observes that in certain instances where we could expect this to happen, such as the earth's weather, the billions of molecules in the relatively closed system of the atmosphere exhibit a tendency to form into massive and highly organised systems like typhoons and whirlwinds. This property is specific to what are called complex systems, systems that are in some degree open to a number of variables. One reason why weather reports are so rarely dependable is that the weather depends on too many factors, from sunspots to local pollution. The mathematicians involved in complexity theory describe what happens in complex systems in terms of errors in the initial data: a very small inaccuracy in a measurement, when applied to a computer model of a complex system, tends to magnify over time and throw the model off track. Applied to the real world, a cascade of microscopic adjustments to the movement of individual molecules can create vast changes to a system like the global climate: in the famous metaphor, a butterfly's wings flapping in China can cause a hurricane in Georgia. In a number of equally complex systems, unexpected patterns of order can emerge from the random interaction of elementary particles. The theory of emergence tackles such problems as the prediction of earthquakes and stock market crashes, even the origins of life and the universe. (Why is all the matter clumped together? How come we got all the carbon when there's nothing but vacuum all around?)

In *The Perfect Crime* Baudrillard turns to chaos theory and emergence at a number of points. In the minuscule adjustments that cascade a system into chaos or into a new mode of order he sees the possibility of a difference that cannot be reduced to the Same. Returning to the theme of natural languages, for instance, he argues that 'languages are not different, they are other. They are not plural, they are singular. And, like all that is singular, they are irreconcilable' (Baudrillard 1996a: 91). The word 'singularity' here derives again from mathematics, where a singularity has the role of defining one function as distinct from another. The term is also used by Gilles Deleuze in opposition to the term 'generality'. According to Deleuze, generality is a way of thinking in which 'one term may be substituted for another', as opposed to 'non-exchangeable and non-substitutable singularities' (Deleuze 1994: 1). A singularity, for Deleuze and for Baudrillard, is a constituent difference, that is, a difference which is prior to the things which, in the Code or in 'generality', it appears to differentiate. Thus languages are singular in the sense that they are untranslatable, each unique, each with specific capabilities that cannot be replicated or cloned, that cannot communicate between one another by the simple and immediate transfer of data. Even though it may be infected by viral communication, by those coded feedback loops that replicate endlessly the same message, the singularity of natural language can fall sick but not die. And in the end, in healing itself, it will 'de-program' the virus that attacked it. Better still, not only will language infect in return the virus of simulation (once again we seem to be privileging writing over television and the electronic), but 'the deregulation of the system will be the work of the system itself!' (Baudrillard 1996a: 91).

Here we have returned to the conclusion of the Gulf War book, where, as we noted, Baudrillard proposed that 'the more the hegemony of the global consensus is reinforced, the greater the risk, or the chances, of its collapse' (Baudrillard 1995: 87). Perhaps this time we can look at the proposal differently. Throughout *The Perfect Crime*, Baudrillard seems to echo some of Deleuze's ideas about the simulacrum. Through the simulation, we are brought to recognise the failure of that 'general' thought that previously grounded our ideas of identity, including the identity of objects. General thought believed that to say 'This is a tree' and 'This is a rock' were equivalent statements, effectively promoting the commodity relation in which the objects 'tree' and 'rock' could be exchanged. If we recognise that both this mode of equivalence and the very identities which it tries to present are in fact simulations, then we can also realise that they are both products of models – especially the model of equivalence central to generality as a way of thinking. And therefore 'the simulacrum is not just a copy, but that which overturns all copies by *also* overturning the models' (Deleuze 1994: xix). Illusion, then, is its own worst enemy: its irreducible difference from language, which is not communicative in the same way, will result in the collapse of the Code. This is effectively an act of faith in the butterfly's wings, for in complexity theory, not only can order emerge out of chaos, but complex systems can also suddenly lose their stability and plunge into turbulence and chaos. Baudrillard believes, it seems, that in that chaos all the molecules achieve their independence from the patterning that held them bound to its model.

As a political strategy, waiting for the butterfly is not particularly invigorating. And as a political goal, chaos is a dangerous ambition. According to Marx, by the mid-nineteenth century we already inhabited a society governed by the anarchy of production. And according to even the most conservative economists, we now live in a global financial system which is beyond control and wildly unstable. In fact, chaotic states like stock market crashes are the reason why global prediction has never been technically feasible. It is simply not possible to define the initial state of the model with sufficient accuracy to ensure that it will produce the correct results. In this sense, the global nature of both Baudrillard and Virilio's arguments themselves falls victim to chaos theory: there is no way of knowing that they have thoroughly accounted for all the possible variables that might, over time, cascade their 'total' simulations into turbulent miasmas. What is possible, however, is to predict more local futures. Virilio here comes into his own as an urbanist, for one of his great themes has been the elimination of the local as a geographical locality. When we speak of a 'local' computer model, therefore, we are speaking not of a place but of an entity like a corporation, just as, when we speak of a battlefield in the context of the Gulf War we are actually talking about a 'theatre of operations' that extends all the way to the audience for that theatre sitting in front of their TV screens to watch it being staged by the militarised media. A company like Microsoft is only metaphorically 'based' in Seattle: its executives are mobile and scattered; its plants, only some of which have its name or are even wholly owned, are dotted all over the world; its customers and therefore its marketing and sales force are likewise global. But Microsoft has to plan for future developments, not least in a future-oriented industry. After the Supreme Court decision in 1999 that the company had acted as a monopoly, the firm has reorganised, and Bill Gates has stood down as chief executive officer. These moves are part of a strategy to maintain the stability of either or both the company as a whole and/or its divisions, should they be forced by law to split up their operations. Shareholders would be furious if there were not also contingency plans for weathering any future depression in the world economy. The world may go to hell in a handcart: the purpose of corporate computer modelling of future scenarios is to ensure that the company does not go down with it.

We are beginning to see that there are aspects of simulation theory which we may need to discard, notably its belief in the totality of simulation as both a phenomenon and an explanatory concept. As phenomenon, it is geographically specific, and does not seem to illuminate the relentless reality of Third World exploitation; while as concept it assumes too much the successful penetration of consumerism into every crevice of life. But at the same time, a judicious deployment of concepts from simulation theory can help us understand crucial aspects of contemporary industrialised societies and the global flows of finance capital. This process comes to a head when we try to comprehend not so much the global management of work as the experience of it and its role in social life. At this stage, it is worth returning to Debord and asking what is the purpose of work in the society of the spectacle. We noted in Chapter 3.i that for Debord, the function of industry had become simply to keep on functioning. As he puts it in *The Society of the Spectacle*, 'The spectacle, grasped in its totality, is both the result and the project of the existing mode of production' (Debord 1977: ¶ 6), and in the next paragraph, 'The language of the spectacle consists of *signs* of the ruling production, which at the same time are the ultimate goal of this production' (Debord 1977: ¶ 7). Any industry – manufacturing, service, office, retail or finance – forming part of the production of commodities is now directed less towards making useful things than towards creating signs.

One thinks of the food industry. Food has become spectacular. It is less a question of what we need to eat in order to survive and thrive, and more a question of signification. Take the quick, prepackaged meals which are sold on the basis of ease of preparation in a busy world, and on tasting 'good'. In fact, they often take longer to cook than a simple stir-fry or a quick pasta. And the 'good' taste is often based on the use of chemical additives and sugar, a taste for which is instilled in even the youngest infant through its introduction in prepared baby foods. The salmonella, E. coli and BSE scandals of the 1990s in the UK are the tip of an iceberg of fast practices. Meat is saturated with emulsifiers to allow more water into the cells and so increase weight at the scales, and with dyes to make it look unhealthily red. The ingredients listed on the side of cake packets read like chemical sludge. Prime Minister Thatcher's early career as an industrial chemist peaked in a contribution to the technology that allows more air to be frothed into the oils used in the manufacture of ice cream. Elvis Presley's death certificate is a paean to the triumph of sign over nutrition. Even health food has become a signifier of consumer lifestyle: the very refusal to eat prepared foods becomes a sign, just as the massive sales of cookbooks and massive audiences for celebrity TV chefs indicates a transition through which we eat no longer food but the simulation of food. The food industry embraces not only agribusiness and food technologists but also nutritionists and haute cuisine. The goal of the food industry in Debord's terms is not eating but the simulation of eating, not taste but the simulation of taste. If computers are ever able to emulate our gustatory senses, they will only be continuing a process begun by the fast-food industries of the mid-twentieth century.

At a more general level, the purpose of work is to produce the signs of work. On the one hand, this means working spectacularly hard so that people will see that you are a hard worker. On the other, it is the familiar argument that ecological concerns, health and safety measures, trade union rights and wages should all be sacrificed in order to keep a firm in a certain locality because people need jobs. Beneath this rationale is the belief that the product of a given factory or office is not to make goods or provide services but to create employment. We work in order to work. Even radical socialist organisations fight not for leisure but for the 'right to work'. Work has become, as Baudrillard has it, 'the object of a social "demand", like leisure, to which it is equivalent' (Baudrillard 1994a: 26). Debord's argument is that this is not a true right, because it conceals the fact that the system only requires us to work in order to be consumers of the very things we have just made, which are themselves the unreal signs of the spectacle. Work itself is a simulation, a repetitive series of motions we go through in order to reproduce ourselves as consumers of signs. This self-scripting repetition has a further function: in Baudrillard's terms, 'the *scenario* of work is there to conceal that the real of work, the real of production, has disappeared' (Baudrillard 1994a: 26).

Digitising work is only a continuation of this same process. There is here a similar history to that of war games. Media historian Friedrich Kittler argues that the war game evolved from the flat checker-board of chess to the sandpit used by Napoleonic generals before becoming computerised. At that point, he argues, 'the matrix algebra of games theory takes the place of Müffling's physical sandbox' (Kittler 1999: 174). Similarly in the world of work: the dissipation of physical labour into the manipulation of signs moves from handcraft, through machine manufacture, to the remote management of datastreams. In the global economy, most observers agree, there has been a shift away from the traditional manufacturing industries and towards services and finance, both in terms of employment and in terms of the cash value of transactions (see, for example, Appadurai 1996; Castells 1996; Coombe 1998). As money itself becomes dematerialised and circulates at ever higher velocities in cyberspace, so too human interactions are increasingly handled through the remote technologies of data management and computer-mediated sales. Word processing allows large blocks of text to be repeated effortlessly without retyping. Mail-merge allows letters apparently addressed individually to be mass-mailed. Repetition of the signs of communication replaces communication, even the restricted and coded communication of a shop assistant with a customer. 'This starting all over again', wrote Walter Benjamin in the 1930s, 'is the regulative idea of the game as it is of work for wages' (Benjamin 1969b: 179). But perhaps even this is no longer true: the contemporary workplace, like contemporary scratch card gambling, never begins from scratch, but from a pre-ordained, pre-ordered state of affairs over which neither gambler nor worker has command. The formula rules. On computers and in call centres on three continents, 'every decision activates a specific set of programmed options, which in turn activate and exclude others' (The Project on Disney 1995: 37). Consumer and 'producer' are indistinguishable: what dominates both is the logic of the pre-scripted dialogue, the illusion of choice between predetermined options, the illusion of helping a caller pick the right one.

Such supposedly interactive systems always protect a certain element of themselves from both the worker and the customer. Neither is allowed access to those deeper levels of coding which, though scripted in at some lost originating moment when the system was designed, have now become so deeply embedded that they have become integral to the system itself. Kittler observes this process taking place in the computer industry, where the user interface and user-friendliness dictate that even the most computer-literate can access only the higher levels of a program. The zeros and ones of machine code, even the READ/WRITE commands of Assembler languages which underlie all software programs, are barred from use. Microsoft, for example, has since 1987 refused to release the Assembler code for its MS-DOS and Windows operating systems. Moreover, Kittler points out, most computers have restrictions built in that keep certain key levels in 'Protected Mode' so that any attempt to alter the way your machine runs will result in it crashing. Kittler reads this as an extension of military encryption, which allows users access to files on a strictly hierarchical basis. The users of such systems are themselves subjected to them, largely because they believe that the basic working of the machine is not for them, even at the moment at which it is being removed from them. Two systems operate simultaneously on most computers: the one you can access and the one you can't. The result, Kittler argues, is 'to entangle civilian users in an opaque simulation' (Kittler 1997: 159) in which we fail to recognise that, while we run the machine, it also runs us. The similarity with the pre-scripted dialogues of multiple-choice menus – and fast-food menus too – is all too apparent: we simulate choice, while the system simulates its absence.

The question of lack of access to the operating system of your own computer is a small element of a larger issue of intellectual property rights. Some companies, monitoring the choices we make in their interactive computer systems, use the input to compile data profiles of their customers. By and large, there is too much data for any human to control: the process is delegated to 'knowbots', small programs which track the user of commercial sites like online book and CD stores and propose books and records that it thinks match previous selections, an example of the removal of decision-making from human managers to mechanical devices so feared by Virilio. These data profiles then become the intellectual property of the store, even though no intellect other than a rather clumsy artificial intelligence has ever known about it. It is very difficult to retrieve a data profile, either as a consumer or as a systems operator. The information exists in a kind of digital limbo, functioning on automatic. Like the protected mode of operating systems, it has simply been removed from the loop and become integrated with the system itself.

The larger issue arises in the question about 'intellect'. Copyright in commodities like Disney icons, pop songs and software packages reside rarely in the artists and engineers who produce them, but in corporations. Intellectual property has become the central tenet of the current World Trade Organisation which governs world trading, and has become a major political lever in cases such as President Clinton's dealings with China in 1998. For simulation theory, this is to be expected: human intelligence has been usurped, first as a legal entity, then as a technical one, by the system itself. More specifically, as we must now argue after the criticisms we have levelled at the totalisation of simulation theory, the systems indigenous to global corporations have automated creativity and freedom. However, armed with simulation theory, we can scarcely go backwards in history and demand the reinstitution of individual authorship as the correct mode of copyright, even though that is the preferred argument of corporate defenders wishing to prolong the current system. There is, however, a challenge to both personal and corporate intellectual property rights that goes by the name of open source. The Windows operating system belongs to Microsoft as a legal entity, and they can choose legally to keep it secret. Open source is a philosophy which has grown rapidly with the spread of the world-wide web, which is itself an example of the phenomenon. The basic programming tools of the Web – notably the file transfer protocol (ftp), the internet protocol (ip) and the hypertext transfer protocol (http) which form its technical basis – were designed in such a way that any user could make changes to them (Berners-Lee 1999). The open source philosophy also guided and continues to guide the development of the Linux operating system and the software that runs on it (Raymond 1999). Both systems use the openness of computer-mediated communication to encourage an evolutionary approach to computer programming, one in which no individual or company can claim intellectual property rights over the program produced.

In some ways this seems like a marvellous model for the future: a form of that symbolic exchange which Baudrillard, in his earlier work, had set up as the opposition to the commodity economy and the society of simulation. It has the traces of play and gift-giving, it abandons individual authorship and corporate ownership, and its openness includes an openness to future development (see Barbrook 1998). But we must be circumspect about every utopia. Open source also demands a certain standardisation, usually in the form of a consortium which vets proposals for fundamental changes to the source code before recommending their release. The power of such consortia is largely moral and professional rather than legal, but nonetheless effective – this is why rival browsers can usually open all pages (although there are some particular software effects that will only work in one of them). One argument for open source is that it produces better software: the open market works on other principles than merit, including corporate muscle and slick marketing. An argument against it is that it introduces into the anarchic culture of computer hacking (in the sense here of those who 'hack' code for the fun of it) that corporate management model of game-playing which simulation theory allows us to see as a further development of the encoding of all aspects of culture. When important players like Netscape, now amalgamated with online and media giants AOL, Time-Warner and EMI, throw open their source codes, we have to ask whether this is a way of recruiting the free-play of freelance hackers in the interests of struggles for market share. Simulation theory helps us see that life is not so simple, but life also shows us that simulation isn't so simple either.

CONCLUSION

8

PESSIMISM OF THE INTELLECT, OPTIMISM OF THE WILL

The history of intellectual engagement with the everyday culture of the last hundred and fifty years has not been a happy one. Pretty much since the dawn of mass media, mass urbanisation, mass migration and mass production, cultural critics have been largely overcome by pessimism. Eco's apocalyptic intelligentsia have staked their claim from Matthew Arnold's *Culture and Anarchy* in 1869 to the panic society of virtual capitalism in Arthur Kroker's aphoristic postmodernism (for example, Kroker and Kroker 1996; Kroker and Weinstein 1994). From the right-wing Ortega y Gassett, from the left-wing Theodor Adorno, and from the liberal centre-ground Jacques Ellul and Neil Postman, intellectuals have marked the period since the advent of photography and the mass-circulation daily press as a cemetery of broken utopias and lost illusions. A certain kind of millenarian thought pervades the entire period, with dire warnings of ends, deaths and losses echoing from the most abstruse philosophy to the most fey of New Age mysticisms. The pessimism of most simulation theory can surely then be read as yet another symptom of what Christopher Caudwell called, in the late 1930s, 'a dying culture' (Caudwell 1971). But Caudwell, who met his own end fighting in Spain against the fascist forces of General Franco, believed that it was bourgeois culture that was on its deathbed. For simulation theory we could say that the state of dying has become the ordinary and indefinitely prolonged position of the whole of society. Like the raddled body of the Spanish dictator, kept in limbo by a life-support machinery over which it no longer has any control, we are free neither to live nor to die but only to keep on existing.

There is something terrifying about the language of our times: blood bank, data bank, memory bank, bottle bank, sperm bank. Are we already overdrawn? Perhaps not yet, but we are invested, and that integrates us into the liquid capital of consumer society. Citing Hitler's dictum that 'Politics is the practical form of destiny', Virilio describes the expert, that compulsory figure not just of science and the military but also increasingly of politics and morality, as 'something like a visionary, a magician who brings the future into view in order to conjure with it and so plays the same role as the digital image simulator' (Virilio 1996: 142). How much more true is that of the expert systems which guide the programming of computer models. As we prepare to be presented with the digitised spectacle (choosing that word carefully) of the map of the human genome, wherein, we are told, our destinies lie coiled at the molecular level, we cannot but fear the moment at which the investments we have made in all the banks are suddenly rendered worthless, not by the kind of inflation that ended the experiment in democracy of Weimar Germany, but by its opposite: the revelation that there is neither choice nor accident, that everything is fated, that the future has been conjured out of existence.

This Cassandra's vision of the disappearing future mirrors Virilio's vision of the lost past. Virilio fears that we have lost space under the impact of acceleration in time, that space is now all past, and even time, at a certain imminent point, will reduce to an eternal present, the speed of light: a flat line on the monitors tending the terminal patient in simulation's intensive care ward. But like all simulationists, Virilio does not imagine a conspiracy behind the media, a cabal of Murdochs, Gateses and Eisners with absolute power over their audiences. Instead, as Geert Lovink argues,

> The idea that the real forces behind or underneath the screen can be revealed is . . . based on the presumption that the media themselves do not have power, but instead are tools in the hands of manipulating third parties. . . . the quest for hidden power not only underestimates this feature of media power, it also sticks to the rules of old power, which has in fact disappeared within the media. (Adilkno 1998: 126)

The media themselves have assimilated the power that once belonged to individuals. Their bosses are in reality their servants too, tied to the laws of repetition that govern the endless replication of the same in the mass media everywhere. Confronting Hans Magnus Enzensberger's demand for a demo-cratisation of the media, Baudrillard argued that wherever that had already occurred, as in the almost universal use of cameras in Europe and North America, people only took photographs of the same things: all weddings, no funerals; all holidays, no fights. We have already assimilated the codes of the media, and the codes have already assimilated us. In the end all our accounts balance, in the plenitude of the zero at the bottom line.

This is perhaps why, once Debord's revolution seemed no longer possible, simulation theory turned its pessimism towards violence. We have noted already at several junctures the ways in which Baudrillard in particular feels the lure of Bataille's orgiastic anti-rationalism and of chaos. The sense of an all-encompassing homogeneity seems to bring about the hysteria of which Baudrillard accuses the mass media, a savage reaction which seeks a response to the supposed ultra-rationality of the simulacrum in the unreason of the body. What is missing in this scenario is an understanding, which

Baudrillard himself has helped evolve, that the simulation is itself neither rational nor irrational, and encompasses both extremes in its de-differentiated embrace. If there is no longer any difference between con-sumers and producers, whether of manufactured goods or of the corporate logic of television, why should we expect to find a distinction between the rational and the irrational? The dominant culture – indeed, simulation theory argues, the only culture – is already savage, blood-stained, stupid and violent enough. Like its own account of television, simulation appears to veer between a theory of nullity and a theory of blind rage, the silent majority and chaos. Faced with this choice, many of us would accept the dangers of passivity rather than risk sinking the world into a splatterfest inaugurated by the revenge of the real. In any case, the regulation of violence as the alter ego of order is already part of the double face of simulation and the information regimes that underpin it. Perhaps passive resistance and waiting for the butterfly is the better option. However, not even passivity quite escapes the double binds of the simulacrum.

Even if we accept the current thesis of cultural studies approaches to television, and try to believe that viewers make their own meanings and pleasures out of the raw materials served them by the media (the most extreme examplar of this view is Fiske 1987), 'the home front, with its superior outlook, is chiefly interested in its own perceptive reactions, not the battle of signs that takes place on screen' (Adilkno 1998: 151). And in fact 'What used to be called apathy, being glued to the TV set, has a become a first requirement for job performance' (Adilkno 1998: 156). In such a perspective, critical distance and play on the images received are only more entertaining versions of the same apathy, versions that are if anything slightly better adapted to the corporate playpens of the new management. When Baudrillard playfully substituted for production the word 'seduction' (Baudrillard 1990a), it was in order to make a new theory of the media. Only objects can seduce (rather unfortunately for feminism, he includes women in the category of objects). The media seduce. Media theory therefore must be more seductive than the virtual object that it theorises. This is the source of his appeal to irony and humour as the royal roads of media theory. Only by being more excessive than the media themselves can we seduce meaning out of the hell of the same. As Paul Patton observes in his introduction to Baudrillard's Gulf War book,

> it is a sort of black humour which seeks to subvert what is being said by pursuing its implicit logic to extremes: so you want us to believe that this was a clean, minimalist war, with little collateral damage and few Allied casualties. Why stop there: war? what war? (Patton 1995: 7)

In Lovink's terms, such media theory is parasitic, not symbiotic: it aims to kill what it feeds off. There are no positive aims: 'Media theory is fatal to media' (Adilkno 1998: 218). But again, as Lovink hints with his observation of the 'superiority' affected by the home-front viewer, irony depends upon the construction of a common-sense agreement about what is logical, just, honest and true, but simulation theory seems to have abandoned these qualities. Besides, as Tom Lehrer, the songwriter, is supposed to have asked on his retirement, 'If they give Henry Kissinger the Nobel Peace Prize, what's the point of satire?' Just as the system already contains violence, so it is only too happy to contain and imprison irony.

There are ways in which, however, an understanding derived from simulation theory and from concepts like seduction and irony can help us understand our society. What is required is a move away from the 'superiority' of home-front critics using their skills with the pen to distance themselves from the simulation they believe is shared by everyone else. Instead, we need a closer look, a more local understanding. I argued in the Introduction that simulation theory begins in the theory of representation, and especially in the observation that representation is never adequate. Now we must confront a different discourse of television, one that respects the singular ways in which it works, in detail rather than as at the level of generality. As Mary Ann Doane puts it, 'Television does not so much *represent* as it *informs*' (Doane 1990: 225). What matters to television is not the reality to which it refers but the contexts in which that reference is taken up. In this instance, US television reporting is far in advance of all but European soap operas. The soap opera, as Robert Allen pointed out, revolves not around events but around characters' opinions about them (Allen 1985). US news reports, especially at election time, are not about events but opinions about perceptions of events. Airtime is devoted to discussions among opinion-makers not about what is happening but about how the strategies for presenting what's happening might be perceived by other opinion-makers in the Pentagon or the Senate or the Supreme Court, and how they are likely to put a new spin on the increasingly remote event itself. In Doane's typology of television time, this is the mode of 'information' and it occupies slow time. 'Crisis', the second step up, is a definable period of time structured as suspense, something which can be narrated as having a beginning, a middle and an end. But the third level is catastrophe. Catastrophe does not have to do with the scale of the event – as Doane points out, the body count in a war is not catastrophic, while the explosion of the *Challenger* space shuttle was. Rather, events become catastrophic when they point to the limitations of television technology: airline crashes that occur away from the camera's otherwise all-seeing eye, or the death of Princess Diana that we discussed in Chapter 6. At the same time, these television catastrophes invariably speak to us of death, of the unsignifiable. 'The catastrophe is crucial to television precisely because it . . . corroborates television's access to the momentary, the discontinuous, the real' (Doane 1990: 238). In this way catastrophe is both the supreme moment of television and the quintessence of its ordinary processing of chatter. Catastrophes will be instantly shrouded in comment, opinion, investigation, speculation. And catastrophes can be planned for. In British news studios, presenters always keep a black tie in their desks in case a catastrophe is announced while they are on air. There are procedures to follow: an address book full of experts to contact, the well-rehearsed handling of phone lines that cut out in the course of the broadcast, a library of maps to be projected into the backdrop of the already virtual studio. There is a mime to go through in which the presenter can withhold information in deference to the sensitivities of the bereaved. Under any other circumstances, we rightly treat such withholding with distrust; in catastrophes, it is a mark of truth. Catastrophic television then uses the absences of death, technological breakdown and partial release of information as proofs of its own actuality and of its connection to the world. Perilously close to the surface, there is just absence. But at the surface itself, there is structure: the logic of information.

To say, as Doane does, that television does not represent but inform has two meanings. On the one hand, it means that television delivers not mediated images of reality but a datastream illustrated with images, diagrams, graphics, hand gestures and facial expressions. To this extent it is a phatic medium – one whose first duty is to address the viewer and keep him or her viewing. TV's secondary function is to maintain the one-way traffic in structured and patterned data. As information, the pattern is more important than the data itself. On the other hand, television 'informs' in the sense that it gives form to the viewer, not so much by inculcating ideological beliefs as by patterning and shaping communication, for example in the regular cycles of the TV schedule. To understand this in terms of simulation we need to note firstly that television communicates representations as information: it uses raw footage and raw news, but structures them into the regulated flows that constitute the logic of information. At the same time, however, in that characteristic double movement of the simulation, television represents communication. In the direct gaze to camera which news readers allow themselves (like no-one else on television except a handful of comedians), TV news mimics communication: it gives us the image and the sound of communication, but images and sounds that are not themselves communication, just as a picture of a tree is not a tree.

It is an important tenet of simulation theory that the depiction of communication has taken over from communication itself. As long as we do not take this tendency in the mass media for a global and total phenomenon, we stand to learn a great deal from it. Communication, I would argue, is a fundamental, if not *the* fundamental, property of human beings. Eco enjoys the definition of human beings as 'rational, featherless bipeds', but even those of us who are not rational and haven't two legs share something a little more than not being birds. Aristotle called humans the '*politikon zoon*', the animal that lives in a *polis*, a city. All the distinguishing traits that have been singled out by theorists, ideologues and psychologists – hunting, farming, city-building, creativity, trade, competition, sex – can be understood as modes of communication. Before any of these can become human attributes, they must also be communicative: there is no society without communication, and if communication once arose out of sex, like the florid displays of the bird of paradise, then by now sex has turned the tables and become one of our most complex and engaging ways of speaking to one another. One thing we need to notice about communication is that it evolves over time. Not only do new techniques come in, like alphabets and photography; new institutions arise in the complex conversation of humankind, priesthoods, armies, legal codes, schools, markets in which communciation shifts and changes form as well as technique. At certain points in history, and in certain institutional environments, communication can be heavily influenced by factors such as feudal loyalties, religious beliefs or command structures. In our times, as I argued in Chapter 4.iii, the richest and most widespread mode of communication is economic. The largest number of relationships into which we enter are mediated by financial transactions: employment, shopping, paying bills, running up debts, borrowing and lending. Even the most active cybernaut couldn't manage to connect to so many people in so little time as the shopper who picks up a pineapple in the supermarket and pays with a credit card. The network of relationships, from national banks to container ship crews, from farmers to shelf-fillers, is extraordinarily complex. Yet at the same time, the content of the communication is pretty much nil. We never see those with whom we communicate, and we can only spend or not spend, buy one product or another. In information terms, this approximates to pure communication, a communication in which the channel is everything and the message is nothing. To say that, in boycotting French wine after the French government's assault on the Greenpeace ship *Rainbow Warrior*, we are 'sending a message to' France, its government, the wine industry or even the store we shop in is wishful thinking. What we are sending is a statistical aberration, not a message. By analogy with non-war, perhaps we should describe this universal currency as non-communication, but that would be inacurate. Communication does take place, but it is a communication to which the communicators are marginal: if the farmer grows a particularly splendid crop or I decide never to eat pineapple again, very little changes. The communicative structure will survive the absence of individuals to communicate between. From the point of view of the network, we are interchangeable, equivalent to any other 'terminal', sender or receiver.

Communication is by no means universally a good thing. John Broughton argues, for example, that we can understand 'bombing as communication' (Broughton 1996: 143). He quotes an essay in which the deconstructionist philosopher Derrida makes the punning point that 'missives' can become 'missiles', that is, that there are ways in which a message always touches the one to whom it is sent, penetrating him or her like a dart of otherness hurled from elsewhere, a pledge of the difference inherent in all communication. Unlike Baudrillard and Virilio, Broughton insists on this difference when he turns Derrida around to suggest that a bomb is itself a message, a signal that, even as it tries to annihilate the other, recognises them as other. Drawing on Bataille at one point in his argument, Broughton posits a viewpoint from which 'the trajectories of munitions reinstate – in however abstract, stereotyped, or dangerous a manner – the desire for communication contact' (Broughton 1996: 146). In the end, however, he must acknowledge that 'The smart bomb may be a symptom of our decline and fall, but it is not a sign of an escape route. The explosive obliteration of the enemy is an act of desperation' (Broughton 1996: 157), a desperation brought on by the closure of communication, the violence which poses itself as an alternative, and the new techniques of subjugation which its wealth of military communications technologies promise to enact in the civilian world. Here is a point at which communication destroys communication, the goal toward which Baudrillard appeared to be striving at the close of the Gulf War book. And yet few of us would agree that this is a suitable outcome. We can agree that communication can be evil. But must it always be? Is there an alternative to this self-destruction of communication in the blind violence of war?

Slavoj Žižek, the Slovenian psychoanalyst and cultural critic, has a radical suggestion. In Lacanian psychoanalysis, symbolisation depends on the existence of an Other, something like God, Truth or, for psychoanalysis, the Father or his Phallus. If all information can be digitised, then this capitalised Other will appear as the totality of databases in cyberspace. In common with Virilio, Žižek now imagines a massive catastrophe occurring in cyberspace, one that disables the Other, and yet which has no effects in real life outside the matrix of computer-mediated communication. So what if, in an era of total digitsation, wars were fought in cyberspace? The prospect is not so remote. Recent years have seen the use of electronic jamming and viral infection of Iraqi computers in the Gulf War, and the disruption of transport and communications, the freezing of bank payments and crippling of energy supplies are all technically feasible as weapons of high-tech warfare ('the economy is the nerve centre of war', Virilio 1999: 328). Such a war has the benefit of not touching anyone in the real world, at least not with the finality of a bomb. Žižek imagines a kind of counter-Hegelian moment in which either cyberwar destroys the Other as root of the Symbolic (and therefore of simulation) or alternatively, 'Perhaps radical virtualization – the fact that the whole of reality will soon be "digitalized", transcribed, redoubled in the "big Other" of cyberspace – will somehow redeem "real life", opening it up to a new perception' (Žižek 1997: 164). In many ways this is evocative of Deleuze's suggestion that simulation can become the overturning of all models. Once the Idea of reality has been overcome, there could be room for reality itself to spread out and take place. In Žižek's version, the simulacrum is not the successful substitution of an imitation for the original, but the idea of origin itself. The concept of reality is what hides reality, as a sensuous experience, from us. If there were a way to trick the concept of the real into the trap of unreality, then the real itself might re-emerge. If Žižek is right, it may be possible to redeem the object; but what of the subject?

Psychoanalysis shares with most psychological models the domain of the psyche, the mind of the individual. But mind is not an individual phenomenon. One implication of taking communication as the primary human characteristic is that in order for a mind to exist – something that has consciousness, that can say 'I', that recognises itself as distinct from other humans – there must be other humans from which it distinguishes itself and to whom it can say 'I'. To say that mind is a phenomenon of language would be too limiting: we think in modes other than verbal, and not all sign systems can be reduced to the model of language. Nonetheless, the principle holds that mind is a phenomenon of communication. We could not think unless we shared language, modes of depiction, narrative structures, recognitions of melody and rhythm, even economic relationships with the people around us. The painful history of 'wild children' brought up without human contact demonstrates that there is no instinct that leads them to speak, sing or draw, only the instincts for basic physiological processes. To paraphrase Descartes, I think therefore you are, and vice versa. Žižek's 'what if' scenario relates to the loss of reality on an individual basis. Even though all individuals would find themselves in a refreshed relation to the real, that would not mean they were able to communicate. In fact, the loss of the symbolic Other leads me to suspect that the survivors of the virtual catastrophe would have lost not only the concept of reality but also the ability to symbolise. Without that symbolic capacity, without the power to communicate, they would have deep and sensuous relations with reality, but not with one another. They would no longer be human.

This certainly seems another possible outcome of the catastrophe envisioned by Virilio. But it also lets us in on another problem with simulation theory. The key problem facing simulationists is that of the disappearance of reality. Throughout this book, I have tried to keep that problem centre-stage. But there comes a point in the theory when we have to say that the question of the relationship with reality may not be the big problem after all. In fact, by looking at Žižek's phantom scenario, I want to point up the fact that making the relation between symbol and reality the major issue is itself the single greatest problem faced by simulation theory. At the end of this journey, I think it is fair to say that reality, if not lost, is nonetheless undergoing a deep change, or rather, the relationship we have with reality is altering profoundly. Perhaps one way of putting the problem in a nutshell is to describe the process as one in which reality and its representations are becoming increasingly homogeneous. To use Žižek's terms, we no longer distinguish between reality and the concept of reality. This of course appears to be the end of history, an ironic conclusion, since so much of the theory since Debord has been an effort to get beyond Hegel's belief that *he* stood at the culmination of the workings of the World Spirit. I feel a rather humbler approach is appropriate.

The problem is that simulation theory has put the relationship with reality at the heart of its analysis. In doing so it has achieved much. It has provided a searching critique of commodity culture. It has given us tools for understanding the dematerialisation of money, the decay of the urban environment, the ecological catastrophe of the automobile, the shoddiness of consumer society, the vacuity of make-work policies and the conduct of war on the battlefield and in the media. But finally the theory, despite its claims to postmodernity, seems to lay claim to a universal account of everything, including the supposedly abandoned completion of grand narratives. The words 'ultimate' and 'final' appear far too often in writings of or writings inspired by simulation theorists, often in phrases that have to be revisited a few years later when the 'ultimate' state of deterrence in the Cold War is superseded by the fall of the Berlin Wall, or when the 'final' state of warfare in the Gulf is superseded by the bitter ground wars in the Balkans. It is this pretense to totality, to final knowledge, that grates, and its source lies in a misunderstanding of the nature of communication.

The purpose of communication is not to describe and define the real. This error arises from precisely that productivist ethos which Baudrillard sought to lay to rest in *The Mirror of Production* at the beginning of his career. Marx, immersed in the squalour and misery of the nineteenth century, can scarcely be blamed for agreeing with his contemporaries that nature existed as raw materials for human industry. That belief was at least as old as Christianity, and has lasted into our secular age in the form of genetic engineering. The emerging ecological consciousness of our times allows us to look with more jaundiced eyes, and to recognise that there is enmity between humankind and the natural environment. It is this consciousness as much as anything that has driven the wedge between us and the real that previously seemed to be our sole possession, to do with as we wished. In his later philosophy, Martin Heidegger began to explore mystical ideas of the land, the hearth, the air as elements of human life that might allow a renewed sense of Being, a reunion with the world such as the ancient Greeks had known in their pre-industrial societies. Similar nostalgic myths circulate in the lionisation of first peoples as mystical receptacles of an ancient union with the spirits of the earth. Baudrillard recirculates them in his recourse to concepts of symbolic exchange. Virilio believes there is a relation to landscape that can redeem the acceleration of culture. Even Debord's concept of alienation rests on a concept of an unalienated humanity. These stories are just that: narratives, even what Lyotard called metanarratives; tales told to hold together some way of persisting, some way of thinking, in the morass of modern life. Like the myth of progress, the myth of a lost reality, though it looks backward into the lost time of the ancestors rather than forward to the unvisitable future of the offspring, is a story, even though it can only be read from the end.

There are other possible sociologies to propose concerning the nature of simulation theory and the reasons why it should have emerged when and where it did. The defeat of all the mighty expectations of May 1968 is surely one of them. For generations brought up on the politics of 1981 – the year of the urban uprisings in the UK – 1989 – the year the Wall came down – or 1999 – the year of the J18 and N30 protests – perhaps these concerns are less relevant. Yet the theory still keeps its persuasive power. Perhaps too it has to do with the gradual removal of intellectuals from spheres of political influence, though one or two – Anthony Giddens in the UK, Michel Serres in France – have managed to capture the imaginations of key politicians. No theory exists in a vacuum. Philosophers are to this extent the same as television producers, technologists or theme park designers: their works bear the stamp of the age in which they were made. For our thinkers, that age was the triumphal moment of consumerism, and they raged against it and still do.

But there is a professional obligation for teachers and writers never to abandon hope. This is why I have named this concluding chapter after a dictum of the tragic Italian Marxist Antonio Gramsci, who spent most of his intellectual life in Mussolini's prisons. The Catholic theologians have for centuries called despair the sin against the Holy Spirit; perhaps this is why the least troubled of our commentators, McLuhan, Eco and Virilio, all have Catholic backgrounds. We can also see in Eco, despite the criticisms I have made of his work, the central problem which simulation theory fails to address, and for lack of which it has painted itself into a bleak corner of its own making. That problem is that the purpose of communication is not to depict the real but to communicate. Communciation is not about the relationship with the real but about relationships with other people. As we have seen in this chapter, communication has its histories and they are often miserable. We have used genocide and inquisition as modes of communication; imprisonment and torture, starvation and disease, and today more than ever debt and weapons are our primary way of speaking from nation to nation. This is why I have found it impossible to end with the generous and humane vision of Eco's recent works in the semiotics of language and the realism of common sense. Firstly, not only is realism still a problem in its own right for simulation, but it is the wrong problem. And secondly, the sinister history of communication has to ward us off faith in the common sense of common folk. Moreover, the rather sentimental faith in ordinary wisdom, which in any case seems suspicious for its approximation to television's ideology of the human family, also lacks a machinery for understanding and expecting change. The same problem haunts the more cognitive version of linguistics associated with Chomsky, mentioned in Chaper 1: what is innate or universal is not open to history. To urge communication as the route forward from the darker visions of simulation is not the easy option; it is harder than waiting for the butterfly. But it does imply a belief in the future, the possibility, indeed the inevitability, of change.

ANNOTATED BIBLIOGRAPHY OF FURTHER READING

Chapter 1

Generations of working-class people have struggled with and been enlightened by the first chapter of Marx's *Capital* on 'The Commodity': the best translation is (1976), *Capital: A Critique of Political Economy*, Vol. 1, trans. Rodney Livingstone, NLB/Penguin, London. Otherwise, still the best introduction to Marx's thought is *The Communist Manifesto*: I use the translation in Karl Marx (1974), *The Revolutions of 1848: Political Writings Vol. 1*, ed. David Fernbach, NLB/Viking, New York, 62–98, although there is an excellent new centennial edition available from Verso. I'm not aware of any beginner's guides to Bataille: the introduction to Botting and Wilson's (1997) *The Bataille Reader*, Blackwell, Oxford, is a good starting point.

Despite the number of excellent introductory texts in semiotics, by and large it is worth reading the originals. Ferdinand de Saussure's (1974) *Course in General Linguistics*, rev. edn, trans. Wade Baskin, Fontana, London, is still a classic, as are Roland Barthes's (1972) *Mythologies*, trans. Annette Lavers, Noonday, New York, and Claude Lévi-Strauss' (1966) *The Savage Mind*, no translator credit, University of Chicago Press, Chicago, both of them masters of prose style. Of particular interest to this study is the more technical Umberto Eco (1979), *A Theory of Semiotics*, Indiana University Press, Bloomington.

Like many German-language thinkers, Freud provided his own introduction in the form of the (1966) *Introductory Lectures on Psychoanalysis*, and the (1965) *New Introductory Lectures on Psychoanalysis*, both trans. James Strachey, Norton, New York. To get a flavour of his thinking in action, read the third section of *The Interpretation of Dreams* (1996), trans. James Strachey, Pelican Freud Library, Harmondsworth. Lacan's notorious obscurantism is slightly less apparent in his seminars, which are now beginning to be translated, than in his *Écrits*: one of the best short accounts of his work is in Chapter 3 of Robert Lapsley and Michael Westlake (1988), *Film Theory: An Introduction*, Manchester University Press, Manchester.

The author's notes on 'Semiotics for Beginners' and 'A Young Person's Guide to the Psyche' can be found at the website associated with this book (http://www.waikato.ac.nz/screenandmedia/staff.shtml).

Chapter 2

A masterpiece of condensation and clarity, Armand and Michèle Mattelart's (1998) *Theories of Communication: A Short Introduction*, trans. Susan Gruenheck Taponier and James A. Cohen, Sage, London, is the best overview of the field for busy students. The history of technology has become a major field of research over recent years. Early classics include Lewis Mumford (1934), *Technics and Civilization*, Routledge and Kegan Paul, London, and Siegfried Giedion (1948), *Mechanization Takes Command: A Contribution to Anonymous History*, Norton, New York. Among responses to Innis and McLuhan's technological determinism, see especially Merritt Roe Smith and Leo Marx (eds) (1994), *Does Technology Drive History? The Dilemma of Technological Determinism*, MIT Press, Cambridge, MA. Two influential recent accounts can be found in Bruce Mazlish (1993), *The Fourth Discontinuity: The Co-evolution of Humans and Machines*, Yale University Press, New Haven CT, and Don Ihde (1990), *Technology and the Lifeworld: From Garden to Earth*, Indiana University Press, Bloomington. A more materialist account of technological development can be found in G.A. Cohen (1978), *Karl Marx's Theory of History: A Defence*, Princeton University Press, Princeton, which analyses the contradiction between the means (i.e. technology) and the mode (e.g. capitalism) of production, and Andrew Feenberg (1991), *Critical Theory of Technology*, Oxford University Press, Oxford. Especially relevant to communication theory is Brian Winston's admirable survey of the economic, political and social constraints on the introduction of new media technologies in his (1998) *Media, Technology and Society, A History: From the Telegraph to the Internet*, Routledge, London.

There are a number of good, readable introductions to aspects of information theory. Jeremy Campbell (1982), *Grammatical Man: Information, Entropy, Language and Life*, Simon and Schuster, New York, is still an excellent overview. Howard Gardner's (1987) *The Mind's New Science: A History of the Cognitive Revolution*, rev. edn, HarperCollins, New York, and Philip Johnson-Laird's (1993) *The Computer and the Mind: An Introduction to Cognitive Science*, 2nd edn, Fontana, London, are both excellent introductions to contemporary psychology and its links to artificial intelligence, computing and linguistics. The best one-volume introductions to linguistics and modern genetics are respectively the extremely readable Steven Pinker (1994), *The Language Instinct: The New Science of Language and Mind*, Penguin, Harmondsworth, and Steve Jones (1994), *The Language of the Genes*, rev. edn, Flamingo, London. More controversial in their fields are the writings of Richard Dawkins, notably *The Selfish Gene*, 2nd edn (1989), Oxford University Press, Oxford, and *River Out of Eden: A Darwinian View of Life* (1996), Basic Books, New York, in genetics, and Daniel C. Dennett (1991), *Consciousness Explained*, Harmondsworth, Penguin, and (1996), *Kinds of Minds: Toward an Understanding of Consciousness*, Basic Books, New York, in psychology.

The best introductions to the work of the Frankfurt School are those by David Held (1980), *Introduction to Critical Theory: Horkheimer to Habermas*, University of California Press, Berkeley, and Martin Jay (1973), *The Dialectical Imagination*, Little, Brown, Boston. Among the many introductions to postmodernism, the most lucid are Steven Best and Douglas Kellner (1991), *Postmodern Theory: Critical Interrogations* (Critical Perspectives), Guilford Press, New York; Steven Connor (1997), *Postmodernist Culture: An Introduction to Theories of the Contemporary*, 2nd edn, Blackwell, Oxford; David Harvey (1990), *The Condition of Postmodernity: An Enquiry into the Origins of Cultural Change*, Blackwell, Oxford; Angela MacRobbie (1994), *Postmodernism and Popular Culture*, Routledge, London; and Madan Sarup (1993), *An Introductory Guide to Post-structuralism and Postmodernism*, University of Georgia Press, Athens. The two most commonly cited among the primary texts are Jean-François Lyotard (1984), *The Postmodern Condition: A Report on Knowledge*, trans. Geoff Bennington and Brian Massumi, Manchester University Press, Manchester, and Fredric Jameson (1991), *Postmodernism, or, The Cultural Logic of Late Capitalism*, Verso, London. Scott Lash (1990), *Sociology of Postmodernism*, Routledge, London, is a more complex and demanding but inspiring account of the interplay between German, French and Anglo-Saxon traditions in the exploration of contemporary society.

Chapter 3

Guy Debord and the situationists have attracted a good deal of interest. One extremely relevant study is by Sadie Plant, who is also one of the leading lights of cyberfeminism. Her book *The Most Radical Gesture: The Situationist International in a Postmodern Age*, was published by Routledge, London, in 1992. The whole text of *The Society of the Spectacle* can be accessed at http://www.nothingness.org/SI/debord/SOTS/sotscontents.html, where you will also find further writings by and about Debord and extensive links.

There is now a substantial literature on Baudrillard. Those I have found most useful are Mike Gane's two books, both from 1991 and both from Routledge, London: *Baudrillard: Critical and Fatal Theory* and *Baudrillard's Bestiary: Baudrillard and Culture*; Garry Genosko's (1994) *Baudrillard and Signs: Signification Ablaze*, Routledge, London; Douglas Kellner's (1989) *Jean Baudrillard: From Marxism to Postmodernism and Beyond*, Polity, Cambridge, and his (1994) anthology, *Baudrillard: A Critical Reader*, Blackwell, Oxford; and Nicholas Zurbrugg (ed.) (1997), *Jean Baudrillard: Art and Artefact*, Sage, London. There is a well-maintained site devoted to *Baudrillard on the Web* (http://www.uta.edu/English/apt/collab/baudweb).

Paul Virilio has attracted less interest in the English-speaking world, but there is an excellent special issue of the online journal *Speed* devoted to his

work at http://proxy.arts.uci.edu/~nideffer/_SPEED_/1.4/articles/. The journal *Theory, Culture & Society* (vol. 16, nos 5–6, October–December 1999) is
a special issue on Virilio edited by John Armstrong, whose collection of
critical esays on Virilio, *Paul Virilio: From Modernism to Hypermodernism
and Beyond*, and anthology of interviews with him, *Virilio Live!*, were both
both published by Sage, London, in 2000. It's worth noting that some early
translations of Virilio are not entirely accurate: my favourite example comes
in a citation of Euler's famous mathematical problem of 'the seven points of
the City of Konigsberg' (1991b), which should read as the seven bridges
(ponts), not points.

   Most of the critical writing on Umberto Eco clusters around either the
novels or the technical writings on semiotics. However, Professor Eco does
maintain a comprehensive website (in Italian) at http://www.dsc.unibo.it/
istituto/people/eco/eco.htm, and there are excellent sites devoted to his work
at Porta Ludovico, http://www.rpg.net/quail/libyrinth/eco/, and at The
Umberto Eco Page, http://www.argyroneta.com/eco/

Chapter 4

Alternative views to those posed in this chapter can be found eloquently
argued in the pages of Armand Mattelart (1996), *The Invention of Communication*, trans. Susan Emanuel, University of Minnesota Press, Minneapolis;
Christopher Norris (1990), *What's Wrong with Postmodernism: Critical
Theory and the Ends of Philosophy*, Harvester Wheatsheaf, Hemel Hempstead; and Roy Bhaskar (1986), *Scientific Realism and Human Emancipation*, Verso, London. Hal Foster's (1996) *The Return of the Real: The
Avant-Garde at the End of the Century*, MIT Press, Cambridge, MA, is an
excellent account of the vicissitudes of the real in contemporary art. The
hermeneutic tradition on which both Rorty and Vattimo draw and which
forms the backdrop to the concept of mediation advanced here owes a lot to
the philosophy of Hans-Georg Gadamer and Paul Ricoeur. For introductory
texts, try *A Ricoeur Reader: Reflection and Imagination*, ed. Mario J.
Valdés, Harvester Wheatsheaf, Hemel Hempstead (1991) and Gadamer's
(1981) *Reason in the Age of Science*, trans. Frederick G. Lawrence, MIT
Press, Cambridge, MA, or his (1986) *The Relevance of the Beautiful and
Other Essays*, trans. Nicholas Walker, Cambridge University Press,
Cambridge.

Chapter 5

Most of the more important work on Disney World is cited in the chapter.
For animation studies, see Norman M. Klein, (1993), *7 Minutes: The Life
and Death of the American Animated Cartoon*, Verso, London, and Eric
Smoodin (1993), *Animating Culture: Hollywood Cartons from the Sound
Era*, Roundhouse, Oxford. While I was preparing this manuscript, a call for

papers for the first conference devoted to Disney Studies was circulating: no doubt there will be more publications on its heels. Mark Dery's (1999) *The Pyrotechnic Insanitarium: American Culture on the Brink*, Grove Press, New York, gives a frighteningly vivid journalistic account of the hyperrealisation of leisure in the USA.

Chapter 6

There were a number of important analyses of military technologies predating the Persian Gulf conflict, notably Jeffrey T. Richelson's (1989) *America's Secret Eyes in Space: The US Keyhole Spy Satellite Program*, Harper and Row, New York, on satellite surveillance, and H. Franklin Bruce's (1988) *War Stars: The Superweapon and the American Imagination*, Oxford University Press, Oxford, which deals with both technologies and the fictions that surround them. Manuel de Landa's (1991) *War in the Age of Intelligent Machines*, Swerve Editions/Zone Books, New York, was in press when the war began. Nonetheless it is an extraordinarily well-researched and persuasive argument that has an importanty bearing on simulation theory's analysis of warfare. Other than the essays cited in the chapter, two important books came out in the following year: Douglas Kellner, who has published extensively on Baudrillard and postmodernity, brought out (1992) *The Persian Gulf TV War*, Westview Press, Boulder, CO, and the same firm also published an important anthology edited by Hamid Mowlana, George Gerbner and Hebert I. Schiller (1992), *Triumph of the Image: The Media's War in the Persian Gulf – A Global Perspective*. On more recent conflicts, especially in Mexico, South East Asia and the former Yugoslavia, it is worth visiting the archives of the *nettime* discussion network at http://www.desk.nl/~nettime/

Chapter 7

There has been an explosion of publishing about computers, the digital industries and cyberculture. The single most authoritative account, theoretically informed but even more shaped by a massive research project into the facts and figures, is Manuel Castells' three-volume *The Information Age: Economy, Society and Culture* (Blackwell, Oxford) comprising *The Rise of the Network Society* (1996), *The Power of Identity* (1997) and *End of Millennium* (1998). Also important are Dan Schiller (1999), *Digital Capitalism: Networking the Global Marketing System*, MIT Press, Cambridge, MA; David Morley and Kevin Robins (1995), *Spaces of Identity: Global Media, Electronic Landscapes and Cultural Boundaries*, Routledge, London; and Stanley Aronowitz, Barbara Martinsons and Michael Menser (eds) (1996), *Technoscience and Cyberculture*, Routledge, London. Sadie Plant, who also wrote on the situationists, is one the more articulate theorists of cyberculture to deploy simulation theory: her (1997) *Zeros and Ones:*

Digital Women +The New Technoculture, 4th Estate, London, is a fascinating book. One of Baudrillard's first translators and the editor of the Selected Writings, Mark Poster, is the author of two important books: *The Mode of Information: Poststructuralism and Social Context*, Polity, Cambridge (1990), and *The Second Media Age* , Polity, Cambridge (1995). My own thinking is influenced by N. Katherine Hayles (1999), *How We Became Posthuman: Virtual Bodies in Cybernetics, Literature and Informatics*, University of Chicago Press, Chicago, and Margaret Morse (1998), *Virtualities: Television, Media Art, And Cyberculture*, Indiana University Press, Bloomington. For further readings in this field, see http://www.staff.livjm.ac.uk/mccscubi/screen.html

REFERENCES

Abbate, Janet (1999), *Inventing the Internet*, MIT Press, Cambridge, MA.

Adilkno [The Foundation for Advancement of Illegal Knowledge] (1998), *Media Archive*, Autonomedia, New York.

Adorno, Theodor W. (1967), 'Cultural Criticism and Society', in *Prisms*, trans. Samuel and Shierry Weber, MIT Press, Cambridge, MA, 17–34.

Adorno, Theodor W. (1977), 'Letters to Walter Benjamin', letter of 18 March 1936, in Ernst Bloch, Georg Lukács, Bertolt Brecht, Walter Benjamin, Theodor Adorno, *Aesthetics and Politics*, ed. and trans. Rodney Taylor, NLB, London, 120–6.

Allen, Robert C. (1985), *Speaking of Soap Operas*, University of North Carolina Press, Chapel Hill.

Ang, Ien (1991), *Desperately Seeking the Audience*, Routledge, London.

Ang, Ien (1995), *Living Room Wars: Rethinking Media Audiences for a Postmodern World*, Routledge, London.

Angus, Ian (1993), 'Orality in the Twilight of Humanism: A Critique of the Communication Theory of Harold Innis', in Brian Shoesmith and Ian Angus *Dependency/Space/Policy* (=*Continuum: The Australian Journal of Media & Culture*, Vol. 7, no. 1); online at http://www.ecu.edu.au/pc/continuum

Appadurai, Arjun (1996), *Modernity at Large: Cultural Dimensions of Globalization*, University of Minnesota Press, Minneapolis.

Asprey, William (ed.) (1990), *Computing Before Computers*, Iowa State University Press, Ames.

Barbrook, Richard (1998), 'The High-Tech Gift Economy', in *First Monday*, online journal, http://ma.hrc.wmin.ac.uk/ma.theory.1.6.db

Barthes, Roland (1972), *Mythologies*, trans. Annette Lavers, Noonday, New York.

Barthes, Roland (1977), *Image–Music–Text: Selected Essays*, ed. and trans. Stephen Heath, Fontana, London.

Bataille, Georges (1988), *The Accursed Share*, Vol. 1, *Consumption*, trans. Robert Hurley, Zone Books, New York.

Bataille, Georges (1997), 'The Notion of Expenditure', in Fred Botting and Scott Wilson (eds), *The Bataille Reader*, Blackwell, Oxford, 167–81.

Bateson, Gregory (1972), *Steps to an Ecology of Mind*, Chandler, San Francisco.

Baudrillard, Jean (1968), *Le Système des objets*, Gallimard, Paris. (*The System of Objects*, trans. James Benedict, Verso, London, 1996.)

Baudrillard, Jean (1970), *La Société de consommation: Ses mythes, ses structures*, NRF Gallimard, Paris. (*The Consumer Society: Myths and Structures*, trans. Chris Turner, Sage, London, 1998.)

Baudrillard, Jean (1972), *Pour une critique de l'économie politique du signe*, Gallimard, Paris. (*For a critique of the Political Economy of the Sign*, trans. Charles Levin, Telos Press, St Louis, MO.)

Baudrillard, Jean (1975), *The Mirror of Production*, trans. Mark Poster, Telos Press, St Louis, MO.

Baudrillard, Jean (1983a), *Simulations*, trans. Paul Foss, Paul Patton and Philip Beitchman, Semiotext(e), New York.

Baudrillard, Jean (1983b), *In the Shadow of the Silent Majorities, or, The End of the Social and Other Essays*, trans. Paul Foss, John Johnston and Paul Patton, Semiotext(e), New York.

Baudrillard (1983c), 'The Precession of Simulacra', trans. Paul Foss and Paul Patton, *Art and Text*, Spring, 3–46.

Baudrillard, Jean (1986), 'The Year 2000 Will Not Take Place', trans. Paul Foss and Paul Patton, in E.A. Grosz, T. Threadgold and D. Kelly (eds), *Futur*Fall: Excursions into Postmodernity*, Power Institute of Fine Arts, Sydney, 18–28.

Baudrillard, Jean (1988a), *America*, trans. Chris Turner (Material Word), Verso, London.

Baudrillard, Jean (1988b), *Selected Writings*, ed. Mark Poster, Stanford University Press, Stanford.

Baudrillard, Jean (1988c), 'The Masses: Implosion of the Social in the Media', trans. Marie Maclean, in *Selected Writings*, ed. Mark Poster, Stanford University Press, Stanford, 207–19.

Baudrillard, Jean, (1990a), *Seduction*, trans. Brian Singer, Macmillan, London.

Baudrillard, Jean (1990b), *Fatal Strategies*, trans. Philip Beitchman and W.G.J. Niesluchowski, ed. Jim Fleming, Semiotext(e), New York/Pluto, London.

Baudrillard, Jean (1993a), *Symbolic Exchange and Death*, trans. Ian Hamilton Grant, Sage, London.

Baudrillard, Jean (1993b), *The Transparency of Evil: Essays on Extreme Phenomena*, trans. James Benedict, Verso, London.

Baudrillard, Jean (1994a), *Simulacra and Simulation*, trans. Sheila Faria Glaser, University of Michigan Press, Ann Arbor.

Baudrillard, Jean (1994b), *The Illusion of the End*, trans. Chris Turner, Polity, Cambridge.

Baudrillard, Jean (1995), *The Gulf War Did Not Take Place*, trans. Paul Patton, Power Publications, Sydney.

Baudrillard, Jean (1996a), *The Perfect Crime*, trans. Chris Turner, Verso, London.

Baudrillard, Jean (1996b), 'Disneyworld Company', in CTHEORY, http://www.ctheory.com/e25-disneyworld_comp.html

Baudrillard, Jean (1998), *Paroxysm: Interviews with Phillippe Petit*, trans. Chris Turner, Verso, London.

Bazin, André (1967), *What is Cinema?*, Vol. 1, trans. Hugh Gray, University of California Press, Berkeley.

Bazin, André (1971), *What is Cinema?*, Vol. 2, trans. Hugh Gray, University of California Press, Berkeley.

Bell, Daniel (1962), *The End of Ideology*, Penguin, Harmondsworth.

Bell, Daniel (1973), *The Coming of Post-Industrial Society: A Venture in Social Forecasting*, Basic Books, New York.

Benjamin, Walter (1969a), 'The Work of Art in the Age of Mechanical Reproduction', in *Illuminations*, ed. Hannah Arendt, trans. Harry Zohn, Schocken Books, New York, 217–51.

Benjamin, Walter (1969b), 'On Some Motifs in Baudelaire', in *Illuminations*, ed. Hannah Arendt, trans. Harry Zohn, Schocken, New York, 155–200.

Benjamin, Walter (1973), *Understanding Brecht*, trans. Anna Bostock, NLB, London.

Benjamin, Walter (1979), *One-Way Street and Other Writings*, trans. Edmund Jephcott and Kingsley Shorter, NLB, London.

Berners-Lee, Tim, with Mark Fischetti (1999), *Weaving the Web*, Orion, London.

Best, Steven (1994), 'The Commodification of Reality and the Reality of Commodification: Baudrillard, Debord and Postmodern Theory', in Douglas Kellner (ed.), *Baudrillard: A Critical Reader*, Blackwell, Oxford, 41–67.

Bloch, Ernst, Georg Lukács, Bertolt Brecht, Walter Benjamin and Theodor Adorno (1977), *Aesthetics and Politics*, ed. and trans. Rodney Taylor, NLB, London.

Bolter, Jay David and Richard Grusin (1999), *Remediation: Understanding New Media*, MIT Press, Cambridge, MA.

Bordwell, David (1985), *Narration and the Fiction Film*, Routledge, London.

Bordwell, David (1989), *Making Meaning: Inference and Rhetoric in the Interpretation of Cinema*, Harvard University Press, Cambridge, MA.

Braudel, Fernand (1972), *The Mediterranean and the Mediterranean World in the Age of Philip II*, 2 vols, trans. Sîan Reynolds, Collins, London.

Braun, Marta (1992), *Picturing Time: The Work of Étienne-Jules Marey (1830–1904)*, University of Chicago Press, Chicago.

Braverman, Harry (1974), *Labor and Monopoly Capital: The Degradation of Work in the Twentieth Century*, Monthly Review Press, New York.

Broughton, John (1996), 'The Bomb's-Eye View: Smart Weapons and Military T.V.', in Stanley Aronowitz, Barbara Martinsons and Michael Menser (eds), *Technoscience and Cyberculture*, Routledge, New York, 139–65.

Bryman, Alan (1995), *Disney and his Worlds*, Routledge, London.

Bryson, Norman (1983), *Vision and Painting: The Logic of the Gaze*, Macmillan, London.

Buck-Morss, Susan (1989), *The Dialectics of Seeing: Walter Benjamin and the Arcades Project*, MIT Press, Cambridge, MA.

Byrne, Eleanor and Martin McQuillan (1999), *Deconstructing Disney*, Pluto, London.

Campbell, Jeremy (1982), *Grammatical Man: Information, Entropy, Language and Life*, Simon and Schuster, New York.

Caudwell, Christopher (1971), *Studies and Further Studies in a Dying Culture*, Monthly Review Press, New York.

Cassell, Justine and Henry Jenkins (eds) (1998), *From Barbie to Mortal Kombat: Gender and Computer Games*, MIT Press, Cambridge, MA.

Cassirer, Ernst (1946), *The Myth of the State*, Yale University Press, New Haven.

Castells, Manuel (1996), *The Information Age: Economy, Society and Culture*, Vol. 1, *The Rise of the Network Society*, Blackwell, Oxford.

Ceruzzi, Paul E. (1999), *A History of Modern Computing*, MIT Press, Cambridge, MA.

Chanan, Michael (1995), *Repeated Takes: A Short History of Recording and Its Effects on Music*, Verso, London.

Chomsky, Noam (1957), *Syntactic Structures*, Mouton, The Hague.

Chomsky, Noam (1965), *Aspects of the Theory of Syntax*, MIT Press, Cambridge, MA.

Chomsky, Noam (1972), *Language and Mind*, enlarged edn, Harcourt Brace Jovanovich, New York.

Connell, Ian (1984), 'Fabulous Powers: Blaming the Media', in Len Masterman (ed.), *Television Mythologies: Stars, Shows and Signs*, Comedia/MK Media Press, London, 88–93.

Coombe, Rosemary (1998), *The Cultural Life of Intellectual Properties: Authorship, Appropriation and the Law*, Duke University Press, Durham, NC.

Critical Art Ensemble (1994), *The Electronic Disturbance*, Autonomedia, Brooklyn, NY.

Curry, Michael R. (1998), *Digital Places: Living with Geographic Information Technologies*, Routledge, London.

Dagognet, François (1992), *Étienne-Jules Marey: A Passion for the Trace*, trans. Robert Galeta with Jeanine Herman, Zone Books, New York.

d'Alembert, Jean Le Rond (1963), *Preliminary Discourse to the Encyclopedia of Diderot*, trans. Richard N. Schwab with Walter E. Rex, Bobbs-Merrill, New York.

Davies, Paul (1995), *About Time: Einstein's Unfinished Revolution*, Penguin, London.

Davis, Mike (1998), *Ecology of Fear: Los Angeles and the Imagination of Disaster*, Picador, London.

Debord, Guy (1977), *The Society of the Spectacle*, revised translation, no translator credit, Black & Red, Detroit.

Debord, Guy (1990), *Comments on The Society of the Spectacle*, trans. Malcolm Imrie, Verso, London.

Debord, Guy (1991), *Panegyric*, trans. James Brook, Verso, London.

de Landa, Manuel (1991), *War in the Age of Intelligent Machines*, Swerve Editions/Zone Books, New York.

Deleuze, Gilles (1990), 'Plato and the Simulacrum', in *The Logic of Sense*, ed. Constantin V. Boundas, trans. Mark Lester with Charles Stivale, Columbia University Press, New York.

Deleuze, Gilles (1994), *Difference and Repetition*, trans. Paul Patton, Athlone Press, London.

Deleuze, Gilles and Félix Guattari (1987), *A Thousand Plateaus: Capitalism and Schizophrenia*, trans. Brian Massumi, University of Minnesota Press, Minneapolis.

Dennett, Daniel C. (1991), *Consciousness Explained*, Penguin, Harmondsworth.

Dennett, Daniel C. (1996), *Kinds of Minds: Toward an Understanding of Consciousness*, Basic Books, New York.

Der Derian, James (1998), 'Interview with Virilio', in *Speed* 1.4, http://proxy.arts.uci.edu/ ~ nideffer/_SPEED_/1.4/articles/derderian.html

de Rosnay, Joël (1986), *Le Cerveau planetaire*, Seuil, Paris.

Doane, Mary Ann (1990), 'Information, Crisis, Catastophe', in Patricia Mellencamp (ed.), *Logics of Television: Essays in Cultural Criticism*, BFI, London, 222–39.

Dorfman, Ariel and Armand Mattelart (1984), *How to Read Donald Duck: Imperialist Ideology in the Disney Comic*, trans. David Kunzle, International General, New York.

Druckrey, Timothy (1991), 'Deadly Representations or Apocalypse Now', in Derek Bishton, Andy Cameron and Tim Druckery (eds), *Digital Dialogues: Photography in the Age of Cyberspace*, Ten:8 Photo Paperback, Vol. 2 no. 2, Autumn, 16–27.

Ducrot, Oswald and Tsvetan Todorov (1972), *Dictionnaire encyclopédique des sciences du langage*, Seuil (Collection Points), Paris. (Encyclopedic Dictionary of the Sciences of Languages, trans. Catherine Porter, Johns Hopkins University, Baltimore, MD, 1994.)

Dyer, Richard (1979), *Stars*, BFI, London.

Dyson, Esther (1997), *Release 2.0: A Design for Living in the Digital Age*, Viking, New York.

Dyson, Freeman (1988), *Infinite in All Directions: Gifford Lectures Given in Aberdeen, Scotland, April–November 1985*, Penguin, Harmondsworth.

Eco, Umberto (1979), *A Theory of Semiotics*, Indiana University Press, Bloomington.

Eco, Umberto (1981), *The Role of the Reader: Explorations in the Semiotics of Texts*, Hutchinson, London.

Eco, Umberto (1983), *The Name of the Rose*, trans. William Weaver, Picador, London.

Eco, Umberto (1984), 'A Guide to the Neo-Television of the 1980s', in *Framework* no. 25.

Eco, Umberto (1986), *Faith in Fakes: Travels in Hyperreality*, trans. William Weaver, Minerva, London

Eco, Umberto (1989), *Foucault's Pendulum*, trans. William Weaver, Secker and Warburg, London.

Eco, Umberto (1990), *The Limits of Interpretation*, Indiana University Press, Bloomington.

Eco, Umberto with Richard Rorty, Jonathan Culler and Christine Brooke-Rose (1992), *Interpretation and Overinterpretation*, ed. Stefani Collini, Cambridge University Press, Cambridge.

Eco, Umberto (1994), *Apocaplypse Postponed*, ed. Robert Lumley, Indiana University Press, Bloomington.

Eco, Umberto (1995), *The Island of the Day Before*, trans. William Weaver, Minerva, London.

Eco, Umberto (1997), *The Search for the Perfect Language*, trans. James Fentress, Fontana, London.

Eco, Umberto (1999), *Kant and the Platypus: Essays on Language and Cognition*, trans. Alistair McEwen, Secker and Warburg, London.

Edwards, Paul N. (1996), *The Closed World: Computers and the Politics of Discourse in Cold War America*, MIT Press, Cambridge, MA.

Eliot, Marc (1995), *Walt Disney: Hollywood's Dark Prince*, André Deutsch, London.

Ellul, Jacques (1964), *The Technological Society*, trans. John Wilkinson, Vintage, New York.

Fisk, Robert (1992), *Pity the Nation: Lebanon at War*, Oxford University Press, Oxford.

Fiske, John (1987), *Television Culture*, Methuen, London.

Foster, Hal (1996), *The Return of the Real: The Avant-Garde at the End of the Century*, MIT Press, Cambridge, MA.

Gardner, Howard (1987), *The Mind's New Science: A History of the Cognitive Revolution*, rev. edn, HarperCollins, New York.

Gelernter, David (1998), *The Aesthetics of Computing*, Phoenix, London.

Giraudoux, Jean (1958), *La Guerre de Troie n'aura pas lieu*, ed. H.J.G. Godin, University of London Press, London.

Giroux, Henry A. (1994), 'Beyond the Politics of Innocence: Memory and Pedagogy in the "Wonderful World of Disney" ', in *Socialist Review*, 23, 79–107.

Gish, Lillian, with Ann Pichot (1969), *The Movies, Mr Griffith and Me*, W.H. Allen, London.

Gleick, James (1987), *Chaos: Making a New Science*, Penguin, London.

Goldman, William (1983), *Adventures in the Screen Trade: A Personal View of Hollywood and Scriptwriting*, Futura, London.

Gomery, Douglas (1994), 'Disney's Business History: A Reinterpretation', in Eric Smoodin (ed.), *Disney Discourse: Producing the Magic Kingdom*, American Film Institute/ Routledge, London, 71–86.

Gramsci, Antonio (1971), *Selections from the Prison Notebooks*, ed. and trans. Quintin Hoare and Geoffrey Nowell-Smith, International Publishers, New York.

Gray, Chris Hables (1997), *Postmodern War: The New Politics of Conflict*, Routledge, London.

Greenberg, Clement (1992), 'Avant-Garde and Kitsch', in Charles Harrison and Paul Wood (eds), *Art in Theory 1900–1990*, Blackwell, Oxford, 529–41.

Hansen, Miriam (1991), *Babel and Babylon: Spectatorship in American Silent Cinema*, Harvard University Press, Cambridge, MA.

Haraway, Donna (1985), 'A Manifesto for Cyborgs: Science, Technology and Socialist Feminism in the 1980s', in *Socialist Review*, no. 80 (Vol. 15, no. 2), March–April, 65–107; reprinted as 'A Cyborg Manifesto: Science, Technology and Socialist Feminism in the Late Twentieth Century', in Donna Haraway (1991), *Simians, Cyborgs and Women: The Reinvention of Nature*, Free Association Books, London, 149–81.

Harrison, Charles and Paul Wood (eds) (1992), *Art in Theory 1900–1990*, Blackwell, Oxford.

Harvey, David (1989), *The Condition of Postmodernity: An Enquiry into the Origins of Cultural Change*, Blackwell, Oxford.

Hayles, N. Katherine (1999), *How We Became Posthuman: Virtual Bodies in Cybernetics, Literature and Informatics*, University of Chicago Press, Chicago.

Hegel, G.W.F. (1953), *Reason in History: A General Introduction to the Philosophy of History*, trans. Robert S. Hartman, Bobbs-Merrill, New York.

Hegel, G.W.F. (1977), *The Phenomenology of Spirit*, trans. A.V. Miller, Oxford University Press, Oxford.

Heidegger, Martin (1977), 'The Question Concerning Technology', in *The Question Concerning Technology and Other Essays*, trans. William Lovitt, Harper & Row, New York, 3–35.

Hitchens, Christopher (1991), 'Realpolitik in the Gulf', *New Left Review*, no. 186, March/ April, 89–101.

Hodges, Andrew (1985), *Alan Turing: The Enigma of Intelligence*, Counterpoint/Unwin, London.

Hollis, Richard and Brian Sibley (1988), *The Disney Studio Story*, Octopus, London.

Holtzman, Steven (1997), *Digital Mosaics: The Aesthetics of Cyberspace*, Simon and Schuster, New York.

Horkheimer, Max and Theodor Adorno (1973), *Dialectic of Enlightenment*, trans. John Cumming, Allen Lane, London.

Innis, Harold A. (1951), *The Bias of Communication*, University of Toronto Press, Toronto.

Innis, Harold A. (1972), *Empire and Communications* (revised by Mary Q. Innis), University of Toronto Press, Toronto.

Jameson, Fredric (1991), *Postmodernism, or, The Cultural Logic of Late Capitalism*, Verso, London.

Jameson, Fredric (1992), *The Geopolitical Aesthetic: Cinema and Space in the World System*, BFI, London.

Jay, Martin (1993), *Downcast Eyes: The Denigration of Vision in Twentieth-Century French Thought*, University of California Press, Berkeley.

Johnson-Laird, Philip (1993), *The Computer and the Mind: An Introduction to Cognitive Science*, 2nd edn, Fontana, London.

Jones, Steve (1994), *The Language of the Genes*, rev. edn, Flamingo, London.

Kant, Immanuel (1983), 'Idea for a Universal History with a Cosmopolitan Intent', in *Perpetual Peace and Other Essays on Politics, History and Morals*, trans. Ted Humphrey, Hackett Pubishing, Indianapolis, 29–40.

Keegan, John (1993), *A History of Warfare*, Pimlico, London.

Kellner, Douglas (1989), *Jean Baudrillard: From Marxism to Postmodernism and Beyond*, Polity, Cambridge.

Kellner, Douglas (1998), 'Virilio on Vision Machines', in *Film-Philosophy: Electronic Salon*, 9 October, http://www.mailbase.ac.uk/lists/film-philosophy/files/kellner.html

Kittler, Friedrich (1997), 'Protected Mode', trans. Stefanie Harris, in *Literature, Media, Information Systems: Essays*, ed. and intro. John Johnston, G + B Arts International, Amsterdam, 156–68.

Kittler, Friedrich (1999), 'On the History of the Theory of Information Warfare', in Timothy Druckrey (ed.), *Ars Electronica: Facing the Future*, Ars Electronica Press/MIT, Cambridge, MA, 173–7.

Kojève, Alexandre (1969), *Introduction to the Reading of Hegel: Lectures on the Phenomenology of Spirit*, trans. James H. Nichols, Jr, Cornell University Press, Ithaca, NY.

Kracauer, Siegfried (1960), *Theory of Film: The Redemption of Physical Reality*, Oxford University Press, New York.

Kroker, Arthur and Marilouise Kroker (1996), *Hacking the Future: Stories for the Flesh-Eating 90s*, New World Perspectives, Montreal.

Kroker, Arthur and Michael A. Weinstein (1994), *Data Trash: The Theory of the Virtual Class*, New World Perspectives, Montreal.

Landow, George P. (1992), *Hypertext: The Convergence of Contemporary Critical Theory and Technology*, Johns Hopkins University Press, Baltimore, MD.

Lanham, Richard A. (1993), *The Electric Word: Democracy, Technology and the Arts*, University of Chicago Press, Chicago.

Lash, Scott (1990), *Sociology of Postmodernism*, Routledge, London.

Levidow, Les and Kevin Robins (eds) (1989), *Cyborg Worlds: The Military Information Society*, Free Association Books, London.

Levinas, Emmanuel (1969), *Totality and Infinity: An Essay on Exteriority*, trans. Alphonso Lingis, Duquesne University, Pittsburgh.

Levinas, Emmanuel (1989), 'Time and the Other', trans. Richard A. Cohen, in Seán Hand (ed.), *The Levinas Reader*, Blackwell, Oxford, 37–58.

Lévi-Strauss, Claude (1973), *Tristes Tropiques*, trans. John and Doreen Weightman, Penguin, Harmondsworth.

Lévy, Pierre (2000), *Collective Intelligence: Mankind's Emerging World in Hyperspace*, trans. Robert Bonomo, Perseus Publishing, Boulder, CO.

Lewis, Wyndham (1968), 'The Art of Being Ruled', in *Wyndham Lewis: An Anthology of his Prose*, ed. E.W.F. Tomlin, Methuen, London, 82–233.

Lovelock, J.E. (1979), *Gaia: A New Look at Life on Earth*, Oxford University Press, Oxford.

Lukács, Georg (1971), *History and Class Consciousness: Studies in Marxist Dialectic*, trans. Rodney Livingstone, MIT Press, Cambridge, MA.

Lyotard, Jean-François (1984), *The Postmodern Condition: A Report on Knowledge*, trans. Geoff Bennington and Brian Massumi, Manchester University Press, Manchester.

MacCannell, Dean (1976), *The Tourist: A New Theory of the Leisure Class*, Schocken Books, New York.

Macey, David (n.d.), 'Guy Debord', reprinted from *Radical Philosophy*, no. 71, http://www.ukc.ac.uk/secl/philosophy/rp/biog/1debor.html

McLuhan, Marshall (1962), *The Gutenberg Galaxy*, Routledge, London.

McLuhan, Marshall (1964), *Understanding Media: The Extensions of Man*, Sphere, London.

McLuhan, Marshall and Quentin Fiore (1967), *The Medium is the Massage: An Inventory of Effects*, Penguin, Harmondsworth.

McLuhan, Marshall and Quentin Fiore (1968), *War and Peace in the Global Village*, co-ordinated by Jerome Agel, Bantam, New York.

McLuhan, Marshall and Bruce R. Powers (1989), *The Global Village: Transformations in World Life and Media in the 21st Century*, Oxford University Press, Oxford.

Maltby, Richard with Ian Craven (1996), *Hollywood Cinema*, Blackwell, Oxford.

Marcuse, Herbert (1960), *Reason and Revolution: Hegel and the Rise of Social Theory*, Beacon, New York.

Marcuse, Herbert (1964), *One-Dimensional Man: The Ideology of Industrial Society*, Sphere, London.

Marin, Louis (1984), *Utopics: Spatial Play*, trans. Robert A. Vollrath, Humanities Press, Atlantic Highlands, NJ.

Marx, Karl (1975a), 'Economical and Philosophical Manuscipts', trans. Gregor Benton, in *Karl Marx: Early Writings*, ed. Quintin Hoare, Viking, New York, 279–400.

Marx, Karl (1975b), 'Concerning Feuerbach', in *Karl Marx: Early Writings*, ed. Quintin Hoare, trans. Gregor Benton, Viking, New York, 421–3.

Marx, Karl (1976), *Capital: A Critique of Political Economy*, Vol. 1, trans. Rodney Livingstone, NLB/Penguin, London.

Mattelart, Armand and Michèle Mattelart (1998), *Theories of Communication: A Short Introduction*, trans. Susan Groenheck Taponier and James A. Cohen, Sage, London.

Mattelart, Armand, Xavier Delcourt and Michèle Mattelart (1984), *International Image Markets: In Search of an Alternative Perspective*, trans. David Buxton, Comedia, London.

Mauss, Marcel (1967), *The Gift: Forms and Functions of Exchange in Archaic Societies*, trans. I. Cunnison, Norton, New York.

Minsky, Marvin (1985), *The Society of Mind*, Simon and Schuster, New York.

Mitchell, William J. (1992), *The Reconfigured Eye: Visual Truth in the Post-Photographic Era*, MIT Press, Cambridge, MA.

Moravec, Hans (1988), *Mind Children: The Future of Robot and Human Intelligences*, Harvard University Press, Cambridge, MA.

Morley, David (1987), *Family Television: Cultural Power and Domestic Leisure*, Routledge, London.

Morley, David (1992), *Television, Audiences and Cultural Studies*, Routledge, London.

Murray, Janet H. (1997), *Hamlet on the Holodeck: The Future of Narrative in Cyberspace*, MIT Press, Cambridge, MA.

Nietzsche, Friedrich (1956), *The Birth of Tragedy and the Geneaology of Morals*, trans. Francis Golffing, Doubleday, New York.

Norris, Christopher (1992), *Uncritical Theory: Postmodernism, Intellectuals and the Gulf War*, Lawrence and Wishart, London.

Oguibe, Olu (1998), 'Forsaken Geographies: Cyberspace and the New World "Other" ', in Melanie Keen (ed.), *Frequencies: Investigations into Culture, History and Technology* (= *Annotations* 4), INIVA, London, 18–29.

Oliveira, Carlos (1996), 'Global Algorithm 1.7: The Silence of the Lambs: Paul Virilio in Conversation', trans. Patrice Riemens, in *C-THEORY*, http://www.ctheory.com/ga1.7-silence.html

Osborne, Peter (1995), *The Politics of Time: Modernity and the Avant-Garde*, Verso, London.

Patton, Paul (1995), 'Introduction', in Jean Baudrillard, *The Gulf War Did Not Take Place*, trans. Paul Patton, Power Publications, Sydney, 1–21.

Plant, Sadie (1996), 'The Virtual Complexity of Culture', in George Robertson, Melinda Mash, Lisa Tickner, Jon Bird, Barry Curtis and Tim Puttnam (eds), *FutureNatural: Science/Nature/Culture*, Routledge, London, 207–13.

Plato (1955), *The Republic*, trans. H.D.P. Lee, Penguin, Harmondsworth.

Poster, Mark (1990), *The Mode of Information: Poststructuralism and Social Context*, Polity, Cambridge.

Prigogine, Ilya and Isabelle Stenghers (1988), *Order Out of Chaos: Man's New Dialogue with Nature*, Flamingo London.

Project on Disney, The (1995), *Inside the Mouse: Work and Play at Disney World*, Rivers Oram, London.

Provenzo, Eugene F., Jr (1991), *Video Kids: Making Sense of Nintendo*, Harvard University Press, Cambridge, MA.

Raymond, Eric S. (1999), *The Cathedral and the Bazaar: Musings on Linus and Open Source by an Accidental Revolutionary*, O'Reilly, Sebastopol, CA.

Rilke, Rainer Maria (1964), *Selected Poems*, ed. and trans. J.B. Leishman, Penguin, Harmondsworth.

Ritchin, Fred (1990), *In Our Own Image: The Coming Revolution in Photography,* Aperture Foundation, New York.

Robins, Kevin (1996), *Into the Image: Culture and Politics in the Field of Vision*, Routledge, London.

Rojek, Chris (1993), 'Disney Culture', in *Leisure Studies*, no. 12, 121–35.

Rorty, Richard (1980), *Philosophy and the Mirror of Nature*, Blackwell, Oxford.

Rorty, Richard (1992), 'The Pragmatist's Progress', in Umberto Eco with Richard Rorty, Jonathan Culler and Christine Brooke-Rose, *Interpretation and Overinterpretation*, ed. Stefani Collini, Cambridge University Press, Cambridge, 89–108.

Saussure, Ferdinand de (1974), *Course in General Linguistics*, rev. edn, trans. Wade Baskin, Fontana, London.

Schickel, Richard (1968), *The Disney Version: The Life, Times, Art and Commerce of Walt Disney*, Simon and Schuster, New York.

Schwartz, Hillel (1996), *The Culture of the Copy: Striking Likenesses, Unreasonable Facsimiles*, MIT Press, Cambridge, MA.

Scientific American (1999), *What Science Will Know in 2050*, Vol. 281, no. 6, December, 30–93.

Seiter, Ellen, Hans Borchers, Gabrielle Kreutzner and Eva-Maria Warth (eds) (1989), *Remote Control: Television, Audiences and Cultural Power*, Routledge, London.

Shannon, Claude E. and Warren Weaver (1949), *The Mathematical Theory of Communication*, University of Indiana Press, Urbana.

Skinner, B.F. (1971), *Beyond Freedom and Dignity*, Penguin, Harmondsworth.

Sloterdijk, Peter (1988), *Critique of Cynical Reason*, trans. Michael Eldred, Verso, London.

Smith, Neil (1996), 'The Production of Nature', in George Robertson, Melinda Mash, Lisa Tickner, Jon Bird, Barry Curtis and Tim Puttnam (eds), *FutureNatural: Science/Nature/Culture*, Routledge, London, 35–54.

Stone, Allucquère Rosanne (1995), *The War of Desire and Technology at the Close of the Mechanical Age*, MIT Press, Cambridge, MA.

Storey, John (ed.) (1994), *Cultural Theory and Popular Culture*, Harvester Wheatsheaf, Hemel Hempstead.

Sturken, Marita (1995), 'The Television Image and Collective Amnesia: Dis(re)membering the Persian Gulf War', in Peter D'Agostino and David Tafler (eds), *Transmission: Toward a Post-Television Culture*, 2nd edn, Sage, London, 135–49.

Taylor, Charles (1979), *Hegel and Modern Society*, Cambridge University Press, Cambridge.

Turkle, Sherry and Seymour Papert (1990), 'Epistemological Pluralism: Styles and Voices within the Computer Culture', in *Signs: Journal of Women in Culture and Society*, Vol. 16, no. 1, 128–57.

Vattimo, Gianni (1988), *The End of Modernity: Nihilism and Hermeneutics in Post-Modern Culture*, trans. Jon R. Snyder, Polity, Cambridge.

Venturi, Robert and Denise Scott-Brown (1972), *Learning from Las Vegas*, MIT Press, Cambridge, MA.

Virilio, Paul (1986), *Speed and Politics: An Essay in Dromology*, trans. Mark Polizotti, Semiotext(e), New York.

Virilio, Paul (1989a), *War and Cinema*, trans. Patrick Camiller, Verso, London.

Virilio, Paul (1989b), 'The Last Vehicle', in Dietmar Kamper and Christoph Wulf (eds), *Looking Back on the End of the World*, trans. David Antal, Semiotext(e), New York, 106–19.

Virilio, Paul (1991a), *The Aesthetics of Disappearance*, trans. Philip Beitchman, Semiotext(e), New York.

Virilio, Paul (1991b), *Lost Dimension*, trans. Daniel Moshenberg, Semiotext(e), New York.

Virilio, Paul (1991c), *L'Écran du désert: Chroniques de guerre*, Galilée, Paris.

Virilio, Paul (1994a), *The Vision Machine*, trans. Julie Rose, BFI, London.

Virilio, Paul (1994b), *Bunker Archeology*, trans. George Collins, Princeton Architectural Press, Princeton.

Virilio, Paul (1995a), *The Art of the Motor*, trans. Julie Rose, University of Minnesota Press, Minneapolis.

Virilio, Paul (1995b), 'Speed and Information: Cyberspace Alarm!' trans. Patrice Rieman, in *C-THEORY*, http://www.ctheory.com/a30-cyberspace_alarm.html

Virilio, Paul (1996), *Le Paysage d'évenements*, Galilée, Paris. (*A Landscape of Events*, trans. Julie Rose, MIT Press, Cambridge, MA, 2000.)

Virilio, Paul (1997), *Open Sky*, trans. Julie Rose, Verso, London.

Virilio, Paul (1998a), *Cybermonde: La politique du pire*, interview with Phillippe Petit, textuel/Seuil, Paris. (*Politics of the Very Worst*, trans. Sylvère Lotringer and Michael Cavaliere, Semiotext(e), New York, 1999.)

Virilio, Paul (1998b), 'Cyberwar, God and Television: Interview with Paul Virilio', conducted by Louise Wilson, in *C-THEORY*, http://english.www.hss.cmu.edu/ctheory/a-cyberwar_god.html

Virilio, Paul (1999), 'Infowar', interview with Derrick de Kerckhoeve, in Timothy Druckrey with Ars Electronica (eds), *Ars Electronica: Facing the Future*, MIT Press, Cambridge, MA, 326–35.

Virilio, Paul (2000), *Polar Inertia*, trans. Patrick Camiller, Sage, London.

Vološinov, V.N. (1986), *Marxism and the Philosophy of Language*, trans. Ladeslav Matejka and I.R. Titunik, Harvard University Press, Cambridge, MA.

Waldrop, M. Mitchell (1992), *Complexity: The Emerging Science at the Edge of Order and Chaos*, Penguin, Harmondsworth.

Walker, Ian (1995), 'Desert Stories or Faith in Facts?', in Martin Lister (ed.), *The Photographic Image in Digital Culture*, Routledge, London, 236–52.

Wiener, Norbert (1950), *The Human Use of Human Beings: Cybernetics and Society*, Free Association Books, London.

Wiener, Norbert (1961), *Cybernetics or, Control and Communication in the Animal and the Machine*, 2nd edn, MIT Press, Cambridge, MA.

Williams, Raymond (1958), *Culture and Society 1780–1950*, Penguin, Harmondsworth.

Williams, Raymond (1974), *Television: Technology and Cultural Form*, Fontana, London.

Wilson, Rob and Wimal Dissanayake (eds) (1996), *Global/Local: Cultural Production and the Transnational Imaginary*, Duke University Press, Durham, NC.

Winston, Brian (1998), *Media, Technology and Society. A History: From the Telegraph to the Internet*, Routledge, London.

Wittgenstein, Ludwig (1968), *Philosophical Investigations*, 2nd edn, trans. G.E.M. Anscombe, Blackwell, Oxford.

Wood, John (ed.) (1998), *The Virtual Embodied: Presence, Practice, Technology*, Routledge, London.

Žižek, Slavoj (1997), *The Plague of Fantasies*, Verso, London.

INDEX